# HOW TO BREATHE WATER

# SHARON BUTALA

# HOW TO BREATHE WATER

Freehand Books gratefully acknowledges the financial support for its publishing program provided by the Canada Council for the Arts and the Alberta Media Fund, and by the Government of Canada through the Canada Book Fund.

This book is available in print and Global Certified Accessible™ EPUB formats.

Freehand Books is located in Moh'kinsstis, Calgary, Alberta, within Treaty 7 territory, and on the traditional territories of the Siksika, the Kainai, and the Piikani, as well as the Iyarhe Nakoda and Tsuut'ina nations.

FREEHAND BOOKS
freehand-books.com

Canada Council for the Arts
Conseil des Arts du Canada

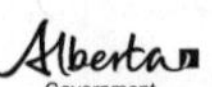

LIBRARY AND ARCHIVES CANADA CATALOGUING IN PUBLICATION
Title: How to breathe water / Sharon Butala.
Names: Butala, Sharon, author
Identifiers:
Canadiana (print) 20250230100
Canadiana (ebook) 20250230119
ISBN 9781990601965 (softcover)
ISBN 9781997534006 (EPUB)
ISBN 9781997534013 (PDF)
Subjects: LCSH: Butala, Sharon, 1940- —Travel—Prairie Provinces. | LCSH: Prairie Provinces—Biography. | CSH: Women authors, Canadian (English)—20th century—Biography. | CSH: Authors, Canadian (English)—20th century—Biography. | LCGFT: Autobiographies.
Classification: LCC PS8553.U6967 Z46 2025 | DDC C813/.54—dc23

Edited by Naomi K. Lewis
Design by Natalie Olsen
Cover photo © hauged/istockphoto.com
Author photo by Jennifer Chipperfield
Printed and bound in Canada

FIRST PRINTING

*For my father, who told me the truth*

*and*

*My mother, who gave me permission*

"... tis a rugged road, more so than it seems, to follow a pace so rambling and uncertain, as that of the soul ..."
**MICHEL DE MONTAIGNE** (1533–1592)

"All my life has been a constant process of obliteration, a turning away from myself and the world."
Jacques Austerlitz in *Austerlitz*,
**W.G. SEBALD** (1944–2001)

"Whether we take water as a symbol of the collective or of the personal unconscious, or else as an element of mediation and dissolution ... this symbolism is an expression of the vital potential of the psyche, of the struggles of the psychic depths to find a way of formulating a clear message comprehensible to the consciousness."
**J.E. CIRLOT**, *A Dictionary of Symbols*
Routledge & Kegan Paul, 1962

"Yet something is added to my interpretation. Something lies deeply buried. For one moment I thought to grasp it. But bury it, bury it; let it breed, hidden in the depths of my mind some day to fructify. After a long lifetime, loosely, after a moment of revelation, I may lay hands on it, but now the idea breaks in my hand."
**VIRGINIA WOOLF**, *The Waves*
The Hogarth Press Ltd, 1931

For fifteen or so years, I walked regularly in the partially wildland park that runs around the City of Calgary's reservoir. In the early years, I often chose times of day to walk when I would be mostly alone there, early Sunday or Saturday morning, later in the day, when most people would be at home at the dinner table. I walked for peace of mind: My husband and I, married more than thirty years and taking for granted many more together, with only two months warning when he was seventy-two years and I was only sixty-six, had died. In his sudden disappearing, I fell into a state of shock; I could no longer shake off the everyday disturbances of ordinary life; worse, I could not move beyond the date and time of his death. I felt as if I had just taken a deep breath to say to him what I needed to say, when he had slammed the door on me – forever. I could not expel that word-and-idea-filled breath, nor could I take in fresh, clear air. Each footstep felt fragile, as if the sidewalk might crack at the impact of my steps, slight as they would be, and I would vanish as he had done, but into some other place than was his destination. I walked day after day in the early morning mist or through frost halos, the trees glistening beside me, sometimes cracking as if an animal had brushed hard against them or they could not bear the burden of the glittering crystals encasing them. I walked, starting with a single thought, but as I moved, the single thought drifted into other thoughts, and the other thoughts into something that was beyond thought, a territory I had come bit by bit to know but couldn't name, a place of sometime sublimity. The path curved between the thickly crowded poplars, the tall pines and spruce, the shrubs that in spring bore sweetly scented flowers and then fruit: saskatoons, chokecherries, pincherries, or those of other wild bushes whose berries no one would eat except perhaps bears or maybe deer.

Often, in those days, because I was alone, I would stop in the middle of the path and gaze in awed silence at the trees on each side, or further into the forest whose living beauty brought me to a halt. Early one morning, as I stood alone in perfect stillness and silence, just as the forest stood still and silent on either side of me, gazing into it I saw a mist descend to weave itself delicately among the trunks and branches, shrubs and grasses. It was not made of water droplets or smoke, but of some material I didn't know, that slowly, as it appeared everywhere, I saw was otherworldly. On another day, I had begun to walk up an incline that would at the top descend into a deep hollow before rising up the other side. There, at the top, I noticed someone coming toward me: A woman: small, her shoulder-length brown hair dishevelled, her heavy outer jacket unzipped, the sides falling away to reveal a dark-coloured inner jacket and on her face, a troubled, inward-looking expression. I barely paid attention, and when I glanced up again, she was gone. I thought at first that she had turned onto one of the narrow trails into the forest, or perhaps was out of sight at the bottom of the hollow. A few more steps, and I realized that the woman I had seen coming toward me who had vanished, was me.

# ONE

# DEPARTURE

## I

Once, some years ago now, I found myself in a cafeteria sitting at a lunch table with a stranger, a young, orange-robed Buddhist monk. In the course of our polite if halting conversation, he remarked, "I always wanted to be a poet." Instantly, I heard myself reply, "I always wanted to be alive." I recall nothing else about what was said during the rest of the lunch, although I remember the look the monk gave me when I said that, his eyes focusing, his gaze more intense, as if I had suddenly become real to him. I was both surprised at myself and for some surely childish reason, innocently, almost sweetly pleased with it; the moment felt buoyant to me, spring-like in its gentleness and, although it should have been, not at all dismaying.

I might have been in my early sixties when that happened. I knew that some basic unhappiness had always lived inside me, but I did not understand its nature, nor know what its source was any more than most people with less than idyllic lives know. I've spent most of my adult life trying to figure out the source of that unhappiness, or else to discover how to bury it forever, more spent on the latter than the former. I'm hardly alone in this pursuit. I'm guessing that most of us die before we understand our always troubling unease, much less find a way to address our sense that we are always in the wrong place, always doing the wrong thing with our lives.

I remember now something I'd forgotten, that when I was an adolescent, teenager, young wife, and mother, a drive so painfully strong thrusting its way up out of my interior, lodging painfully in my solar plexus, crying out *I want, I want, I want*, would overcome me before sinking again, leaving me gasping and – it did not then bear looking at. And yet, even when I was twelve years old, I knew that this yearning was about something more than I already had, some unspecified good for which I had no name.

That voice stopped, eventually, and I'd forgotten it, but the equally puzzling words that years later I had spoken: *I always wanted to be alive,* hung on. I asked myself, what does *being alive* mean? Why did I think I was not alive?



## II

Sometime around late March or early April of 2021, a friend told me that she had decided to take a week out of her busy life and in July drive to Winnipeg, about thirteen hundred kilometres from Calgary, where we both lived. She was eager to see the Museum for Human Rights there, and while in the city, she thought she would try to find the homes of family members who had once lived in Winnipeg, including her parents, but especially that of her paternal grandparents, with whom she had spent an indelibly happy week when she was five years old. Would I like to come with her? I agreed at once, but our departure seemed so far off in time, anything could happen in the months between, so that I thought little about it, while she, not a born-and-bred prairie woman as I am, began studying various routes and mileages, choosing where we would stop each night, and searching for points of interest to visit.

I took little part in the planning. It was her trip, I thought, we'd do whatever she wanted, I was only along for the ride. Anyway, the trip would only last a week, I knew the way and where to find gas, hotels, decent meals, and help if we should need it, as we drove across sparsely populated southern Saskatchewan and Alberta and into Manitoba, which had been once part of, although no longer was, the area called the Palliser Triangle, historically famous for its low annual precipitation and poor agricultural soils.

As an aging widow living alone, I didn't often get out of the city anymore, except when I flew somewhere, and with flying so much more uncertain during the COVID pandemic, I'd stopped making my usual visits to relatives and friends. That I didn't have to make any decisions about this trip made it even more appealing. With my husband's death fourteen years earlier, I felt plunged overnight into too much responsibility; I could not believe sometimes how hard merely living turned out to be, especially in the early years of my widowhood, always accompanying an overlay of guilt about what I thought might be bad decisions, not the ones he would have made. Or else my lifelong sense, especially when I was young, that I didn't know how to live my life and it seemed that others, from teachers and friends to divorced or dead husbands, did.



As I aged, I found myself becoming more solitary, spending my time alone, writing, reading, watching TV, mostly because I wasn't born in Calgary, didn't go to school there or work there, nor had I shepherded children through school there, so my range of friends and acquaintances in the city might be wide, but generally it was shallow. Added to that, my close relatives and old friends, all in different cities and provinces, were dying one by one. I was solitary so much of the time, though, because I found life outside my condo harder and harder to manage, while seeming less and less worth the effort.

Besides the uncertainty that I might not be, in a general way, good enough as a person, as the years of my youth slowly wore away, I had developed a cloud of amorphous anxiety, which enveloped me, that I couldn't beat my way through, and that constrained me more and more in terms of where I went and what I did, whom I saw and where I saw them. Eventually I faced that my fear was probably the result of events in my life going back into infancy that hadn't been resolved, weren't even acknowledged much less precisely examined in the way they needed to be to dissolve them, and that had left that residue of unease that grew with every passing year, and was becoming more unmanageable. After my husband's death and my move to the city, I had adopted the practice of refusing to think of those things – at all. Ever. The ones that made my heart rate increase or my chest hurt or made me act like a crazy person if I thought about them: suddenly standing up for no reason, muttering under my breath; if alone, tossing things, swearing at them; if walking, running a few steps. The ones that, if they leaked up into my conscious mind, I pushed back down as hard as I could, and smiled, and carried on. I got so good at refusing them that I no longer even noticed when I did.



I was proud to have finally gained control of my emotions, so much so that I no longer even cried. The older I got, and although strange to me, the more moved I was by people in trouble, especially children or young soldiers in war whom I saw on television. Then my vision would blur with tears, and puzzled, I would let them; I couldn't make sense of them, as if a part in me that knew what it was doing while "I," whoever "I" was, was separate. I saw dimly that those tears came from being older. The old know how cruel life can be and how little can be done about it. But cry over my own remembered pain? Not a chance.

Added to the anxiety that bedevilled me was that I felt myself growing more fragile physically, my mind seeming to me less sharp and quick at the same time as I could no longer wave airily away the certainty of my death. All of this at a time when I no longer had anyone nearby on whom I could rely to help me with the steadily accumulating things I now couldn't do by myself: driving after dark, driving on freeways or busy or strange streets, getting things fixed, lifting even medium-heavy things, walking fast, dealing with the always changing, ever-puzzling computer tasks. Odd things too: for years after my husband's death, I couldn't cook or bake properly. Most older widows happily abandon the monotonous routine of meal making, but even when I tried, I who had once been considered a good cook, no longer was. My muffins or cakes fell, and my forays into cooking the simplest dishes flopped, until I gave it up and ate out of cans or boxes of frozen food.



In July of 2021, when my friend and I set out on our trip, I had spent over half my life as a rural or small-town person. The other part, a little less than half, I'd spent in cities, mostly Saskatoon, but also Halifax, and after my husband's death Calgary, at a time when it was burgeoning. According to Stats Canada by 2021 Calgary had a population of nearly 1.3 million, and for people like me it was growing ever more unmanageable. I hovered on the dividing line between the two worlds, and yet, if the truth were told, I had never fit fully into either one.

But when my friend asked me to go with her, flooding through me at once was the memory of high summer on the prairies: the dry heat, shimmering up from the land, breeds glistening mirages sometimes breathtakingly upside down in the sky, the briefly green grasses that the further south you go stay green for even less time, beside them the wide fields of various kinds of wheat, barley, oats, rye, canola, which all the time I was growing up was called "rape" from the ancient Latin word *rapum* for turnip because it belongs in the rapeseed family, and also peas, mustard; all of them shading through cream to the brightest yellow to burnt gold, with the occasional field of blooming violet-blue flax intervening. All this against the flat cerulean sky, or its bright cornflower colour, or its sun-or-ice-bleached white; at night, its luminous indigo hinting of realms not known, realms to come. The sky here *is* the landscape, while the narrow band of land around you that your feet are anchored to speeds away in all directions to the furthest, lowest horizon, out at the edge of the earth. The air full of the scents of ripening wheat and grasses and whole fields of sweetest-smelling hay, the dank tang of wet clay and roadside sloughs, and even of asphalt roads softening in the baking sun, while the powdered white earth of "alkali" flats spins upward, ghostlike, and, thinning, whisks away.



I was past eighty: I believed this trip would probably be my last chance to immerse myself in that world I'd left behind years earlier, which I continued to dream about and to long for in unexpected, piercing flashes every day. Just to see it, to smell it, to *live* in it one last time. That was all I wanted. And to do it not from the back seat, mutely, as is usual for the aged widow, who, out of kindness – I'm decidedly in favour of kindness and endlessly glad to be its recipient – is taken along on outings, but instead with an agreeable companion to whom in ways that mattered I was an equal. Surely, I told myself, an elderly person has earned the right to leave behind for a week the too-often public humiliation that is her lot in an ageist world, the steady roll call of deaths of friends and family, and the loneliness that doesn't leave even in the midst of crowds, which is at root existential.

Still, thinking back, I might have been dubious that the trip would actually happen. There was no reason for my uncertainty: since my husband's unthinkable death, I had begun to expect ambiguity and steady change, and to assume that nothing would come about as I had thought it would. The truth is that slowly I had begun to live more profoundly in dreams, reverie, and memory than in my formerly lively, action-filled world. Year by year, the prairie life I mourned was slowly transmuting in my mind from precise pictures of events – rodeos, brandings, roundups, dances in country halls, trailing herds of cattle, combines whining across fields, fowl suppers, conversations in kitchens, barns smelling deliciously of horses and manure, corrals full of bulls, worn-out houses, animal sightings – deer, coyotes, badgers – rarely, moose or elk, or even more rarely, cougars – stories heard and so on – to hazier, detail-less pictures. Now, when passing by in a car, if I saw wild prairie grass in a ditch, or caught a glimpse of a bright lichen-covered rock in a field, I'd quickly look away. Unless details needed discussing, from our first conversation about the trip on I rarely thought about it, but if I happened to, it was without emotion other than a little prick of pleasure at the prospect, again, of the fragrant, radiant prairie.



July arrived; the day of our departure drew near. I put a few clothes and toiletries into a small suitcase, added two woven-straw sun hats, one fitting neatly over the other, and a few books in a box to drop off at an antiquarian bookseller's shop along the way. And then it was Sunday morning, my friend pulled up to the door, I stowed my bag in her trunk, my books and the hats on the back seat, got into the car beside her, and we drove south, out of the city.

## III

I never, at any point until then or on the trip, planned to, or even thought that I would write a book about it. I didn't take a proper camera with me; I didn't take a notebook and pen much less my laptop. I wanted only to be in the countryside in summer, even if merely racing through it in a car. As a writer, because of certain circumstances, I hoped I'd finally emerged from the period in which I couldn't let a single thing go as merely life; it was, all of it, fodder for my writing. I was curious to see, even hopeful about how life would be if I went back to seeing all things in each day without the intensity, the filing away of the tiniest things for future use, but casually, as I thought non-writers did. I was also going to leave behind, or try to, the career concerns that had occupied me every day for nearly fifty years. A time out of time; that's what I was looking for. It was at least a year after our return before the idea of this book lodged in my brain so firmly that I couldn't dismiss it.

I have decided, in homage to Cervantes, who, in his book about Don Quixote, that half-mad, fully wonderful traveller, invented the name around 1600, that I'll call my travelling companion "Luscinda," but using the modern spelling, Lucinda. At first, I thought about pretending I was alone. Then I toyed with the idea of turning her into somebody she wasn't and our travelling relationship into something it wasn't either. Maybe introduce a little excitement: Arguments? Fury? Fist fights, maybe? Glasses of wine being thrown in faces? One of us leaping out of the car determined to walk the rest of the way, one of us having a meltdown and needing to be deposited in hospital overnight? Intimate, shocking revelations about our private lives that would cause us to wonder if being alone in the car with the other person was a good idea? I imagined the scenes I would get to write, the nutty dialogue, maybe even screaming and hitting, more scandalous because between women, one of them elderly. But I was thinking of Bruce Chatwin, who mixed fiction and nonfiction in his 1987 memoir, *The Songlines*, and was roundly criticized for it, although nonetheless, his book was a bestseller and also, with quibbles, a critical success.

I squelch that, she is my friend, and anyway, I can't lie in a memoir, not to mention that that is probably a cliché in road trip books. I was going through models of road trip memoirs in my mind. Jack Kerouac's *On the Road*, published when I was seventeen, kept nudging its way in, but I hadn't liked the book, felt no relationship to it, and in places it shocked me. Each time Kerouac's book crossed my mind I erased it at once. Bill Bryson's excellent travel books were not what I had in mind either, nor any number of wandering-around-the-universe titles, those by male writers, anyway, physical books, too often about brave but ironically viewed Great Adventures in hard-to-reach, scary places. They had a focus that was all wrong for the book that was forming dimly in my mind. Lucinda would stay the Lucinda I thought she was.



When my husband entered his final illness in 2007, I'd been a writer since 1978 and had published seventeen books. In the last years before his illness and death, when he had retired from ranching, although we still had a few animals around us and he continued raising his hay crop to sell it, my writing life had become almost my only life. When I wasn't writing or doing housework or ranch-wife's jobs, I read constantly and with the same seriousness with which I wrote. That phase of my writing life ended in June 2007 with his cancer diagnosis, and I cancelled all my summer's literary commitments in order to be with him. Barely two months later, he died.

Fifteen months after that, I moved to Calgary to be near my son, daughter-in-law, and grandchildren, after years of seeing them only rarely, fully expecting that there I would resume giving readings, presenting at festivals, being on panels, making the occasional speech, and teaching workshops around the country. This didn't happen, though. The invitations mostly dried up, I guessed because, at least at first, organizers thought I wouldn't be much good if lost in grief, which was probably true, but as more time passed and I failed to publish another book, with what seemed to me was stunning rapidity, they forgot all about me. At the same time I thought, never mind, the literary life will all be mine again as soon as I finish another book, which I was sure I soon would.

Through this long period of not exactly grieving, but more of being in a mild but steady state of shock, a sort of footless disorientation from this new life I'd been thrown into, mixed, weirdly, with excitement at having all the richness of the city at hand after so many years of repressing my longing for it, and the constant need to alter position as I fumbled to find my place in my new world, I continued to follow my old writing regime. Mostly, though, the loss of my husband and what for thirty-three years had been my way of life had knocked me right out of myself, so that I was not myself, never mind my writer-self.



Then, seven years after my last book, when I was seventy-five, I published my seventh novel, *Wild Rose*, then a memoir, another novel, a short story collection, and lastly, when I was eighty-one, an essay collection, and had finished a novel, my ninth, called *Leaving Wisdom*. It was as if in the seven years I'd spent relearning how to write at the same time as I also struggled to find myself or maybe to create a new self, all my stories had piled up inside me until one day they came tumbling out at the speed of light.

Then, as with other seasoned writers, I found the publishing world had moved on without any more need for me and my work, and, worse, when I read lists of Canadian writers being paid attention to, not only was I no longer on them, and although I read steadily, I frequently didn't recognize a single name on those lists.

When I got in my friend's car that morning in July 2021, the awful truth was dawning on me that I'd probably reached the apex of my career around the time of my husband's death, and, even though I was writing as well as ever and as interested in the literary world as I'd ever been, I was beginning to be afraid that my struggle to regain lost territory might be futile. I kept telling myself, I'm a writer, that is who I am; I write books. I was beginning to pick up hints that literature itself had moved on, although for a long time I brushed that off, too. But I couldn't avoid the knowledge that I wasn't going to grow younger next year: I was going to grow day by day more out of step with the fashionable world; I was going to end up dead. And I wasn't ready for any of that. No, I was thinking, if I'm not a writer, I don't exist; I have to keep fighting.

That was what I'd been worrying over night and day, half-sick that it was true, and I was done, still angry, and avoiding telling anyone else what had happened so as not to humiliate myself any more than I'd already been. Then Lucinda asked me to go on a road trip with her, and with relief I said yes. I would leave the fear for my writerly future and the approaching *new* grief behind while I sank into the beauty of prairie and its wildly changing or steadily peaceable sky, its smell of sage, its sounds of wind sloughing through grass and the bright, brief songs of the little ground-nesting prairie birds. I'd come home refreshed, doubts squelched, ready to dive back into the literary world with my old excitement and determination.

Unlike me, a child of boreal forest and plains, Lucinda grew up in the perpetually humid, vibrant greens of British Columbia's temperate rainforest, the Pacific's tang always in the air, and had never spent any serious time examining the prairie itself in any depth. I didn't ask, and we didn't talk about this, but maybe, like most Canadians, she believed the southern prairie to be a uniformly flat, barren, boring landscape, without any interesting or dramatic stories attached to it. I wondered if the possibility of boredom, which non-prairie dwellers constantly referred to, caused her to ask me to accompany her. Or, maybe she thought I could open up that blandness for her, give it life that she could otherwise only guess at. Most likely, though, she just wanted an amiable companion and friend to chat with and to share the driving.

I didn't even think of bringing along a camera: What would I take pictures of anyway, having lived nearly all my life within the circumference of the roads we would be travelling, the places and scenes along the way were not just permanent in my memory, but were my memory, they were what I was made of? By anybody's definition I was old, and although I'd spent a long time doing my best to forget my own life as the only way to survive the unpromising present, I thought that on the trip, I wouldn't be knitted into the prairie again, but could just look at it, as if I were in an art gallery or a museum. I thought I could stick with the unending knowledge of it that country people possessed, which I knew a little from my long sojourn on it. For most of one week I'd be free of the steady roar of the city, because, though I tried, and even in my deliberate forgetfulness, I'd never stopped longing for the silence of the country broken only by wind and birdsong, the distant yodelling of coyotes, the thrilling rarity of hard rain singing slantwise against the roof, of wind-driven snow pounding the windows, and in spring, the steady lowing of the bulls ceaselessly pacing in the corral below the house, or the thud of horses' hooves against the earth as the herd swept by racing from things I couldn't see.

We knew that 2,600 kilometres was a long distance for such a short time, but I had vowed to be the most agreeable companion possible, so I didn't mention it. Maybe Lucinda had determined that she would be the best possible companion to me, too, both of us writers and widows, and despite our nearly twenty-year age difference, our already proven compatibility.

As we drove out of Calgary that morning, we were cheerfully eager to leave. Neither of us could quite believe that the city had become our home, and although Lucinda would soon leave, I felt forced to accept that it would be my home for the rest of my life. Calgary, and not Saskatoon, the city I called my hometown even though it wasn't. I hadn't gone back because whole household moves are expensive, my capital was dwindling, I wasn't earning anymore. Besides my family members were gone from there by death or design, and also, nobody had cured Saskatchewan of its often-horrendous winters, and I had no husband to lighten its burden. I'd built a life in Calgary, I had a doctor, dentist, ophthalmologist, bank, and hairdresser, and dreaded, at my advanced age, starting again in another city, even if that's where I truly belonged. I knew that every single time I was there, something from my far past confronted me, and I thought that I couldn't live with the steady reminders of my past weakness, the multitudinous mistakes of my youth striking me every time I walked down a sidewalk. That was what I told myself. Even after my main reason for being in Calgary, my beloved family, picked up and left for Ontario, I stayed on in brisk, teeming Calgary and tried to enjoy it, while avoiding thinking of my past or my future.



## IV

I was eighty years old that morning, in a few weeks would turn eighty-one, and as I wrote this, would soon be eighty-two. By the time I finished this book, I predicted, if I was still alive and did finish it, I would be eighty-three, maybe even eighty-four. I was going the way of the elderly, although more slowly than most, and still appeared younger than I was. Or so people kept telling me, and every time someone did, I crossed my fingers, wondering how much longer this impression would last. Worst of all, I suspected that I'd lost an inch in height, a catastrophe for a woman barely five feet tall at the best of times. I found I was now often described as "tiny," or was I always, once I grew up, having been a "tiny" child, and just refused to credit it, because, amazingly, I didn't feel tiny?

As a writer, I wanted to give the lives of the so-called common people, the poor and working classes out of which I came, the nobility, wisdom, and strength usually denied them. I admired, for example, the work of Norway's Knut Hamsun, Australia's Patrick White or (now Lesotho) Basutoland's Olive Schreiner (*The Story of an African Farm)* or Chinua Achebe's *Things Fall Apart,* and Canadian Gabrielle Roy's *Bonheur d'occasion* (*The Tin Flute*), among many others. I was schooled in humanism, and as a writer remained a realist. But I chose finding and telling what I recognized as the truth, in the clearest, plainest language I could, as my goal. I had no idea then how very hard that goal would be to reach.



## V

We were driving in Lucinda's unglamorous Toyota sedan. Our destination was Winnipeg: Winnipeg was fine with me. That historic city was full of my relatives, but mostly those on the French, my father's, side. I had two elderly aunts left there, although before I finished writing this book, I would have only one, my hundred-year-old Auntie Cécile having died, who said to me, when she was a hundred years old, that the way to extreme old age was "Work! Work hard!" as she had always done, a recommendation about which, despite her living to a hundred, I remain dubious. My slightly younger Auntie Germaine, though, would remain clear-headed, still bright-faced and beautiful and a role model for me as I aged.

I had first cousins, too, although far fewer than I once had, and I didn't know them well, our mother's family having been the go-to relatives all my childhood, mostly because our father's family were francophones. Our mother didn't speak French and wasn't very forgiving of people who did. We children lost out terribly by not learning French at home, and yet I can't blame someone for having had an upbringing that embedded lamentable ideas in her that she knew no reason to rid herself of and, not seeing how the world was moving on, failed to recognize that her own children were half French and deserved to know the language.

Sometimes, now that I'm old, I think that for much of our childhoods our mother was a very angry woman, often a despairing one, too, now and then taking out her anger on her children — nothing that would have gotten her arrested, but a subject we remaining children don't talk about. Although I've suddenly remembered sitting around with my girlfriends from school when we were twelve or barely thirteen, naming the awful things our perfectly decent and usually well-meaning mothers did to us. This era was before today's gentler, more tenuous mothers who seem to coparent with their children. We were shockingly, strangely emotionless in our telling: *She hit me with my skipping rope because I left it on the floor; She called me a slut and swore at me; She made me stay outside when it was twenty below.*

Our mothers' rages back in 1952 were awful for us to witness and often ended with any one of them suddenly or slowly forgetting us, her anger not having been at us in the first place, or not exclusively so, stumbling away, falling into a chair to break down sobbing, and even though she had just screamed at us, said we were useless and stupid and lazy, had assaulted us, we would then try to comfort her, because as much as we hated her unfairness and feared her rage, we couldn't bear witnessing, in our powerlessness, her pain. This, we seemed to be telling each other, is what we, kids merely – although we didn't feel "mere" – had to endure in our childhood homes, and for us, fortunately, none of it was too terrible, we could manage it. We knew kids who dealt with so much worse: Our friend whose father truly terrorized her, those who didn't get enough to eat, those few with petty-criminal fathers and alcoholic mothers who abused them while failing to protect them from the adult world. It was a very odd, a very adult moment in the lives of girls who were essentially still children; a confirmation among us of our understanding of our place, and of the patience required for us to get through to adulthood.

There remains something mysterious about that scene when we were still children, reminding me of J.M. Coetzee's novel about Jesus's upbringing (*The Schooldays of Jesus*, 2016), where Jesus, called "David," is not only sometimes unmanageable, but also often shows a depth of knowing not given even to most grown-ups. Although I doubt the Dalai Lama would agree, I think that person who *knows* exists inside all of us, but we are satisfied to fulfill the roles given to us by custom, regulations, and advice and don't go looking for anything else, and in the process, devalue any other news that rises up from who knows where. Yet sometimes children, perhaps because closer to the source, can still find that source, but must remain silent.

The morning we left, the temperature was a reasonable low twenties, but by the time we travelled a couple more hours it climbed to thirty, sometimes spiking higher, with the sun shining relentlessly in a high clear sky. We headed south down

Macleod Trail and made a left turn onto what used to be a single-laned paved prairie road leading in and out of the city, now called Stoney Trail after the Stoney/Nakoda people of the area, and is four to six lanes wide, and unnervingly fast for someone who had spent more than half her life driving in the countryside or in small towns, until we left the city limits behind, and the highway narrowed to single lanes each way. We headed east for a hundred kilometres until we reached the Trans-Canada Highway at the town of Gleichen. Located beside the town is the headquarters of the Siksika Nation, also known as the Blackfoot Confederacy, some of whose reserve we just passed by and partly through. For the first while we were mostly silent, we definitely weren't singing in the ebullient way of people heading out on a much longed-for holiday, or leaving behind forever a place that made them unhappy.

The cool summer day my first husband, our little boy, and one of my younger sisters drove away from Halifax after four years there, two of us adults not yet thirty and the third just past, we were singing as loud as we could some old cowboy song about the prairie, maybe "Don't Fence Me In." We were prairie people born and raised; we found that lack of a view in Nova Scotia, only steadily in-your-face dark forests and hills, uncomfortable and annoying. We hadn't been able to get used to the fact that only at the beach could we see the view, and at that, only a whole lot of forbidding navy blue, frigid Atlantic stretching out all the way to England and now we were at last heading back to the wide sky and endless vistas we'd been born to. We shouted more than we sang; after our four vista-less Nova Scotia years, we were going home.

Now, in July 2021, we were just two quiet, although far from dead widows rolling down the highway in the high heat of summer under the immense prairie sky.

The route I prefer goes past Gleichen, which was named after Count Edward Gleichen or else his son, Lord Edward Gleichen, because one of them was an investor in the Canadian Pacific railroad. We reached Gleichen after the first hour, Brooks after the second, and the small city of Medicine Hat after the third. I've always enjoyed that first hour once I'm past the city limits, because the highway is slow and runs past fields and a few houses and occasional turnoffs to villages or towns you mostly can't see from the road.

The second hour is a blank despite all the times I've driven it: few dwellings in view, mostly grazing land with cattle and occasionally a few horses dotting the fields. Or else it's farmers' crops, but in your vehicle racing along the highway, it's like watching TV; it's impossible to feel connected to the rural life on the side of the road. That part of the trip, if you're lucky and have an agreeable companion, is good for chatting.

Past Gleichen, we saw jacks pumping oil occur here and



there, and perhaps travellers who didn't come from oil and gas country would have found them interesting. My years in Calgary had given me the occasional fascinating, if sometimes horrified, glimpse into the oil and gas sector, including the people who said blithely, when asked what they did, that they were in oil and gas. It seemed everybody had been or was in oil and gas. And practically every male I met, if not a writer, was either an engineer or a geologist or a lawyer in oil and gas. I had met a fair number of female executives, too, and I always wondered how they could bear that industry, how tough they would have to be, or maybe cleverly manipulative, likely compensated, nonetheless, with huge salaries.

In Calgary, hidden behind groves of trees, or long stone or iron fences with high gates or around certain corners where people wouldn't usually drive, or on seemingly unapproachable buttes or escarpments within the city, were the mansions of the superrich, those either in oil and gas or who got their wealth in trades that oil and gas depend on. I knew some of the wealthiest had become so in other ways, such as cattle ranching, having begun in the early days when land was cheap, or else all the usual, fairly dull and yet precarious ways people get rich, like wealth management or real estate or even white-collar crime.

My route had always been to head straight to Medicine Hat. Lucinda, being sensible and in no rush, thought three hours of driving without a stretch and a bit of a walk-around was too long, so somewhere along there we stopped for a bathroom and coffee-buying break. Aha, I must have thought, there are other ways to do what I've done several dozen times no longer even thinking about it, and I perked up a little, or as Leonard Cohen put it, a tiny crack appeared in my brain and the light sneaked in. I always wanted to tell him that sometimes it's the other way around.

I suppose I wondered about talking to Lucinda about my past—my *real* past, that is, the one that exists in a place I mostly choose not to go, down into the blackness that exists inside us all—better not to go there, better never to go there. We were on a holiday, and no airplanes, passports, vast quantities of money, endless lines or crowds of people or jetlag were involved. What could be better?

But a few days before Lucinda and I left, toward morning I dreamt I was in a worn, slightly shabby, once-white-painted kitchen. It was not one I recognized but that had a forties feel to it: cupboards covered with thick layers of glossy once-white paint now yellowed to a cream and nicked and scratched with wear. The thick, once-shiny paint of that particular colour has always been a symbol of poverty to me. I was standing at the counter a few steps to the right of the place where the wall and counter made a right-angle turn when I heard the sound and felt a fat drop of water fall precisely on the centre of the top of my head.

The drop quickly became a stream of drops; I looked up in alarm and saw a dark, water-stained perfect circle the size of a quarter in the ceiling directly above my head. The drops were coming from its midpoint. As I stared up, the surprisingly large tear-shaped beads of water were beginning to come so fast that they would soon be a stream; there was a deep pool of water behind the stream; although I couldn't see it, I knew it was there and that there would soon be a deluge from it onto me. I remembered that I lived at the top of the building, so where could the water be coming from? I vaguely thought, from the heavens, but awake, I realized that it must have come from the crawlspace just below the roof: the attic, where we store old things, where we store our memories.

Then, still dreaming and knowing I had to do something at once, I fell into a panic; things began to blur, I couldn't see well, and I tried to remember the person I was supposed to call two floors below, who would find a way to stop it. But I was so panicky I couldn't remember her name or how to reach her, and still the drops of water increased in number, came closer and closer together, were now a stream beginning to soak me.

I woke dry and in my own bed, with pale early morning light leaking in around the curtains covering my large bedroom window and its view of rooftops and ponderous tall conifers, the dream still vivid, the perfect, stained circle the exact tobacco-colour of prairie slough water, the unusual largeness of the drops, how they came faster and faster until a stream, how I panicked, how in my panic my vision blurred, so that everything was light-coloured – pale yellows and greens and creams: the colours of an early spring landscape, or of high summer on a drought-seared, sun-cured shortgrass prairie.

# TWO

# WIND

## I

In the years when I still travelled twice a year to the area where our ranch and hay farm had been in southwest Saskatchewan, for the sole purpose of visiting my husband's grave, it was de rigueur that I take my first bathroom, gas, and snack break 300 kilometres from Calgary at Medicine Hat, a city of about sixty-three thousand people. I would turn in at the mall just off the highway, where all such needs could be satisfied in one stop. But when Lucinda and I approached where I'd always turned north, the exits off the highway were new, I didn't know them, and I hesitated about which one to tell Lucinda to take. We would have sailed on by, but ever-vigilant Lucinda picked the right sign, took the exit, and there we were, passing the mall and heading down Dunmore Road into the city's downtown. We made a left turn at one of the last streets before the river to see the municipal buildings along the South Saskatchewan River; how lovely that area is in summer where there are some very old, interesting buildings. If we'd kept on backtracking west along the river, we would have seen the many beautiful houses, a few from as early as the late nineteenth century.

Then we went back to the mall, where Lucinda bought coffee at the food court, and I bought a drink, too, but I've no memory what it was or whether we took our purchases to the car to drink while driving, or if we sat there in the mostly empty food court for a while. I saw not a single person I knew there, even though in the past I nearly always saw several. Not because I know Medicine Hat people, but because the rural people of southwest Saskatchewan and southeast Alberta use the city as one of their "market towns," so on any given day you might run into your neighbours and acquaintances at the mall's food court. The ease of that trip, the smooth roads, the light traffic, the brilliant weather, our amiable, undemanding relationship, the lack of pauses to see obligatory sights, just whatever came up on the way, still pleases me to think of it.

I only wrote about it just short of two full years since we made that drive, and I'd made no notes and taken no pictures, and as Lucinda bought the gas, keeping a tally so that we could settle up when we got back home, I had almost no paper trail to prove what I said was true. It was odd, the way that imagining us both in the food court at the mall compared to having no doubt we were there are almost the same thing. If I had only vague mental pictures, did it really happen?



I could ask the same question about the whole of my life. I suppose that's why people take photos; some are said even to run out of burning houses passionately clutching photo albums while leaving behind passports, cash, pets, and sometimes even children – the unending, urgent need to prove one exists. That the past happened, and in the way we say it did: grandfather slowly backing his team of giant Clydes, or were they taffy-coloured Belgians? out of the barn, the exotic, giddy-making smells of the garage where my dad worked seventy-five years ago, grim childhood hours of weed pulling in the vast and, on the prairie then, essential garden, whose produce prairie families lived off all winter, the moist black soil crumbling and sticky, clinging to fingers and palms like sweet cake. How different the soil in the southwest, where I spent thirty-three years and that we were driving through: pale, hard, and dry.

In July of 2021 the temperature was racing up the thermometer, although having taken no notes I don't know how high it reached, and, looking at Environment Canada's archives, you do not begin to get the sense of how suffocatingly hot it was. Not for the first time, I was grateful that the humidity must have been about as low as possible without causing spontaneous combustion of people, buildings, and cows: prairie heat—as if you'd been placed in a bright, spacious, searing-hot oven.

## II

When we started out that morning, I'd been reading a 1957 translation of *Don Quixote*, by Miguel de Cervantes, an almost exact contemporary of Shakespeare. I can't remember why I started it, but it was so enjoyable I couldn't stop reading, and pretty soon Don Quixote and Sancho Panza and the Don's determination to be a man of sublime heroism and unflinching honour had taken up residence in my mind. Less obsessively, so had Emily Carr's book of drawings, cartoons really, illustrating a trip she and an equally intrepid older sister, Alice, had taken north into the watery green wilds of British Columbia. They had gone there not just to see for themselves the unspoiled rainforest, but to record the art of the Indigenous people of British Columbia's northwest, with which Emily seems to have been fascinated and also intensely stirred at an artistic, even spiritual, level. The two, Cervantes and Carr, wrestled for first place in my mind even while I thought that neither set of travellers bore much resemblance to me and my friend. I couldn't say, not even at the time, why they had such a firm grip on my thoughts so that I could hardly shake them.

I kept returning to Emily Carr and her life as we know it from her voluminous writings and some good biographies. Heartbreaking stuff, I found, probably because I was a woman, too, once a girl, like Emily, and one also with longing and hope to achieve something with art. I was thinking how very much a proper upbringing damages people, stifling their natural impulses and at the same time failing to teach children anything useful about how the world works, so that once released from parental power, a young person strikes out in the world, often in rebellion and ignorance, in all the wrong ways, with wildly inappropriate ideas about what to expect. It takes a very long time for a so-raised person to find a workable balance in life. I think this was true of Emily, a child of a stern and proper Victorian/Edwardian British upbringing, and in some ways also true of me. And yet, I thought suddenly with pure love of my parents when they were young and poor, also with longing and pity, much as if they were characters in a book I was reading, and not the very material out of which my soul was made.



Impossible to forget Emily Carr, especially if you're a Western woman-artist, or the purely wonderful Don Quixote, but after a bit, the British writer-curator-intellectual Bruce Chatwin came back into my mind. His *The Songlines* recounts his drive through Australia's outback, discovering for himself the Aborigines' ancient songlines. I'm thinking that is what Emily Carr did seventy or more years earlier, but in her own barely-charted-by-the-settlers country, and although she wrote about that trip and others, she is mostly remembered for her paintings and sketches of the First Nations dwellings, their villages, their activities and especially their art: masks, baskets, canoes and totem poles, not her books. And now she is excoriated by some for appropriation, although for a long time she was thought remarkably brave when, with the sublime confidence borne of the British culture she was raised in, even though born and raised in Victoria, BC, she risked so much to follow her creative urge.

But the wonderful Lucinda and I had no such momentous goals, we were travelling for fun, out of curiosity, and for relief from everyday life, so I can't say why heroic journeys were so strong in my mind. Maybe irony was nudging me slyly. Although Lucinda's desire to find the place of her parents' meeting and marriage and of a time of indelible childhood happiness was also the product of a need for soul-fulfillment and, even without a work of art as its product, was not only meaningful, but beautiful. I'd asked my husband, for my sixtieth birthday, when I was close to the age Lucinda was in 2021, to take me back to my birthplace and the place of my first years, when we were encamped along the edge of the boreal forest in Saskatchewan. People from the family who'd been our closest neighbours when I was a very small child took us to visit the now houseless sites. That trip proved to me that I was indeed who I said I was, who I had always believed myself to be. I came back as satisfied as I needed to be, having no need to return.



Now, thinking of Chatwin and Carr and their companions, and of Don Quixote and his intrepid servant, Sancho Panza, and having ceded authority to Lucinda, so that she was firmly in the lead, although she didn't know or think that, and I was the trusted companion, made me laugh. She and the Don weren't a perfect match, because she is sensible and efficient, nor I and Sancho Panza, as I, even though not wanting to be the leader, balked at being the subservient one: Could it be that I was Quixote and she Sancho? Me, given to tilting at windmills, forever seeing or hearing things that weren't there, and with a tendency to lecture about honour out of a vision of the world a good hundred years out of fashion? But then, Lucinda was a leader by nature, strong and able, and yet also a very good poet. She would have made a terrible Sancho Panza.

Lucinda's desire to ground her own life and her love of fun, even her occasional willingness to go off track to follow an impulse (where I tend to nervously back off from both, remembering a friend's Ukrainian grandmother's dictum, *laugh laugh you're going to cry*) wouldn't describe Sancho's attitude. And whenever Quixote sailed too high above the stolid track of reason, Sancho could jolt the Don back to the hard facts of the moment. In fact, it is often hard to tell which one was the leader, even though one appeared to lead and thought unquestioningly that he did, and the other always followed, except when he didn't. And, as a result, there isn't a funnier, more enjoyable book on the planet.

As I took the first step in trying to think about how to write



Lucinda, I couldn't help pondering the controversies evoked by *The Songlines*. One was that Chatwin described his travel mates as a Russian and his girlfriend, sometimes even quoting the Russian. Later, it was discovered that Chatwin had been alone on his journey. In her writings, Carr claimed she was fifteen and alone on her first trip north, when she had actually been closer to twenty-eight and travelling with her sister. Both had broken memoirists' contract with their readers, that in nonfiction we are telling what really happened, that we have not made things up.

I noted to myself that we teachers of memoir can make all the rules we like about how to write them, but writers will break them; the best will invent their own forms. In the end, Carr's fib is trivial beside her paintings. As for Chatwin, whether the two Russians were on the trip or not is of no consequence to the truth of the book: that is, to the remarkable story of the Aborigines' songlines. As Farley Mowat once said when caught up in a similar controversy, "I never let the facts get in the way of the truth."

Then, how do you distinguish fiction from nonfiction? As a writer of both, and with the well-known vagaries of memory, and always trying to follow the first imperative to write well, I suspect there is little difference anyway.

### III

We arrived in Maple Creek around three-thirty in the afternoon, when the day was at its hottest—suffocatingly, head-swimmingly hot, the unbuffered sun crisply violent against our skin. The streets were deserted, you'd think not a soul lived in Maple Creek, but to begin with, there just aren't that many people in Saskatchewan, its population hovering around one million for many years, over it in good times and below it in bad ones, all rattling around in the province's 652,000 square kilometres. Statistics Canada's latest report places the provincial population at just under 1.2 million, probably an all-time high, while Alberta comes in at 4.5, British Columbia at 5.07, and Manitoba at 1.3 million. The total for the four Western provinces is about twelve million people, where Ontario and Quebec weigh in at close to twenty-five million. That most of the votes are in central Canada explains so-called "Western alienation." And in Maple Creek, in that perishingly hot Sunday afternoon in July, anybody with any sense was somewhere cool. Still, driving into a seemingly deserted town gives an odd feeling, the stuff of novels and films, and in the middle of the COVID pandemic as we were then, it crossed my mind that maybe everybody was dead. Or maybe that was just because we were people whose trade required vivid imaginations.

After driving slowly up and down streets, we found our B&B, unloaded our belongings, noted how carefully the proprietors had considered our every need, then saw the fans set everywhere that led us to discover we did not have air conditioning. I usually stayed in the small, fairly new inn on my trips between Calgary and my old home, but Lucinda's preference tended to be B&Bs if they were available. I recall hesitating at first, wary of what I felt was the intimacy of a B&B as opposed to the relative anonymity of a hotel, but having little experience with B&Bs, and trusting Lucinda, I'd raised no objection, and was in fact mildly curious.

Already this trip was breaking my long-established habit of focusing on the journey's destination and not the journey itself, innocuous and placid as it was. I was awakening to possibilities I'd long discounted as pointless or unpleasant, and the actual changes – a different time to stop, a different place to buy coffee, a B&B instead of an inn – were trivial and not the point: Their effect was to jar loose a set, dozy world that for me had too often been merely things to be endured in order to get to where I was going.



What I had fixed on concerning the B&B was the name of one of the proprietors, who I guessed was the daughter of a certain ranching couple whom I knew, liked, even admired. I was foolishly pleased about this, as if it proved my claim that I'd once lived in the district and knew people there, as if everybody in my circle back in the city thought I'd invented my thirty-three years in the area as a rancher's wife.

In any case, we never saw the proprietor, but a day or two after we'd left Maple Creek, I received an email from her telling me she'd found a necklace in the rug when she was vacuuming and had put it in the mail to my Calgary address. In fact, in 1976 Peter had given the necklace to me as my wedding present.

It was a fine gold chain with each of three tiny diamonds with miniscule gold rays fanning out around them set at intervals on the chain. I was more than a little chagrined to realize I hadn't even known it was missing. I forgave myself: lack of sleep, a strange bed, the unremitting heat of the night. But imagining the day I would have searched for it in my small store of jewellery and not found it, I felt a stab of shame and then grief for the day so many years earlier when the man who would be my husband for so many years, with a shyly embarrassed look on his face, gave it to me.

We decided to spend the rest of the day touring the Saskatchewan side of Cypress Hills Interprovincial Park, only thirty kilometres south of Maple Creek, although the road rises all the way through mostly fields of native grass – we were in ranching country – occasionally introduced grasses, or possibly planted hay including alfalfa, which is a legume and an herb and not a grass. Now I was the driver, and, because this was my home country, I could do it in my sleep. But I'd been gone thirteen years by then, years that suddenly seemed to have flashed by and, in that moment, to have been a long, bland nothingness, while my life as a countrywoman, now that I was back in it, was unstoppably vivid, a complex mixture of pictures, images, voices, scents, and sounds, recalled completely and with attendant emotions and sensations. I could scarcely bear the force of it, gritted my teeth, and shut the memories down.



In the years after I left, I'd stayed overnight in the park only a couple of times, although I had often stopped there to eat a sandwich at a remote picnic table under the trees. Then I would go for a solitary stroll among the lodgepole pines whose branches didn't start until maybe twenty feet up their straight trunks, trees that can grow to 160 feet in height, and under which there was no brush, only extended spongy layers of pine needles littered with cones. I would listen as I walked among them, savouring the clean scents that drifted around me of pine and soil, feeling the air as filled with life that I could not see or hear but that wafted delicately above or beside me before slowly thinning or moving away. Calmed and stilled, I would continue down the bumpy road driven, once you passed the park entrance going south, mostly by locals and the occasional tourist. Or my older sister and brother-in-law, after landing in Medicine Hat, driving in their rented car, half-lost and anxious in the absolute country darkness, on their way to be with me, my husband having died late that afternoon.

Still, nothing much I could see had changed since my last visit as I drove us around the interior of the park, sometimes on gravel roads, remarking to Lucinda on historical facts or brief memories of places Peter and I had been. For instance, the time we joined a couple of my city relatives for a New Year's Eve dinner and dance at a hotel high in the forest, and how eventually a couple of young men arrived together. They were wearing their best: shined-up riding boots, new riding jeans, fresh western-cut shirts, and with discreetly colourful scarves knotted just so around their necks. They were alone, and very young, clearly hoping to find single girls or at least a party. Seeing them, my relative asked me if they were the real thing, or only drugstore cowboys.

"Oh, they're the real thing," I said, keeping my mouth firmly shut on the question of real cowboys and their code of honour, for the most part a belief system that in practice, in my opinion, had more to do with their perception of their own manhood than the women it was in part directed at. We drove past a couple of private cabins about whose owners I might have told stories, but I passed by, resolutely saying nothing. Maybe I'd been gone too long; I didn't care anymore. The owners were usually the prosperous elite of the area, and although my husband and I were never a part of it, they and their tiny subculture had always interested me. Particularly what I saw as their understanding of urban life from maybe their years at college or their prosperity that allowed them to spend time in cities if they wanted to, and out of which they'd adapted mostly urban style that had mixed in with their country habits of decorum and the country way of breaking that decorum.

It occurs to me now, although it didn't at the time, that those people had aged, too, that some of them had died, or lost their health or their money, that other bad things would have happened to some of them; the emotion they had aroused in me, a confused envy at their tightness as a group and all the fun they seemingly were having that I wasn't, no longer applying. I didn't try to explain any of this to Lucinda. Leave that to the sociologists, I thought, although I couldn't imagine a sociologist being interested enough to study them, because they were, of course, all white people, with roots firmly in the settler generation and, if they were not resolutely heterosexual, few ostensibly knew of homosexuality, and it was never mentioned.



What a strange world the country is, I mused, now that, through television and better roads and vehicles, it is so mixed in with urban values that it's not recognizable for what it used to be, not even from 1976, when I first went there to live. Now I was once again a city woman. Sort of. In truth, I confess I was a hybrid, or else I was neither; I was something else, something uncomfortable, like an artist. It made no difference that fame and fortune both eluded me; at eighty-three I had learned to yawn in the face of most of that. I urge the reader interested in this question to read Coetzee's *Summertime.*

The stories I might have told as we circled around the village of summer cabins were simply facts about the lives of people I barely knew and whose stories mostly didn't affect me. I imagined telling Lucinda what I knew: No, she would be bored; it wasn't nobility that kept me from saying anything; it was my desire not to lose my audience, and just maybe, just a little, the ordinary facts of those ordinary lives bored me, too, even though they also fascinated me when I enhanced them a little, polished the details, found exquisite language in which to tell them, or better for me, I went off the rails and began to search out the unfathomable mystery at the bottom of the places where people make life-settling decisions, to try to lay out the desires, to speak of the suffering that mostly goes unspoken of, unrecorded, unmitigated other than by time. To puzzle over the endless tumult of human souls. I was never "of" those people, I knew it, a stubborn part of me never wanted to be, and trying to be a writer, endlessly watching and thinking, made my alienation more irremediable and more profound.

But I decided to say nothing of what I knew to Lucinda. Once I took a visitor on a drive past a row of small houses, each on its own few acres on a country road, and on a whim told my passenger the story, the parts that were general knowledge, of each household as we drove past. I was trying to do something that had little to do with entertaining my guest, who must have been astonished, not to mention bored, and as I told story after story as I knew them, instead of stopping when I thought my visitor might be getting restless or common sense intervened, I grew more and more interested, bordering on the obsessive: I couldn't have said why I was doing this or what was it I was searching for.

Of course, twenty or more years later, I knew that I'd been puzzling over the enigma of our lives; I was subconsciously drafting a novel: I was thinking, everyone's life is made of story – the experts tell us that humans need narrative, the need for narrative is built into us, we all struggle to find a coherent narrative for our lives even if we have to invent one, moving things around and leaving out the parts that don't fit or hammering them into shape until they do.

But Virginia Woolf, in 1917, in "The Mark on the Wall" wrote: "As we face each other in omnibuses and underground railways we are looking into the mirror; that accounts for the vagueness, the gleam of glassiness in our eyes. And the novelists in future will realize more and more the importance of these reflections, for of course there is not one reflection but an almost infinite number; those are the depths they will explore, those phantoms they will pursue, leaving the description of reality more and more out of their stories, taking a knowledge of it for granted, as the Greeks did and Shakespeare perhaps . . ."

But despite Woolf and her at least partial correctness, and despite Salman Rushdie's declaration that "If [Milan Kundera] is right . . . the realist tradition is doomed to a kind of endless repetitiveness," and further, that "we must turn to irrealism and find new ways of approaching the truth through lies" (*Languages of Truth: Essays 2003–2020*), in the face of postmodernism I remain a hopeless humanist, and also a realist in love with exploring human consciousness and character and turning facts or semi-facts or ideas into meaningful, coherent narratives.



But that sweltering late Sunday afternoon in Cypress Hills Park, I was remembering how, almost fifty years earlier, I'd made my first visit here on another too-hot, too-dry July Sunday, and how I hadn't been able to understand why the park seemed, at least then, to have an almost mystical place in the lives of the people of the area. Having come from forests myself, born in Nipawin, Saskatchewan, and taken at once into "the bush," that is, the edge of the boreal forest to where my father, for a brief period including the births of four of the five of us in the hospital in Nipawin (Cree for "a place to sleep," the town incorporated only three years before I was born) had had a sawmill, I should have understood the attraction of trees.

Many years later, long gone from there, I saw that the land we settlers tore apart and called our own must have been the hunting and gathering land of the Swampy Cree people, to the extent that traditional First Nations people thought of land as theirs. Probably their descendants were and are those now living on the Red Earth Cree Nation Reserve established in 1875 by Treaty 5, east of where, about sixty years later, our government had invited us whites to settle, and where we would find swamps to avoid or drain, trees to cut, their stumps and roots to be dug out and burned to clear land for farming.

I remember at the edge of a field a long row of tangled stumps, limbs, and roots piled high over my child's head, smouldering and stinking, the earth itself dripping from the roots, the roots wrenched out of the soil giving off their own smell of death, the occasional flame flickering upward, as a neighbour, in the established method of burning, tried to rid his field of the last of the detritus. All of it the unending back-breaking labour of pulling the stumps and roots from the earth and piling them at the edge of the cleared field, in those days and in that place done usually with horses and in the midst of tormenting hordes of mosquitoes and black flies. That which began as the Creator's precious gift to the Swampy Cree.

I was still close enough to the places of my birth and earliest childhood that when I first saw Cypress Hills Park, at about six hundred metres the highest point between the Rockies and the Labrador Peninsula, I was unimpressed. Trees – so what? But they were lodgepole pines – there are no cypresses in the Cypress Hills – and once I saw a half-ton truck on the

Trans-Canada between Gull Lake and Medicine Hat travelling east pulling a half-dozen long trunks of lodgepole pines fastened together at one end where they poked up above the roof of the cab they rested on, their length fanned out and fastened to a small, wheeled cart, so that, by their deliberate teepee shape, I knew they were harvested for a teepee or a First Nations' lodge. This sight had thrilled me: a connection to ancient history, alive and not ancient after all.

It was a long time before I came to appreciate what Peter told me about the park, that it was so high it had its own micro-climate, that the glaciers hadn't reached to the top, that therefore plant species grew there that didn't grow on the prairie below, because they'd been scraped away by the glaciers ten to fourteen thousand years ago, and that the grassland people went there on the hottest summer Sundays to lounge around on the grass and eat chicken and watermelon and have a beer or two, because at that time of year the park was as many as twenty degrees cooler than the prairie below, such a relief after living and working for days in the unrelenting, parching heat.



Every July during the seventies when I first visited the park, we used to get about two weeks of plus-forty-degree temperatures, just when the ranchers, indeed, anybody with some hay land would be out haying. Most people didn't have swathers with air-conditioned cabs then; Peter hayed in that heat with a large umbrella attached to his tractor and his wide-brimmed straw hat as his only protection from the sun, and nothing for protection against the heat that he claimed to love. Imagine the women trying to keep the house cool, the kids from sunburn and sunstroke, the babies and toddlers from heat rash, standing over the boiling potatoes and roasting meat in the oven to provide the calories the men needed to keep up their strength for the real work.

But sometimes, during that period of intense heat, when Sunday came, many men would park their haying equipment or do their irrigation sets so they could leave for a few hours, and the women would pack lunches, and families would drive up into the relief of the relative cool and shade of the park. But what I came to love was never the forests of the park, but from its highest points, the unobstructed prairie nearly two thousand feet below, rolling out for miles in three directions to the low, building-free horizon, so that the view, as prairie artist after prairie artist has seen, became mostly the enormous, constantly changing, riotous or serene sky, the prairie a narrow ribbon below it, fading and pale, glistening now and then, as the sun cast its rays across the early spring green, then pale-yellow grass of summer.

That late Sunday afternoon in July now two years ago, I drove us to the top of the park along narrowing roads turning to gravel as we went higher until we'd reached the lookout point at the northwestern edge of the Hills with its sharp drop to the prairie. We parked, got out, and stood still, gazing at the prairie billowing out below, at the dots of cattle and strokes that were horses grazing peacefully in the grassy abundance that, far away from us, blended into sky. I said, "There's a man in Maple Creek whose grandfather owned that land below us. I wonder what made him sell it." The same man was descended from someone further back, a North-West Mounted Police officer who'd come west on the original great trek in 1873 and '74. That status belongs to the highest, truest level of prairie society, at least in that region: to descend from a Mountie who'd come west on the trek called the March West. Charles Wilkins called it *The Wild Ride* in his book by that name; Griffiths and Cruise called it *The Great Adventure*, both titles likely also referring to the endeavour of the early policing of the West.

Otherwise, around the province, the proudest heritage came from descending from the earliest settler family in the area. This particular bit of hubris has faded since the colonists' myth of the empty, unused land that they would finally make productive as God intended has been deconstructed in the light of First Nations' far greater claim and the recognition at last of the horrifying abuses they suffered. And also in the light of the current climate crisis, this being a subject far too big and with too many controversies, especially in the midst of agricultural country, for me to tackle here.

At some point on our journey, I remember telling Lucinda about that trip by the North-West Mounted Police, bits and pieces: the trouble they had because they didn't know the prairie, how they ran out of food, got dysentery from drinking the wrong water, had to establish a sick camp, how their animals were starving and dying because the Mounties, mostly recruited from the British Isles, Ontario, and Quebec, thought that only the green grass in the wet patches was any good, when in fact the nutrition was all in the great expanse in every direction of dried, pale grasses that we saw below us stretching out to the horizon, and that, in their ignorance, they scorned.



"One of the things you have to get used to," I must have said, "if you're going to live in Saskatchewan's southwest or the southeast of Alberta all the way to the foothills, is the wind." Odd that I should have been thinking of wind, because there hadn't been a breath of it since we'd left Calgary. Such stillness is rare on the southern prairie; prairie people treasure it at the same time as, if it isn't at dusk or sunrise, both of which are often utterly calm, it makes them uneasy, as if it has to be the stillness before the cataclysm, and when it's so very hot as it often is in the summer, you feel the wind as the only thing that makes the heat bearable. Newcomers hate it, but prairie people are used to it; unless it's extreme, they barely notice it, while new arrivals can find it impossible to live with and often leave because of it. Life in the southwest, I may well have said to Lucinda, is a constant adaptation to the wind, including the stoicism after it has done its worst damage to your life, destroying sometimes even crops by causing them to "lodge," never mind taking down your trees and smashing your buildings.

If, as the song from the popular television comedy out of Saskatchewan called *Corner Gas* goes, on the prairie you can see your dog run away for days, you can see the weather coming, too. One day Peter and I drove to Lethbridge (five hours west of us, a city with a population of about one hundred thousand) for the annual summer fair, Whoop-Up Days, named for the whiskey fort called Fort Whoop-Up, the notorious goings-on that in 1873 helped create the North-West Mounted Police. One of history's ironic footnotes is that when the Mounties, after their gruelling trip, arrived at the fort eager to finally demonstrate their policing skills, all the residents and hangers-on, having heard of their coming, had lit out from there and not a soul was to be found. The fort was empty. But the frontier name sticks, and you can still see where the fort was along the valley near the confluence of the St. Mary and Oldman Rivers near Lethbridge.



Peter had bought tickets to the grandstand show headlining the country and western singer Janie Fricke. Fricke was a crossover from the mainstream; she doesn't do what I think of as the worst of the country and western singers' vocal mannerisms (peace to those who love them) and with her marvellous voice, she was a joy to listen to. We heard her pure, strong soprano soaring out across the miles of near-silent prairie. Even the gophers must have poked up their heads from their burrows to listen.

Her crew had set up a low stage with tall amplifiers, various cables, musical instruments, microphones on stands, and other unnameable gear. The stage itself was set at a carefully calculated angle so that nobody, musicians or audience, would be blinded by the intense red-orange rays of the setting sun, and so that the musicians and singer had their backs to an enormous, early evening prairie sky, unblemished and glowing with the near-magical light that prairie dwellers never find anywhere else on the planet.

The concert began. For almost an hour, those of us who lifted our eyes from the stage below us saw what at first was a dark dot miles away on the far distant horizon and behind the stage as it appeared to approach us slowly, but actually was moving very fast. Nobody that I know of warned the musicians even as the dot became, perhaps, a storm cloud, still miles away, but coming ever closer, and closer still, growing in size, although never massive, while at the last possible minute there were a few warning shouts from men in the audience to the people on the stage, too late, and then – wham – it was on us.

Or rather, it was on the people and equipment on the stage, racing from behind them, as if with conscious intent, unstoppable, catching them full blast, completely unaware. A huge, dust-filled, plowing, grey and blue-black narrow ball of wind and dirt, relentless, deviating not one millimetre from what seemed from the moment it appeared on the far horizon to be its goal. If it had come in to the right or to the left only a few yards either away, it would have missed the stage and the audience on the bleachers; we were stunned at its accuracy; how did Mother Nature pull that one off? It had been the only mark in the entire endless, giant sky, as if a prairie God, or maybe it was First Nations ancestors, had taken offence at all that ridiculous electronic caterwauling violating the prairie's purity, and had decided to blow the racket-makers off the prairie. Thinking of their steady low drumbeats, moccasin-clad feet rhythmically thudding against the grass, the coyote-like cries of the singers. *That,* they were telling us, *is the true prairie.* Could some very annoyed medicine man/healer have conjured up that ball of wind? First Nations people have plenty to be annoyed about, and we were a few miles from more than one reserve. We white people are fools when we discount that kind of power.

In slow motion, the huge speakers started to fall over. I recall at least one of the musicians trying to hold one up, while the stands got hit next, while we covered our faces and our beer, protecting children's faces, hanging onto our hats, turning away at least our torsos so the stinging dirt wouldn't hit us straight in the face.

Prairie people all, nobody got angry or started looking for the villains responsible for this, nobody pulled out a six-shooter or an AK-47 and shot out the sky as they might have in the fabulous USA, or at least as movies and television would have us believe. We just waited for it to pass; if we'd stood, we sat back down again, found our hats and pulled them down more firmly, wiped our faces, brushed ourselves off, laughed along with the half-frightened, half-amazed children, and waited for the program to get rolling again. Which it did, if I remember accurately, after some righting of gear but not even a short break. Crazy! But also, awesome.

And yet, one afternoon on our hay farm down in the Frenchman River Valley, we saw something dark approaching at the bottom of the southeast sky just above the rim of the valley. I went outside to see if I could make out what was coming, while Peter and his friend came from the Quonset where we stored machinery and equipment and Peter kept tools and where he worked on his tractors, baler, swather, all-terrain vehicle, snowmobile, and whatever else we had in the way of machinery in those days. We three, some distance apart, stopped on the road,

I on one side of it and they on the other, which ran between us from the entrance to the house's yard down to the barn and corrals just above the Frenchman River, where it made a lovely, placid loop around the yard. I was closer to the house and poised to race back into it: Peter and his pal, to my left and behind me as I stood looking into the southeast sky, were ready too to run for the Quonset if things got dangerous.

As the wind drew closer, I saw it was pink – a wall of dusky-pink wind and dirt – not a flashy hot or a pale peony pink, but a dulled brownish pink, and thickly opaque, like a pink smoothie, and coming so fast that the poplars behind me began to whip, and even the caraganas, also behind me to my right, were starting to snap and dance in expectation. It was coming straight for us, sweeping down the hillside to the valley bottom, crossing the narrow river, slamming the corrals, bending our *steel* corral gates and panels, upending steel-rimmed feeders, blowing away anything not fastened down and a few things that were.



We ran, I for my kitchen, the two men for the wide-open mouth of the Quonset, a crazy thing to do, but being rural men, they believed in their own toughness, and they were totally curious, and had lived in the heart of nature all their lives – this was something exciting and new, this weird wall of wind – they didn't want to miss a thing, so they could compare notes with their friends later on coffee row. Or else add this anomaly to their already vast store of knowledge about the prairie. And if there were a cure for such a thing as this breathtakingly precise, freight-train wind, being rural men, they were probably already planning it.

From my kitchen window I watched it roar on up the yard through, in that naturally treeless land, our beloved stand of poplars, breaking off their limbs, even their trunks, collapsing them so that we couldn't get in or out of the yard until they were sawed up and taken away. Then it was gone, heading northeast up out of the valley, beyond us.

We found later that it had taken the roof off a steel building on a farm southwest of us and on the flatland above, and went on to take out another one – brand new, just finished – at a farm site a couple of miles northeast of us, also on the flatland above the valley. Strangely, it might have deviated a little in its path when it swept up through the corrals, missing the barn beside them, then funnelled itself up the gravel road between the house and the Quonset, missing both of them, and right between where the three of us had been standing, crashing down our trees, before racing across the hayfields, up the northeastern valley side and taking out that new long metal shed.

Later, I would be amazed by the quantity of greenery those few poplar tree-trunks had held up, and that we so loved for their shade and the pretty way their leaves turned, rustled, or clapped delicately, or shone like small moons, or were dappled or dark or bright. They smothered our deck, crushed my flower-beds, buried the passage between the groups of trees, all those wonderful green leaves and smooth grey-green branches in mere seconds piled up now, over my head, all the way to the roofline of our one-storey house.

In the abrupt ensuing silence, the atmosphere seemed to crackle, and an odour filled the air, a smell new to me, that came from the trees, the branches piled up, smashed and criss-crossed, the trunks broken, their ends jagged, the interior wood still fresh, and pale, creamy to near white, damp with life, and I thought – how could I not? – that this was the life-blood of the trees as they lay wounded, scintillating in the air, it was the smell of their dying, so that I stood still breathing in that smell, in wonder and pity.

Later, the meteorologists would identify this as a "plow wind," meaning that it travelled in a straight line, unlike a swirling hurricane or rotating tornado. If I'd been struck at the Fricke concert by the accuracy of the wind as if guided by an unseen hand, once again I – we – were mystified by the way it ran up the lane hitting the corrals but missing the barn, deviating to miss the men in the Quonset, yet not so far as to strike me just slamming the kitchen door behind me, then deviating back east again to tear the roof off that brand-new long shed a couple of miles northeast of us. As if it wasn't interested in doing *us* serious damage. But what a ridiculous idea, I thought, and think now, but with fingers crossed behind my back. Were not those trees serious damage?

Years later, we would see this phenomenon again, but at the ranch out on the open prairie once, and then twenty years later only me, because Peter was gone by then, same location, a second time. I swear the prairie has a soul, although it might be not the very land itself – but instead, that of the millennia of ancient peoples who lived, hunted, slept, and prayed on it, and made the points, stone circles, hammers, and axe heads we still found on it, and during or after the glaciers when the great herds of buffalo, sixty or so million of them, swept across it and left behind sometimes their skulls (all gone when I was there) or the casings of their horns the same way that I could get up in the morning and find at the bottom of the kitchen steps the transparent, roughly scaled skins of snakes lying on the cement pad, but the horn casings were half-buried in the blown dirt. How I loved that place. Everything about it. Such lives, such a long gathering of beings for whom the prairie was who they were – surely, they make a soul with its own desires, needs, beliefs. We should honour this, although we do not.

And that soul knew what fit and what did not. When the Nature Conservancy of Canada and various other groups, including the people of the Nekaneet Nation north of us in the Cypress Hills and a few government officials, held the inauguration ceremony of our ranch becoming the Old Man on His Back Prairie and Heritage Conservation Area, owned and run by the Nature Conservancy of Canada on July 18, 1996, it was out on the prairie. The site included a sweat lodge at one of the highest points on the grass, but near the single road running through our land so that everyone could find the place easily. The minute that the ceremony in the sweat lodge concluded, that same ball or wall of wind came whooping across the prairie, again from the southeast (as had the one at the Janie Fricke concert), was on us in seconds, and it blew all the hides and the blankets that had been pulled so taut you couldn't work a finger between a hide and the outdoors right off the dome-shaped willow frame. People went racing to the north, east, and west down the hillside trying to catch the pieces, and that was the end of the outdoor ceremony, because next came a downpour.



It soaked us all and meant that many people got stuck in the mud on that gravel road trying to get down to the community hall about five or six miles from where the ceremony had taken place, and where it would carry on with a feast and more ceremonies and speeches. At the end we had a round dance: ranchers with bemused half-embarrassed smiles on their faces, the Nekaneet people relaxed and easy, and a lot of us dancing with them in pure delight. Some feeling that we were being allowed in on a great secret that we had always, privately, wondered about but could never ask.

And then, amazement after amazement, twenty years later the second ceremony to celebrate the success of the Old Man on His Back Prairie and Heritage Conservation Area was held, this time in the ranch's house yard rather than out on the prairie, and in a big white tent erected about twenty feet from the new building the Nature Conservancy of Canada had moved onto the place with a meeting room and living quarters for the scientists who came in the summer to study the flora and fauna. It was to be a bison barbecue, and we were all hungry for that, maybe fifty or sixty of us from dignitaries to neighbours – we couldn't wait to scarf down those bison steaks. We sat inside the tent on folding chairs in three long rows down both sides of the long folding tables that every church hall in the country has, and the first table began to be served. The food was good, the talk was great, we were all hugely happy because we did this impossible thing, and twenty years later it was still working! Such ebullience, a kind that only being out on the prairie all of a fine June day can infuse in people.

And then, it happened again. This time it came from the west – a few people had seen it coming, but the land rose a bit in that direction, so the view wasn't great, and we were having too much fun, didn't pay attention, and then – whammo! We were hit again, this time with a wind so strong that it blew the food off peoples' plates, it blew away folding chairs, it partly knocked down the big white tent where we'd been sitting, and the driving rain came with it. Some NCC person who had kept his head in all the turmoil shouted to us to run for the new building with its deck that ran across its front and was right beside us, and so we did. Or tried to: the wind and rain were so powerful it was more than we could do to actually run. We pushed ourselves against the wind, we shoved ourselves sideways as the steaks flew off our plates, and our desserts and hats vanished across the prairie and things flapped and flew around us. Oh my God, it was fun! We couldn't stop laughing!

We crowded into the small building then, soaked, water dripping off us and leaving puddles everywhere on the brand-new floor, and we made our speeches, although we cut them short, and a funny thing – with Peter gone – I seemed to be one of the very few there who remembered the same thing had happened twenty years earlier. Only then, it was the sweat lodge coverings that blew away and anything else lying around on the ground and within the ancient stone circles where the women of the Nekaneet had been sitting. Had the Ancient Ones said again, as they had twenty years earlier, okay, it's done, now move along? "It is finished," as the Elder of Elders, or "healer" as the people described him, Red Bear, had said to me when I asked him to explain that first wind that blew away the hides and blankets covering their sweat lodge. The University of Saskatchewan built a building when he died and named it after him. I've written more about this in *Wild Stone Heart: An Apprentice in the Fields,* including more that the Elder said to me, more about his dream of how the ancestors felt about this handover of land.



All of us, the first time and twenty years later, the second time, were so happy, so exhilarated, so filled with delight. Pretty dumb, eh, you'll be thinking, but I think we felt acknowledged as nature lovers, loving nature in a more intense way than most nature-loving people; we *felt* the prairie and the wind and rain and the blowing grass with our deepest beings as if we were – sometimes, luckily, when it laid down the law like that in the middle of our good time – a *part* of it, and we all knew who, in the end, was the boss, and it wasn't us. And we were okay with that, so great were the rewards of it.

And I'm now going to admit that maybe not all of us *loved* that storm, but I counter that by saying that the mood inside the cramped, wet meeting rooms was a warm, laughter-filled, cheerful one. Nobody was angry about what had happened, we varied in mood from laughing with it to just maybe – there were a couple of people from the Eastern Canada there – hiding our fear of that uncontrollably powerful, water-filled wind. When you are born and raised and make your living all your life in the natural world, weather feels different to you than it does to people who spend most of their lives indoors and who, sadly in this modern world, get a taste of nature only a few weeks each year.

Meanwhile, back in Maple Creek, about sixty miles north of where those ceremonies on what had been our land were, Lucinda and I were in bed at the close of the first day of our journey, but I don't think either of us slept much. It was simply too hot; the day's heat, having condensed and built up under the roof, didn't dissipate all night, and, in that appalling heat the fans weren't up to the job – it was so hot I'm not sure air conditioning could have done a lot better. But the fridge had in it everything a person could ask for: cereal, yogurt, cream, fresh fruit, and there was a coffeemaker and coffee, a toaster and bread, and a very nicely appointed bathroom, and comfortable beds, so in every other way, the place was great.



We drove around the town of Maple Creek, which had been settled in 1882 and incorporated in 1903 – called, colloquially, Cow Town, as was Calgary – with me at the wheel, before we headed south on Highway 21, this time past the park entrance and on for about another eighty kilometres until we reached the junction where the highway went east to Eastend and west to the town of Consul and then on south to the Willow Creek border crossing into the USA.

The next border crossing west of Willow Creek is called Wild Horse; a long-dead cowboy, an old man then, told me a tale of roping a gone-wild "bank horse" there when he was a young man, and how it bucked its way down onto the dry white lake bed and out and up again and around in circles, up and down, before it gave up, my cowboy-friend still on it, and settled down to the business of rounding up cows. It turns out a bank horse is one repossessed by a bank from a rancher-cowboy for non-payment of loans and turned loose by the bank on the prairie, where such horses then ran wild in herds. Who knows how long this horse had been running free before my friend needed a new saddle horse, his old one having gone lame. The horse he roped and mounted might never have been broken or might once have been broken and, wisely, objected to having to go back to work.

At the T-junction we would turn east for the roughly sixty-kilometre drive to Eastend. But first, about sixty kilometres south of the park gate, we had to stop at a flat, unplowed place leading off the road, in country parlance, an "approach," with, directly ahead of us and on each side, farmers' fields. A herd of about twenty pronghorns were grazing maybe twenty metres from us. They were once called antelope or pronghorn antelope – *Antilocapra americana* – now we must call them only "pronghorns," as they aren't related to the African antelope. It was Lucinda's first close look at them, so I pulled up so that she could study them and take some photos with her phone. I'd advanced the car very slowly so as not to disturb them, and we sat quietly, Lucinda smiling, though probably not even realizing she was, as she watched them.

I told her I'd once seen a herd of over eighty of them, but that people said years before their gatherings could be as many as two hundred. "Habitat destruction," Peter had explained to me. "Farmers plowed up so much prairie that they have to go further for food." Over the years, we began to see them further and further north from what had been their home territory, places like the Butala ranch roughly thirty kilometres south from where we sat gazing at the pronghorns, and a further sixteen to the Montana border. Nearly all the land that had been ours was native prairie and, at a bit over thirteen thousand acres, was large enough to contain such a big species.

When I saw one or two of them far from large stands of native grass, grazing in a ditch next to a farmer's field, I always had an internal flinch. What was this beautiful creature doing, munching tame, that is, planted, often non-native, not local, grass in a ditch beside a busy road when it should have been out skimming the prairie sixty or more miles south? The plowing of land had turned an iconic prairie creature into the equivalent of a homeless person digging in other peoples' garbage, turning it into a scavenger. Then I felt angry, and sad. In my life, the only things I ever saw stop the advance of the plow, besides drought, were government programs and the marketplace. Nowadays, though, environmental programs were gaining a degree of power to influence such decisions. After a few minutes I backed the car up onto the road again, pointed it east, and drove on.



But at a certain stretch of highway a few miles from where we stopped to watch the pronghorns, I couldn't help but brake and point to where the land flowed south for thirty or so kilometres to a wide stretch of low hills, which melted into a soft aqua and mauve, rising thinly to meet the bottom of the endless sky. That day, and in that light, you couldn't see where the hills stopped and the sky began, the blue-green fading and melding into the pale blue. But, as your eyes rose, the sky gradually turned to a deeper blue, and then, higher, became bluer again, and although you would have to lean out of the car to see it, at its apex, in the high heat, it melted into an intense near-cobalt. Pointing south to that pencil-thin range of low hills, I said to Lucinda, "*That's* the ranch."

That may have been the first time that my heart gave a lurch, and I had to swallow, my lighthearted approach to our trip less firmly in place than it had been, as I put my foot back on the gas and we drove on toward the village of Eastend, not much different in size at around a population of six hundred than it was the day I first arrived there forty-five years before. Although, after the nearly complete Tyrannosaurus rex fossil was found a few miles down the valley from our hay farm, tourists and scientists alike arrived, and the population swelled for a while; a few new businesses opened, mostly small art galleries and antique shops before, gradually, people forgot about the T-Rex, or else a new one was found in the northern states, and excitement about the one near us diminished again.

I'm driving through relentless heat, but I'm thinking about mud and snow, and ruts in muddy snow, and half-ton trucks rocking back and forth in the deep furrows, their tailpipes spewing pink and mauve exhaust into the dark and cold, snow blowing hard past their lights, and the laughter of men in their ragged-wrist heavy denim, thickly lined work jackets, and their worn boots, and the jingle of harness and spurs and the pungent smell of manure in the corrals. I'm thinking of those days. I'm thinking of Peter, who became my husband for more than thirty years, and how everything changed then as it once had when I was a child, and our family left the countryside for the city. And how, after he died, as surely as if I'd committed a crime, and as in myths and fairy tales, I was ejected into the world, a woman on the edge of old, left to gather up the tattered shreds of her once-whole life and knit them back again, if she could. Because in truly rural communities, anyone not born there is almost never fully accepted. With no one to support or protect her other than her husband (who rarely even notices how she is treated by people he has known all his life) after his death, widows are pretty much abandoned. Although, of course, I admit to being an extreme example because I wrote books about their home and their lives that actually got published and sometimes even made the Canadian bestseller list. I should have understood how that would ostracize me. I don't think it even occurred to me that I should choose another subject. I had no other subject of such potential power and uniqueness.

One of the first of many of the stories I heard about happenings in the village before my arrival was how a young man had arrived as pastor for a church, and how he had been harassed and hounded by some people who were, I believe, his parishioners, until one morning when the town got up, he was gone, his belongings gone too, the front door of his house left wide open. He was just . . . gone. When told, I thought how distressingly awful this was, and smugly, *that will never happen to me.* And yet, I had read Shirley Jackson's "The Lottery," and should have known better.

Thirty-some years later I would leave almost the same way, not even taking my furniture with me or saying goodbye to anyone but a handful of people, almost all newcomers too. I'm reminded today of a young woman who came around the time I did, also as bride of a local young man, who was well treated, not only because she was a decent, pleasant, intelligent person, but because the family she had married into not only did not participate in any nastiness, but would not have tolerated anything else but kindness and generosity toward her.

During the last week of Peter's life, when he was in the palliative room of the hospital in a nearby town, I arrived every morning by seven or earlier and stayed with him until evening visiting hours began, when, despite his eventually asking me to stay, I refused, because I did not want to see the people who would come to see him, or deal with the unpleasantness inevitable for me around them. This, even though in mere days, although I did not know that then, he would be gone forever. I no longer cared about my wifely reputation or the demands of duty. He didn't know, for example, that a pair of women sat with me and two or three other visitors in the waiting room across from the palliative care room where he lay dying, and chatted together, but refused to speak to me.

I'm sure he told the other visitors who came in the evening that I had had to go home to feed the horses in the corral, which was true, a reason instantly acceptable to country people – animals and crops just about always come before people in the country – and although the horses might have waited a couple more hours, I was beyond tired, afraid, struggling not to despair, and in pain anticipating this unthinkable loss at the same time as I pretended that it wasn't already happening. I knew that when his visitors were with him, Peter didn't need me, and I simply could not do what convention expected of me: sitting there smiling politely, maybe once in a while interjecting a comment, otherwise being ignored, and Peter never noticing. And I, as usual, giving him full benefit of the doubt because he was too ill to think straight, much less carry on a reasonable conversation. I wonder, now that he is dead for sixteen years, if he has figured out yet what life there was like for me, and how enraged I sometimes still am about it.



I suppose this is another example of my lifelong practice of running away from situations I couldn't fix. I no longer knew why, at such a time, I should endure the slights. I suppose, irrational as it is – or is it? Grief therapists would know – a part of me was angry with Peter for abandoning me by illness and death, but also, irrationally perhaps, for not saying one word about how I should live when he was gone. Other widows have told me they had felt the same way, despite their circumstances being different from mine. If not for the dreams after he was gone when he came to see me night after night, I would still be in a secret rage at him for dying. But even in dreams he never did tell me how I should live, which I know was a question about some other thing I still can't name. That was a conversation he could never have had, not because he couldn't think it, but because his survival had always depended on not speaking any but conventional words, and pushing down everything else. For years after he died, my anger at him was such that I couldn't even grieve, and I was angry about that, too, until finally I came to see that being in a state of not-grieving was also grieving.

And I wonder now if maybe I knew not only that Peter was dying, but that very soon, in a week, perhaps only days, he would be gone forever, and that then I would not be able to stay where I'd lived for the last thirty-three years, would have to go wherever I could find to go, to a future I couldn't bring myself to imagine, and once I was gone, other than my loss of Peter, I would be free of all the rest that had caused me such misery for so long. In my confused terror, disgust, and unacknowledged profound sorrow, in my rage, not even realizing what was going on in my subconscious, I was already detaching from all of it. Even from Peter himself, whose coming absence I couldn't bring myself to think about, and whose present suffering was mute and gallant, not to be shared, as he had refused to share so much else of his inner life, even though now I was beside him from early morning to early evening every single day. At last, it seems to me now, I was naming things for what they were. Or sixteen years after the events of that week and the thirty-some years that led up to them, was I finally naming them all for what they were?

In writing this book, I tried at last to find a "narrative conception" of my own life. Hard to do, when, as an acquaintance had just said to me, “You’ve had about five lives!” And I replied, “Yes, and I’m ready for the next one to start,” and only after she’d been gone an hour or so, realizing the “next one” would not be the move to a different city, the “right” city finally, as I so often thought of doing but never could locate, or acquiring another husband and moving to his, I hope, palatial house, or even, perhaps, somehow returning into my Palliser Triangle past.

I see now that the last move, or what I thought then would be my last move, wouldn’t involve trucks and burly men, or the ridding oneself of condos or land, hay, or cattle. Instead, without belongings or companions, I’d pass through the invisible membrane from this fleshly state to a bodiless one in the surely blissful city of the not-dead, but the departed, on the other side of what we thought was reality.

# THREE

# FIRE

## I

Lucinda and I were sailing merrily east on Highway 13 on the last stretch into Eastend, over the curving, bumpy, black-topped road, past the farms and grazing land of former acquaintances or sometimes friends, past deserted farmsteads of long-dead people – stories everywhere we looked – splaying lazily out on each side of us. We went past the first side road leading north to Ravenscrag, with the tops of the craggy, buff-coloured buttes visible near the once-village lit up in spots with brilliant white. The white spots, so bright in the sun that nobody could miss them, are a puzzle to strangers, so, never one to miss an opportunity to tell a story, I said, "Those are clay deposits, such good quality clay that it used to be transported to Medicine Hat, where there had once been more than one factory that made clay goods 'for various purposes, including irrigation and sewer pipes and tiles and eventually pottery, but in the beginning, bricks.' Many tons of them."

In 1883 a very large natural gas field was discovered under Medicine Hat. The largest well, drilled in 1904, made industrial activity cheap and transformed the small city into an industrial centre for all of Alberta. The clay outcroppings we were looking at on the valley walls of the northern Frenchman River, which was originally called the White Mud, exist in pockets along those valley walls. In the Eastend-Ravenscrag area, if you knew the trails, and all the local people did, you could easily follow them into the places where the clay was mined, loaded into trucks and carried away to Medicine Hat. I was at first fascinated by this activity, but in all my years there, and despite the tire tracks and evidence of excavation, I never once saw a truck being loaded with clay, nor met or passed one on the highway that I recognized as such, so that the whole business had rather the quality of myth to me, the excavation sites resembling abandoned archaeological digs, but different in that in the high summer sun they radiated an otherworldly white.

The roads in and out of Ravenscrag were gravel, and neither of us wanted to risk a flat tire, so we kept on going northeasterly toward Eastend on the road also called the Redcoat Trail, because it follows, although in the opposite direction than we were going, the track the North-West Mounted Police took on their trip west to provide law and order to the North-West Territories. They left Dufferin, Manitoba, south of Winnipeg at the American border, on July 8, 1874, and about thirteen hundred kilometres later arrived in Calgary, Alberta, or the fort that became Calgary in the North-West Territories, which became, in 1905, partly, Alberta. Their route mostly crossed the grasslands and south of the highway that we were currently driving on.

Here I quote from Wikipedia: "275 men" (otherwise given as 300 men), "310 horses, 143 draught oxen and 187 Red River carts and wagons," plus "two field guns and two mortars . . . cattle to use as food, and mowing machines for making hay." The haying equipment was to make hay to feed the animals.

The story of that near-impossible trek includes those hardships I've already listed – dysentery from drinking bad water, the establishment of a sick camp, animals starving because they were set to grazing on the green grass when the dry yellow grass had all the nutrients – plus the torment of insects, the increasing shortages of food, the deaths of many of the horses from illness and starvation, and of the cattle killed for food. The Mounties desperately needed more horses and cattle, which were very hard to acquire, requiring that one party head north to Fort Carleton and another south to Fort Benton, Montana, to try to buy more.

I find myself wishing Canadians would do more mythologizing of our past, although historians agree that the trek was replete with mistakes and unnecessary suffering on the part of both men and animals. Nonetheless, out here in the West, we love that tale; we cherish it, even when it also makes us laugh ruefully. It is honoured especially around Maple Creek, Saskatchewan, fifty-six kilometres northeast of Fort Walsh, where for a time the North-West Mounted Police had its headquarters during one of the early West's most critical moments: the demise of the plains bison in the late 1800s, which left the First Nations people starving, and how something like three to five thousand of them, accounts vary as to the number, camped around Fort Walsh in the hope of receiving desperately needed food and supplies from the Mounties. In the 1870s, the government was terrified that if so many First Nations people stayed massed in southern Saskatchewan, "Indian Wars" might take place, as had happened in the United States. Canada was only ten to twelve years old then, and fragile, and couldn't fight such a war without the danger of its collapse. Indian Commissioner Dewdney, later Lieutenant-Governor of the North-West Territories, made a strict policy that no food would be given to people whose chiefs had not signed the treaty, and what could the chiefs do as their people lay dying of starvation around them, some of them begging their leaders to sign so that their children and other loved ones might eat?

Part of the signing or "taking treaty," as they put it, was that the people were forced to leave their traditional area to go to reserves east of Regina or north of the South Saskatchewan River, an enforced move that would soon result in Indigenous children being torn from their families and forced into residential schools, the far-reaching results of which would soon overwhelm most other First Nations' news.

If you want to know more about the West at that time, read William Francis Butler's 1872 *The Great Lone Land,* or Isaac Cowie's 1913 *The Company of Adventurers: A Narrative of Seven Years in the Service of the Hudson Bay Company During 1867–1874 on the Great Buffalo Plains with Historical and Biographical Notes and Comments,* or Sam Steele's journals, or books and articles about him, one of Canada's great, if largely unsung heroes, who entered the NWMP as a staff sergeant in 1873 to go on the founding March West, rose to Commissioner, and was eventually knighted. This tiny list barely breaks the surface of the heartbreaking, detailed stories about that heroic for Euro-Canadians, and tragic for First Nations, time in Canadian history.



At the top of the long hill into Eastend instead of proceeding easterly, Lucinda and I turned back south, drove up the steep hillside, bumped over a cattle guard, parked on the small patch of mowed wild grass, got out, opened the creaky black iron gate, and entered the Eastend cemetery. At the top of the cemetery where Peter lay, there was a wide view to the west of the town's reservoir, and beyond it Ravenscrag and its deceptively shining clay buttes. Below us was the village and north, beyond it, across the Frenchman River and gazing up the far valley wall, your eyes were stopped briefly by the T-Rex Museum before sweeping up the yellow grass to the sky.

Lucinda stood, looking down with interest at the houses and streets and trees, and the narrow highway we had just turned off that runs through the town and at its far eastern edge, leads up another steep hill, this one caused by the valley curving southwest there toward our once hay farm and on for more miles to the place where the T-Rex was excavated over several summers. That hill takes you up onto the flatland above and runs on east across Saskatchewan and into Manitoba, where the highway number changes.

Even though taking this long detour and stopping here must have been my idea, I remember that looking out over the town and the river, I felt bored. Maybe it wasn't so much boredom I felt as a sort of prickly, indeterminate irritation at the whole place, all my memories of it pushing and pulling each other around in my brain while I batted them away, one after the other, impatient at having to think about the place and my past in it at all. I remember pointing out the various sights below us. Then we turned to Peter's grave.



His sisters picked his plot, their view being a more romantic one than mine: I would have put him along the caragana hedge to give him some shelter from the incessant wind and the winter blizzards, the bane of people who live their lives outdoors and much of the time on horseback, as he did. An old cowboy said to me, a man I was told had once been known as the toughest man in the area, the highest praise possible in that rural world, as he lounged in his rocker in front of his television in his small, overheated house in Eastend, "I been damn cold most of my life; I'm damn well gonna be warm now."

I made a half-hearted effort to brush off the dust from Peter's headstone and to scrape away bird droppings. This was the first time I hadn't brought water and a scrubbing brush and had no flowers to set at the base of the stone, but this didn't seem a proper visit anyway, because I wasn't alone, and it wasn't very early morning, my usual time for visits to Peter, or whatever Peter might be now, before anyone was stirring in the village below where we stood in the sun. I felt no connection, no sense of spirit around me, and after a moment when we both stood in silence, we walked away, down the slope to the other half of the cemetery, and I showed Lucinda Peter's parents' graves.

We walked through the headstones, stopping at the row of tiny white crosses with the names of children engraved on them. They had died a hundred or so years earlier, and we wondered how: Diphtheria? Whooping cough? Measles? Or perhaps by fire, as fire killed too many people in their barely insulated settlers' shacks, which were heated by wood or coal, or in desperate times, as Peter's mother had once written for *The Western Producer*, with dried cow dung referred to as "cow chips."



**II**

I sometimes used to start adult classes I taught in memoir-writing by asking the students, "What is your deepest secret? Write it down!" At this, a frightened, near-panicked look would appear on the faces of a few of the students. Most would look merely engaged and thoughtful, others would freeze, staring at me as if they couldn't believe the request, that they couldn't answer it, or did not dare. After maybe five seconds, surprised myself, maybe even a bit alarmed at the reactions of a couple of the students, I would say, "No, no, don't! Don't write down anything. I was only trying to illustrate that if you are going to write a serious memoir about parts of a serious life, that is, all lives, that's how deep you will find yourself having to go."

Relieved exhalations would follow from different corners of the room, some laughter, or, sometimes, rarely, fleeting annoyed expressions. The question was only a tactic, but at the same time, I was serious, although I knew that only one or two of those students would ever go that far, at least in writing. Their revelations on the page might well be only the final reader-mystifying distillation of the material of many sleepless nights, maybe even years of painful struggle that their readers would never know about. And, I would be careful to point out, it is possible to never reveal a single intimate detail about the writer's own life and still be a successful memoirist. Or, to simply lie all the way, and at least in terms of sales, still be a successful writer. I'd never seen any sign that the venue where I was teaching wanted writing teachers who were not serious seekers after the truth, however each might define it. In my experience, the students who wanted casual, pop-culture kinds of teachers: Seven-Steps-to-a-Bestseller kind of teachers, did not come to that beautiful island venue for instruction.



Recently, when I told a knowledgeable acquaintance about my exercise with the students, I read disapproval into her hesitation in replying. Maybe she has never been where I've been, I thought; or maybe if she had been one of my students, she would have been one of those people with the alarmed stare. And perhaps, I thought, I should not have picked such psychological-emotional themes for my own writerly material, never mind to suggest that others should do the same. Which must have been the reason in those days that giving the students barely time to let the question sink in, I immediately told them that the question was a ploy, that nobody should respond to it.

I could imagine that afterwards students might have talked to each other about the question, maybe even about the range of possible answers and thus were thinking in a deeper way about what it means to write a memoir. Even in the private sessions with each of them, I don't think any student ever spoke to me about that strategy and its effect on them. Only someone, in our private meeting, telling me about a realization that a family member had deliberately set the house fire that killed all but one other family member who was away for the night, and the absolute secrecy in that family that had always surrounded that truth. How, as she told me, the air in our small room grew heavy and dark. How we struggled against it – that thick darkness – believing it could be overcome, believing that it *must* be overcome. That the story *must* be told. But there would always be a few writers who had already figured out that secrets were where their lives lay: In the writing exercises, especially in scene-writing, the stories students told were sometimes so visceral, so disturbing and clearly, we thought, autobiographical – child abuse, domestic violence, gender dysphoria, drug addiction, war memories – that none of us knew how to react to them other than with spontaneous sympathy while also trying to maintain an appropriate degree of detachment. Always remember this is a class on how to write a memoir, I would say; I am not a psychologist, this is not a therapy workshop. What about the writing?

But some scenes were so visceral that the punch they delivered to everyone was proof enough that the writing was working. How sometimes, not often, we forgot detachment and wept for the storyteller. Now some of those stories come back, and I am almost as overcome by the tellers' suffering as I was the days when in class I first heard them.

We need to find a way to tell our stories. But you can't tell your life story if you don't know what it is, and most of us don't, not really, no matter how good we might be on places, dates, names, and versions declared as the truth by family members.

My memoir work has been, whether I meant it to be or not, to figure out what my story is. And although I've avoided it before, I'm aware that like most women, my story cannot avoid being about my mother.

I don't remember my four sisters and myself ever having deep discussions about our mother. That didn't begin until we were all mothers ourselves, full adults dealing with our own lives, diverse and often difficult as they've been. Then we would think about our mother's influence on us, how in terms of our relationship with her, each of us had a different mother. Now that I have only one sister left with whom I can talk about our family's past, when we were going over our mother's weaknesses and mistakes, I am the one who said, "But she was always there, and she wasn't drunk or high on drugs, never locked us in closets, almost never hit us, and never beat us." My sister could only agree, but I had effectively ended any chance of a real deconstruction of what it was like to grow up under her rule and her enormous influence in making us what we were.



But she did beat me and only me and only once, when she caught me, at five years old or possibly younger, striking match after match against a cast-iron pot-bellied heater standing in the small frame house where we lived briefly in a pioneer village set against the forest. As each one flamed and died, I let it fall to the floor, so that she found me standing in the midst of the evidence of my crime: a circle of burnt matchsticks.

I'm not sure I knew what a major transgression this was in the pioneer world where often whole families were wiped out by fire, where the final conflagration, the house fire, the barn fire, was the one prospect that terrified everyone more even than bear attacks, being chased by wolf packs, being lost in howling blizzards, or the threat of starvation. Nor would today's children understand how omnipresent open flames were in the lives of pioneering people, for light, for cooking, for heat, or how we saw our parents strike matches and set things – the lamp wick, the kitchen stove for heat and cooking – on fire over and over again every single day. Today's urban children would see only the open flames of birthday-party candles or maybe summer barbecues, or lit candles at the dinner table or possibly, once in a long while, the bonfires that so fascinate everyone except those already scarred by fire. I was four or five years old, and at least in part I was striking matches out of a child's wonder and curiosity at the miracle of fire.

But also, today, examining that memory, I think I did know what I was doing and how forbidden it was: I am sure that I was already full of rage at the unfairness of my mother's daily treatment of me: I think I wanted to burn down the whole world, I wanted to destroy it all by fire.

And yet, I was – I am – so traumatized by that beating, even though I wasn't even hurt, I was so shamed both over my



crime and the unheard-of humiliation of the punishment, that in my entire life, I have told only one person of it. It happened many years ago, but crying, I forced myself to say it. Even that disclosure failed to help me, and I have never mentioned it again until now.

Aha! I tell myself, and that was *my* deepest secret? That puny thing? When I know people who as children were nearly killed by their violent fathers or mentally ill mothers? Why is it that after nearly eighty years of not being able to tell people about it or even tell it out loud to the four walls am I now able to? It occurs to me now that of course it was a recurrence of the earlier betrayal when as a toddler I was sexually abused. In my mind there is no doubt that that was what happened to me, although everyone who knew of it is dead, and there is no way left to prove my allegation. That beating from an otherwise moderate disciplinarian, although strict mother, destroyed my child's illusion of absolute safety; it was a further blow against my unthinking belief of my inherited place in the world, when the last shred of my notion of myself as a deserving child like my sisters, was pressed down to a thin, barely discernible line at my feet. And, I think in wonder, that damage isn't fully repaired to this day.

In writing a conventional memoir, the real problem is how far do writers go in telling the most intimate parts of their lives? How much should they reveal? And more, what can you say, both legally and ethically, about other people whose influence altered your life, usually for the worse?

I used Nabokov's memoir, *Speak, Memory,* not just to demonstrate one possible structure, but also to point out that memoirs aren't always about scandalous personal things in the writer's life: having a sexual affair with your father, your misspent, drug-raddled youth, your parents using you as a sex slave for other men, violent fathers or mothers, or a parent who spent the memoirist's childhood in prison for murder or bank robbery, or a parent who committed suicide virtually in front of the author as a child – all of these are the subjects in memoirs we could name. Sometimes a memoir is about some impersonal force – war, famine, disease, pockets of cultural craziness (life in a cult, or in the CIA) – made personal by the author's participation in it and suffering, or elevation by it. Nabokov didn't tell intimate personal secrets, and despite this, I don't think there is a more famous or successful memoir. "Consciousness in the light of history," is how American writer Patricia Hampl described memoir, and Nabokov's book demonstrates the power in this. "In the light of history" is the part often either left out or not considered by first-time memoirists.

One solution found by writers is to write a novel instead of a memoir, carefully disguising the perpetrators so as not to be sued or harassed; another is to write all of it, always emphasising that they are telling the story from their own point of view, that others will disagree and even accuse them of lying, will maybe throw a rock through their living room window, take potshots at them, set fire to their house, or use social media to destroy them, but to maintain at all costs that what they have written is only – only! – the truth as they remember and understand it and, always, that it is their story, they have the right to tell it.

I used to respond with astonishment when some of my readers found the emotions and experiences I had told in my books to be too revealing. "You have made yourself vulnerable," they would tell me, and I would ask, "Vulnerable to what?" I viewed literature then as a way for people to understand the forces in their own lives and those of others; it seemed pointless to me then to write if you had nothing to say about one individual's pain, if you chose to avoid the deeper truths about individual consciousness. I wondered, shuddering, if they were worried more of their own repressed and denied stories being revealed than of mine. But I had received only expressions of gratitude for validating readers' experiences in their own lives, and for helping them to see that they were not alone, and not unworthy because they were merely who they were – themselves.



And for also insisting that there are other ways of knowing the world beyond time and distance measurements, and the revelations of photographs, microscopes and X-rays, elaborate computer mathematics, or other scientific ways of knowing. It took me almost thirty years before, having lost my indignation, I revisited that remark and realized what the speakers really meant when they said I'd "made myself vulnerable": They meant: You have revealed your craziness.

I reread, for the first time in at least twenty years, *The Perfection of the Morning: An Apprenticeship in Nature*, the memoir in question, and I was angry with myself for not having seen it clearly when it was first said to me. I was also, and for the first time, somewhat abashed by what I had written, and worse, sorry to find myself again staring into the dark face of my weakness, when the book had felt to me at the time as an attempt to reach a kind of purity of truth about a major shift in my life and my feelings about it (when I moved from the city and a university life to the far country to live as a rancher's wife). Nor did they seem to recognize the simple curiosity of a writer, in my case the unquenchable need to get to the bottom of my own psyche, as far as I dared to go, and to understand my own emotional-psychological dynamics, to understand not only my new life, but also my own past life as it was increasingly revealed to me by comparing it to my new circumstances: being alone so much of the time; adapting to a strange place and strange culture that my marriage had brought me to.

Peter was a distant relative. We met when he came to stay with us (my young son and me) for a few days while he attended a large animal clinic at the university's Vet Med school. He invited us to visit him on the ranch, an invitation I had no intention of accepting, but my son, dying to see cowboys and horses and a real working ranch, begged me until I gave in. One weekend staying in that beautiful country, watching the men rounding up cattle on horseback, and I was hooked. For good.



I thought the story of *The Perfection of the Morning* was about building a relationship with nature; I thought it was about discovering more than the comfort and healing to be found in nature, but much further, nature's real power and wisdom. Eventually I became willing to lower my sights a little and think not of an omnipotent power, but instead of contact with ancient ones and with perhaps local spirits of a place, called by the Romans *genius loci*, daemons, all omnipresent in nature but not recognized as such by most non-First Nations people because of having the wrong attitudes, focusing on the wrong things, or being purely, determinedly materialist in viewpoint. Or too frightened by the teachings of our prevailing cultural views, taught by experts, to acknowledge the sometimes-contradictory evidence of what they had *personally* felt or seen.

In my case, nearly all of the many readers who wrote to me via snail mail or email about the book were women, and they responded by telling me their own, similar experiences in nature. And I wondered then and continue to wonder if women could accept what I had written because traditionally women haven't held power, haven't needed to close in their boundaries of self tightly in order to focus on survival, material things, and the competitiveness inherent in those goals. And anyway, it was men who remarked whether in writing or not that I was crazy, with the exception of those who worried that I had made myself vulnerable. I thought that insisting on that point of view toward my book was their loss, and a product of the very things I was complaining about: scientism and materialism.



As for others who might appear in my memoirs, I used to say from my start as a writer that the lives of my family members were off limits, although I've made one exception, and the two involved are both dead now. I took it for granted that decent people didn't wreck other people's lives, and I thought that even my own small, unremarkable world was so full of wonderful stories that I didn't have to steal the stories of the people closest to me to have something sufficiently interesting to write about.

But in the revisiting of life that the old seem to need to do, often we see events in a new light, we think differently about them, even allow ourselves to conclude different things about who we are and who we have been. We revise our life's narrative. That done, we, or at least, I, find it easier to put it all away.

## III

Done with this journey of thinking through my life, I refused to think about the past anymore, refused to share "remember the time when . . ." stories with my remaining sisters, wouldn't get into anything more than a cursory discussion of our parents, shied away from rehearsals of old stories. I can't even remember them, I would say! I even claimed in an essay in *This Strange Visible Air: Essays on Aging and the Writing Life* (2021) that I did not remember the past, that I had put it away forever, and was mightily pleased with myself about it. Psychotherapists who might have heard of this must have laughed their heads off, but I remember reading somewhere about Buddhist monks, whose wisdom I respected, who said that. I thought this stance a nobler one than constantly going over the past, blaming or celebrating others, or sinking into it, smiling dreamily or glaring furiously as I sat by the window, seeing nothing of the present as it passed busily by.

More truthfully, the past assailed me, would not let me sleep, nor see the world with new eyes each morning. It was a quagmire threatening to suck me down into it, from which I would never free myself, never be whole, never be a free person in the world. Should I say, *never be alive*?

I decided to live as if none of it had ever happened. I had become so successful at this approach that I had emotionally pretty much frozen solid; my hope was to stay that way forever. Was that what Paul Bowles, author of the classic *The Sheltering Sky*, did? He has been reported as cold, unemotional, distanced, a state my best efforts have never quite taken me to.

But even with my hesitation and uncertainty, and as I struggled to remember the places Lucinda and I had gone and what had confronted me there in terms of my younger life, it was as if somehow along the road, I had torn a rent in the fabric of my self-protection. And since our trip, I kept reading, thinking, trying to remember details, small scintillations of memory have begun returning, details of no particular consequence nor any deep emotion, just small remembrances in quick flashes of this or that out from my life. In squelching my responses to the major events in my life, I'd also ripped away the daily texture of my life, and I pondered that, puzzled as to whether that loss mattered or not. But every little flash surprised me again into realizing I *had* been alive, all along I *had* had a life like everyone else.

Eventually I realized that our trip would make a good frame for another memoir. This seemed delightfully obvious, and I began to think of how I would write it. For a long time, I hesitated, probably in fear that the result wouldn't just be prairie history, geography, and culture I'd be writing, but my own, and although this hesitation wasn't clear to me, I must have been afraid. More than once I thought of the dream of the dripping water that would drown me, if I let it. I put the idea away and turned to other writings.



Rather like the time that Peter and I were flying in a small plane, he beside the pilot who had trained him to fly and I alone in the back, where there was room for another passenger or two. We had flown only a short distance when we entered a bank of impenetrable fog or mist or cloud; we could see nothing out any of the windows but the same even, flat greyish-white matter that cloaked all the world from us. The pilot, who had trained pilots in World War II, shifted in his seat, straightened, grasped the steering wheel more firmly with both hands, telling us the cloud rose too high and too low to fly over or under it, muttered something to my husband as he pointed to an instrument on the dash that I understood represented the horizon line, and flew us for two more hours with intense, silent concentration, to our destination where the cloud cleared and he was able to land easily.

And I? The moment I understood that our situation was perilous, that our lives depended on the pilot not losing his concentration or his sanity, did I sit wide awake behind him tensed with fear, keeping my eye on the instrument panel? No, I fell like a stone into sleep and did not wake until we were about to land. It might be said, with regard to my memory, that as I wrote my third memoir, it was now time to wake up; time to land.

**IV**

One night in Swift Current, Peter and I were to speak at a conference. I remember no other details about it, only that the talk was about the land and our just-completed arrangement with the Nature Conservancy of Canada for the Butala family ranch to become the Old Man on His Back Prairie and Heritage Conservation Area. I began our presentation by reading a description of the area around Swift Current down to the American border from the Palliser Expeditions' papers (1857 and 1859), as reported by its leader, James Palliser. He wrote of the sand that was everywhere, in some places so deep that one of the expedition members got his cart stuck in a deep patch and, while he was trying to free it, was attacked by a bear and had to kill it. We don't know how, but probably with a gun. I didn't want to mix that story up with the one the conservationist Richard St. Barbe Baker (1889–1982) told about his settler-uncle killing an attacking bear with a shovel, which so thrilled him it brought him to Canada.

The night we spoke in the 1990s, plains grizzlies, once plentiful in the area Lucinda and I were driving through, had been extirpated for about a hundred years, although there were rare reported sightings as late as 1960 and only in remote areas such as the Pasquia Hills, a few hundred miles north and east of us but not far from where I was born. And as for that sand, you can still visit the Great Sand Hills in southwest Saskatchewan near the Alberta border, where the dunes, ever changing as sand dunes are, can be thirty to sixty feet high.

Then Peter talked about what had happened to that landscape since, and about our project. Afterward, some of the audience said how fascinated they were, having never before seen so visceral a picture of what fifty years later their ancestors had begun to turn into placid farm or grazing land, and how they never truly imagined the wild their homeland had once been. How do you turn sand into farmland? In that area, after settlement around 1900, I conclude you've just been lucky with the rain. That is, outside of the actual sandhills.

Palliser probably arrived after years of drought; the Henry Youle Hind expedition travelled through the area in 1858, roughly the same time as Palliser's first expedition, but came to a different conclusion. The first explorer said the area south of the South Saskatchewan wouldn't support agriculture; it became "the Palliser Triangle," extending into southern Alberta and Manitoba; the second was enthusiastic about its agricultural potential, but historians now conclude that the two expeditions had different mandates and didn't cover precisely the same territory: nearly two hundred thousand square miles, larger than some countries and only slightly smaller than the gargantuan state of Texas. Think of how each expedition had only three to five men on horseback to cover it all; think of how focus and point of view is everything—even in science. And what governments might choose to do with that knowledge depends on political goals: The British government at that time wanted to fill the West with settlers to ensure its hold on the territory and so had a tendency to listen to Hind rather than Palliser, to the eternal regret of far too many devastated, impoverished, and eventually desperate settlers. And yet, today nearly all that area that was once grassland is either grazing land or farms, no matter how precarious making a living in agriculture can still be, despite improved seeds, better and larger machinery, more careful farming techniques, and chemical fertilizers and insecticides.

I decided I wouldn't write my book in the familiar form of memoirs, that is by finding a theme and telling it chronologically, but instead I would tell my story in an associative way, in no particular order, just letting myself go into whatever thoughts came up as we drove through familiar country territory or stopped or passed through the towns along the route Lucinda and I drove on, through the plains, the super-hot, drought-ridden summer of 2021. The plains that happened, more or less, to encompass my life from August 24, 1953, when I turned thirteen years old and we drove into the metropolis of Saskatoon (population then about fifty thousand) and sat in a car parked on main street waiting for our father, gone on errands. Waiting, we children looked wonderingly out the car window, in my case trying but failing to see "the city," my vaguely formed notion of it that, in total innocence of cities, I held in my mind.



As I've written, I have no photos of the trip, nor any written observation or reflection about it, and now, try as I did to explain this careless disregard of my writer's process, I was beginning to know I was nowhere near finding the real reason for this week-long dereliction of what was the writer's duty: To pay *attention*. To *notice*. To think about, to mull it over, never to forget. Then to turn it into words.

## V

I came from a family of five girls. Although I was second oldest, I was the worker of the five of us, doing more housework and babysitting than anyone else, because one was off doing other things, one was disabled, and the remainder were too young;

I was also the one who, when we were in elementary school, was given the most responsibility for our disabled sister, who came just after me, every day in winter pulling her to school and back on a sleigh. I didn't consciously know I did more of the work – although, how could I have missed it? – until a relative mentioned it to me recently as something she had noticed when we were young. When I thought about it, I made excuses for my mother about this: She had two smaller children at home and couldn't take our sister to school, our father left early for work and came back late, and our older sister, three grades ahead of me, was going to a distant high school in a different direction.

Our mother was strict, even rigid, in her adherence to the social norms she'd had drilled into her as a child by her strict, born-in-1883 mother – she likely wasn't her mother's favourite child any more than I was hers – and she was always working from sunrise to long after sundown. She even made all our clothing, and when we were young, twice a day spread a blanket on the table for our polio-stricken sister to lie on in order to do her prescribed exercises with her. I don't know how she did it, we women of my generation say of our mothers, shaking our heads in awe and pity.



But she was often, at the least, unkind to me. I was young when I saw that she did not love me, but I'd never understood until I was old that I had lived my life in that realization's shadow.

It was not until she was dead thirty-five or so years that I began to see that she wasn't the wonderful, loving, all-wise mother of sentimental movies and bestsellers, not even underneath the short temper and disinterest caused by a mostly unhappy marriage, her broken dreams, and the life that was her own that she couldn't live because of her breathtaking workload and the sense of duty women of her era had been taught as inviolable. But she once said to others about me, when she had visited Peter and me in the country, "Sharon sure gets through a lot of work in a day," and how surprised and proud I was. I liked being responsible and necessary and, also, appreciated for it, rather than constantly criticized as I'd been in my first marriage and even though the work I did there was hardly what I had dreamt of for my life, either.

All my life I've made excuses for my mother, but recently I have allowed myself to think otherwise for the first time. Skip the excuses: she was often awful, which is not the same thing as saying she was a monster. I tell myself that she gave her life over to us, but then I add, it was just that she didn't enjoy it much and often seemed near despair. It occurs to me that at least three of the five of us didn't feel sufficiently loved or noticed by her, although I could be wrong about that; with two dead and one lost in dementia, there is no way to verify my claim.

She was certainly the dominant one in our household, and if she said something was so, it was so, and that was that. It took a long time to grow out of her rigid ideas of what was appropriate and what wasn't, what we could do and couldn't do, the way her authority suppressed our natural adventurousness, so that we grew up too ignorant of the world, as she had been brought up herself to be. We had only the most naïve ideas of how to make our way in it, the latter mostly based on her by then-archaic ideas about how women should live.



We were carefully trained for a world that no longer existed, fine if you came from a prosperous home, absurd if you were part of a working-class community and probably destined to stay there, where you would have to make your own way without resources other than the bolstering of an overweening pride our mother had inherited from her mother. On her deathbed she had a dream telling her of her mistake with us. She was near tears as she whispered to us, "I should have let them in; I should have let them in." Children muddy, ragged and hungry, begging to come in, and she refusing because "I'd just washed the floor." She understood what her dream meant; we older daughters knew, too, but we didn't discuss it because she was dying and despite everything, we loved her.

Then, each one of us grew out of her reach, slowly her transgressions washed away, and it is only in disquisitions like this one that my old hurts and unfulfilled yearnings return. My remaining sister with whom I could still converse and I would say to each other about our mother: She made the meals three times a day every day, saw to it that we ate them and drank our milk, went to bed every night at a proper hour, then got us off to school without fail, wearing clothing she had made for us herself. How bad could she be, considering the things we read about or see in movies that other children have suffered? We would have defended her with our very lives when we were children, because she was our mother, and every single day she tried to be that, however badly or well.



I want to give her full credit where it is due: Sometimes she spoke gently to any one of us, when we told her of playground hurts or teachers' cruelties, or when we asked hard questions that she knew it was too soon to answer, for instance, when I asked what "rape" was, fumblingly pronounced by me as "rap-ee" with a short *a*. I'd read it in the paper. She said she would explain it when I was older, although when that time came, I had already found out. She was indelibly loyal to us when we were in trouble with people who were not our family, whether we were guilty or not. She comforted us when we needed comforting; I don't recall her cuddling us, although I think she did my sisters, but not me, and how I longed for her warm, saving touch but did not ever receive it. I wonder now how much cuddling she received as a child, and knowing our grandmother, I suspect not much, and think that must have been part of our grandmother's ethic: once children weren't babies, you did not overdo the hugging.

How I would sometimes, in grade school, get sick so I had to stay home, just the two of us, and lie on the sofa all day or upstairs in a bedroom hoping she would hold me in her arms, but she was always in the kitchen or the garden or upstairs making beds. During those times, several when I was nine or ten, I wound up in hospital for a couple of week-long stretches when I did get some of her attention. But she had three children younger than I was at home, the youngest at the most two, and I remember her visiting only once.

My chief memory of her then is of sitting beside my hospital bed in her good clothing, legs crossed elegantly at the knee, her elbow resting on her hand, holding a burning cigarette shoulder high, not speaking, and gazing off into the distance. It was likely a Sunday when she came, because my father would have been at home to watch the others. In the hospital I suffered alone through some miseries such as endless blood drawing, that sort of thing, as the medical staff tried to figure out what was wrong with me. My illness would begin with a cold; swiftly it would go into my chest; I would run a high fever, have trouble breathing. Then the doctor would come, and I would wind up in hospital. I never thought I was faking, nor did the doctor or nurses: I wasn't faking, I believe now I had made myself genuinely ill.

Eventually, I would get better and go back to school and, in a day or two, catch up on what I'd missed. I understand now how my life got so weird, messed up, for a long while calamitous with pain. Even as I know all too well how trivial my mistreatment was in a world full of orphans living on the streets, children routinely beaten, starved, murdered, used as drugged child-soldiers, sex slaves, and the abuse of those, even their hunger that went unacknowledged, who sat in the same schoolroom with me. Nonetheless, by her treatment of me she set me apart not just from my own family, but from myself, although it took me many years to see that. And many, many more to take charge of it, if I ever have.

Our mother changed after our father died at sixty-seven of leukemia in 1973, too young I see now, and as age came upon her, a softening occurred, permanent sorrow appeared in the lines of her face, and in her eyes there was a steady glimmer of pain. Sometimes when she looked at one of us, she radiated love, not something we often experienced as children that I can remember.

Then our mother was so beautiful in spirit, that we were, all of us, full of forgiveness; we gave it unconditionally, without thought, as we sat at her bedside as she died of the breast cancer that had moved into her bones, and she drifted toward and into that silent no man's land, then through it, and then beyond the final boundary, out of our grasp. When I revisit that part of my childhood when I did not have my mother's heart, my rage is gone, but the scar remains, although it grows fainter every year.

# FOUR

# BONES

## I

I cannot visit my husband's grave in the cemetery at Eastend, someone so important in my life, unless I'm alone. I stood and stared at the handsome chunk of granite with his name carved on it, and, while Lucinda looked around, I made that desultory effort to wipe off the dust and bird droppings. No strange birds appeared or sang, no butterflies came, and there was no worker on a tractor cutting grass or straightening leaning headstones, all of which had happened before. Peter himself was also not there.

I'm thinking now that of course our pact had been fulfilled by then, the ten years of twice-yearly visits I'd promised after his funeral, or rather, that we'd agreed on as an appropriate demonstration of my loyalty to him and to all I owed him, and a final rounding off of our years together that began with our wedding in 1976 in the courthouse in Saskatoon.

It seemed to me that Peter agreed with this, although he was dead. I felt him and his opinions in the air around me; I never doubted his presence in those days, and most widows don't, either. Strange things happen around deaths of spouses in long marriages, at least to the women who are left behind, those who hear things—music that no one else can hear, voices whispering to them, sometimes maliciously, dead husbands sitting quietly in the living room reading, their presence so palpable widows get out of bed to inquire as to what they want, or inexplicable thumps or tapping in their homes that they had never heard before. The marital conversations and arguments continue for years, although one is living and one is not. And the dreaming! So intense and so seemingly real. Put all those experiences on grief, we're told, dismissively, but we do not, because we know what we know.

"I have the spot next to him," I told Lucinda, and I could feel my mouth go wry when I said it, my face, I'm supposing, betraying my bafflement. That I should end up here? In any condition, much less dead. Even though I love the prairie, and the wind, the enormous sky and the kingdom of the sun and the grass more than I do trees and shadow. I don't want cremation and what's left of me being carried away by the four winds. My never-ending longing for home is too great; even in death, I tell myself, I need a place to call home. It troubles me to think that my husband gets to stay home for all eternity while I, as with all widows who leave their own homes when they marry, no longer have a place that I can truly call home.



We visited the gravestones of Peter's mother and father before we left, his father's tall headstone ending in a Celtic cross and beside it his mother's, a flat headstone in matching dark-flecked pink-orange granite, polished and shiny. Nothing fancy for her, although she was a remarkable, if difficult, woman. I wonder if that's what people will say about me when I'm dead, the second attribution cancelling out the first. But nonetheless, I go on thinking about my life and sometimes dreaming mystifying dreams that if ever decoded will perhaps show me what my puzzling, upside down, moderately bizarre life has been about.

## II

Lucinda and I had come on the Redcoat Trail, and we would travel on it a few more kilometres. One of the men who was responsible for marking out the Trail, Everett Baker (1893–1981), born and educated to university-degree level in Minnesota, chose to come to Canada after graduation and spent the rest of his life in this country. He introduced the idea of placing historical markers along the NWMP's path across the southern prairies when all of it but then-tiny Manitoba was part of the North-West Territories. We had two of those markers on our land at the hay farm, one on each side, on the grassy banks above the Frenchman River. We were proud of them, although I'd heard that some of the farmers along the way had used their giant equipment to pull those on their land out of the ground and toss them away, because they got in the way of their summerfallowing, fertilizing, seeding, or harvesting rounds. I might have heard that some of them replaced the markers along the edges of their fields, but I'm just guessing about that; I might have made it up.



Baker, a man of high intelligence and unusual vision, and also of some charisma, or his subjects wouldn't have taken time off their work or smiled so openly and naturally in his pictures, for years took photos of ordinary people, including First Nations people, at their daily activities all over Saskatchewan, starting around 1940 and up until his demise. One of his pictures is of my husband, his father, his mother, and one of his two sisters. Peter stands with his sister and his mother who are holding the reins of the men's saddle horses. It occurs to me that Baker might have asked them to do that for a quirkier picture, and that is why they're all grinning. The photo was taken in 1953 and is in a collection of Baker's photos selected by Saskatchewan historian Bill Waiser (*Everett Baker's Saskatchewan: Portraits of an Era*, Fifth House, 2007). That book is one of my favourites. By the time I saw the picture, I was pretty familiar with that world from Peter's and his mother's stories, but this was the first time I'd seen a photo in the midst of the family's daily life. Usually photos of the time showed only young men working with horses or cattle in the corrals or riding across unending fields of grass, females elsewhere, not in the shots. I notice that the photo was taken in the same year my family and I arrived in Saskatoon.

Peter had considered Baker a friend. Peter took me to the nursing home where Baker, who would have been in his late eighties, then lived. He came out of his room in his wheelchair and responded in a friendly, even gracious way to our introduction. But what I mostly remember about that meeting, besides Baker's friendly openness, was that through his open door I could see his scholar's bookshelves tightly packed with books, a sight rarely seen around 1980 in the "old folks" homes of that area. I think of him in his wheelchair, the shelves of books behind him, his smile, and wonder if I could figure out how to end my life so well. Standing at my husband's grave, I wanted to thank Baker again for his genuine humility that made the photos possible, and for his clear view, to know as he must have, that his record of Saskatchewan people in the early days of our province, would one day be so precious.



I didn't dare think too hard about my husband, though, not even at his grave in the cemetery high above the village, wild grass all around and then crops and then the sky. All the ways we live life, every one ending in death.

I was recognizing once again that I was old by anyone's reckoning, and that the Fates themselves, the Moirai, were gazing coldly down on me, spinning, as they had watched my hospitalized husband. He was ill, he was dying, now I visit his grave. Just like that. I'm thinking of: "Life changes in an instant / an ordinary instant," and from the Episcopalians' graveside service: "In the midst of life we are in death," both quoted in Joan Didion's excellent, wildly bestselling *The Year of Magical Thinking*, the first a repeated refrain, but that for Didion was a life learning. Oh, that cold, detached, arrogant, headachy, brilliant woman, Didion, finally coming up against Life.

But, at last, when Lucinda and I left the lilac-fenced cemetery and drove down the long, steep hill to the highway leading into Eastend, the town named by Superintendent James Walsh of the North-West Mounted Police because, even though in the extreme southwest of today's province, it is located at the east end of the Cypress Hills, I found myself dropped back into my sprightly, feelingless mode. Considering all the years I'd spent mostly only ten miles from the village, and bought my groceries in it and for a while saw the doctor there and attended meeting after meeting there, I suppose it was surprising that, beyond showing off the Wallace Stegner House that I'd helped to develop as an artists' retreat, I had so little to say to Lucinda about it, and little desire to stop anywhere except at one friend's house. The friend is twenty years younger than I am, but in certain ways wiser and smarter, a gifted woman, but one who (in my judgment) has been unlucky in life. We used to be good friends when I left the area a year after Peter's death, and at a certain level I thought we still were.

We three sat together in her secluded, wild garden and, as far as I can remember, talked mostly about the local news. Then the three of us went to Jack's Café for lunch, where I discovered to my chagrin that the Greek family who had launched the café in the early twentieth century along with the launching of the town, generation after generation owning and running it, were no longer its owners, and the new owner told me he was Filipino.

But the brightly coloured mural of the history of the community painted close to twenty years earlier by the amateur-painter wife of, I guess now, the second-last Greek owner, was still there, along the walls above the booths, an illustration moving, booth by booth, decade by decade, through the history of the area to the near-present time: herds of buffalo to ranches, cattle and cowboys to vast farms and small towns, to oil derricks dotting green fields. If the first – no more Greek owners – kind of stunned me, the second, that the mural remained, did the same.

### III

We ate lunch there, Lucinda and I said goodbye to my long-time friend, and then we continued to our next stop, with me at the wheel. I debated and took the high road up out of the valley where the town sat, and then, a few miles south, went back down into it via the long, too-steep hill. More than forty-five years earlier, when I'd first had to drive down that hill when it was thick with loose gravel, it had scared me. But, this time, down we went, slowly, so as not to slip or slide, past the spot where late one December afternoon, Peter had been driving down the hill in his three-quarter-ton truck, pulling a twenty-foot flatdeck with a small tractor chained on it.



Snow and ice were everywhere, the gravel road was rutted and icy, the ditches on each side snow-filled and deep. The flatdeck started to jackknife, Peter couldn't straighten it out, and so the loaded flatdeck and truck headed for the snow-filled ditch. Fast-thinking Peter got his door open and leaped out just as the whole thing plowed, driverless, into the ditch. Fortunately, neither truck nor flatdeck turned over, but there was no way possible to simply get back in, turn on the motor and drive the rig back up onto the road.

No cell phones then; I guess somebody came along and gave him a ride the two miles home, or else he walked what was, luckily, a short distance to a neighbour's and asked for a ride. Later, when it wasn't yet fully dark, I went back with him to see the situation, but the next day when he had rounded up help to rescue the truck, flatdeck, and tractor, I was at home typing, so I never saw how they did it.

Now, I often think how much I've missed because I was typing, and typing, and the world I was creating or, I thought, representing, seemed more important than actual life, even if the latter did involve my husband almost getting killed. Well, I told myself, remembering how the truck cab's bright blue had looked black in the dying light, dusk starting at four in the afternoon at that time of year, I believed then that you could be a writer or you could have a life; you couldn't quite do both. And firmly, or as I sometimes think, by default, I grasped writing and hung on. Maybe it was a bad decision, but I wasn't a roaring success as a rancher's wife or a community member either, and the choice was, as in so much of life for most of us, a double-bind situation I was stuck with. I suppose that I felt a lot more real when I was writing than I did when I was on a horse chasing cows, a lot more like my true self than what my life in that place was unearthing.



Lucinda and I made a right turn at the valley bottom, soon began to drive through what had been our land, our *place*, our home, made a couple more turns and drove into the yard of what I still think of as my house, even as I write this, fourteen years after I'd sold it to a friend and her husband as Peter, when alive, had urged me to do if anything happened to him — never specifying what "anything" might be. He knew that I'd never be able to live alone on my own land in that community where, as with all agricultural communities, men believe without even noticing they do that in the end all land belongs rightfully to them, never to women. I couldn't let it lie fallow; I couldn't, more likely, choose to do the work myself instead of writing books.

The deck along two sides of the house had been changed, and the short length of cement sidewalk in front of it at the kitchen door, that a friend and I had laid, was gone, and now a wheelchair ramp ran along the end of the sun porch Peter and I had added maybe two years before he died, over what had once been my first and best flowerbed. The ramp was a surprise, although it shouldn't have been. I knew how ill the new owner's husband had been, and I knew that, on the mend at last, he had come in from outside where they had both been working all morning feeding their cows and sheep, probably both lambing and calving at the same time, there was a crash, and he was dead. At fifty-seven. On my living room floor, except it wasn't my living room anymore, a fact I will never be able to believe even though it is ridiculous not to.



I stood there for a minute gazing at the spot where I guessed his body would have been, and remembered him, a man I had thought so highly of and had liked so much. A good end, I guess people would say, after so much suffering, gone in an instant, although I doubt he would have believed himself to be wholly gone.

I had been in Perth, Australia, the day the change of ownership took legal effect, and Peter, although dead, urged me to buy a bottle of fancy wine to mark the occasion, and I bought the cheaper one instead and still regret it. Almost the only vestige of my reign left in the house was the gorgeous warm dark grey still on some of the walls. And the kitchen's paint colour called "mandarin" that the husband of the new owners, to my surprise, never failed to say how much he liked, although the painter insisted on calling it "peach" despite the light tang to the shade; I couldn't get him to say "mandarin."

Still there, years later, those colours I'd chosen with such care, that I could only stare at in bewilderment even though I chatted normally, walked around, and mentioned this and that with a smile on my face. If I could have, what would I have admitted to? What would I have said? Screamed? Torn my hair? Fallen to the floor weeping over the calamity of losing that life, not just my husband, but the small, intense part of me that still lived and glowed even after he died? Or for the things that were happening that I didn't know about while I was concentrating on painting the kitchen walls mandarin, never a banal peach, and the hallway that rich, deep grey hinting of the beauty of twilight and of darker realms.

Or else was shut in the bedroom-turned-study typing. Reading books. Thinking. Gazing out at the wind-tossed lilacs against the low white-painted log house next door that had been our first home, or at night at the southern stars above the hills, following the mysteriously moving tiny white or reddish lights in the depthless cobalt sky while he sat half-asleep before the television, or in spring, was down at the barn checking to see if a cow had delivered yet, or would need his help. And sometimes, my help, too, or, if even with the two of us she couldn't deliver, loading her and taking her to the vet, or phoning the vet to come.

Then, as the newborn fell to the straw on the barn floor, Peter would turn gentle, clean its mouth, rub it, drag it close to its mother's head to be sure she took it, and if she didn't, if she refused, or something bad had happened to her somewhere along the way, or it was a viciously cold night even in the barn, he would carry the calf up to the house and warm it in the half bath by the kitchen door before he took it back down to its mother and tried again to get her to take it.

First though, we had gone down to the corrals and barn, and behind them to the river still moving lazily down its channel with the high bank on the far, south, side where swallows nested in holes in the soft clay cliff and the lower, accessible grassy bank where we stood, which rolled out a little way between the corrals and the shallow brown water as the river meandered softly by in its grass-edged channel.

"There used to be a lot of milkweed along here," I remember remarking, gazing down the now sheep-cropped bank to where the corrals behind us followed the river's contours to curve away from us, the far bank rising above us, where years before on the top of the low hill that rose a further ten feet above that nearly twenty-foot-high bank, to my awed delight, I'd found tiny fossilized seashells. They'd been left behind maybe fourteen thousand years ago, when the glaciers melted and, where we stood on the grass in the high sun, there had then been a mile-wide rushing river of freezing water that would have mounted many yards above our heads. Maybe even another mile above us; I didn't know how deep the scientists said it had been. All that was left of that glacial floodwater was this narrow stream between high banks flowing placidly, quietly along, by our feet.



"Still is," the owner said, referring to the milkweed, the three of us widows, in our fifties, sixties, eighties, but I could see no sign of any, remembering the pleasure of the highly scented globes comprised of many small pink blooms arranged in a sphere a few inches across rising above the tall grass, and the monarch butterflies who loved them. And the owner's young husband, whom I'd cared for too, the finest man, trained to a deep knowledge of his people's ancient spirituality, who had once taken Peter and me to see "Okotoks," Siksika for rock, the massive glacial erratic now split in two (nine metres tall, eighteen metres wide and forty-one metres long) for which the town of Okotoks, Alberta, was named, dead on the living room floor. The sweet lambs in the barn sucking greedily from a bottle Lucinda, at the widow's offer, was holding for them. Lucinda teasing me because I'd mistaken round hay bales in the distance for cattle, but I'd been looking up at the field I'd written a book about (*Wild Stone Heart*), and had many strange experiences in it that had altered my life and when she'd asked, "What's that?" pointing, I'd only glanced over and said absently, "Cattle," and looked back to the field above on our left because, when this place was my home, they would have been cattle. Or sometimes big round bales, I admit it.

But I knew that I could never tell her one true thing about the things I knew, the things my mind was full of when I studied that field, which stretched upward about sixteen hundred feet or was it twelve hundred, measured once by an archaeologist with a topographical map, to flat farmland above, searching for certain rocks, the one that was nearly waist-high on me, glossy black basalt, the only large basalt rock on our hay farm, with places where flakes of rock had been chipped off to make arrowheads or maybe spear points, all called "points" by the archaeologists. Or for the places where I knew the fat bull snakes coiled lazily on shale shelves high on the cliffside warming their, in that pose, seemingly ringed selves, reddish-brown markings on tan, in the high hot sun. Or the place where the rocks were laid so that, an archaeologist suggested, they once might have been the guidelines used to send buffalo over a buffalo jump. That valley wall was high enough and steep enough to have been a small buffalo jump, and below it, a Nakoda Elder, some years ago, had found a few bones, but not many. Or the many cairns in the field under which almost certainly lay, some of them anyway, the bones of the dead. Cree, Siksika, whites can only guess, although in the nineteenth century, this area was known to be the border between the two nations. Skirmishes and even battles took place there that only Indigenous Peoples know the stories of. There is also a stone turtle outlined on a low hilltop with a path delineated by carefully placed stones on each side leading up to it.

I think now only of lying in the grass staring up at the sky, watching the hawks circle, and much higher sometimes a pair of golden eagles, moving black dots swimming through the palpable blue, while far below I lie on the stiff yellow grass, a light breeze carrying the scent of sage and wildflowers caressing and cooling me, and I, immersed in beauty.

And I wonder how much of my own need for beauty came out of my childhood in the Catholic Church, even though it began in a church so cold you could see your breath, set in the midst of a northern forest, a small, raw-wood frame building empty of all decoration. At first my need must have been awakened by the mystery of the service, and later of the glowing colours of the priest's robes, colours seen nowhere else in my small-town, small-city life, and later again, in one church at least, the interior walls and ceiling covered in murals of angels and cherubs and the Way of the Cross and the Annunciation, the Virgin Birth, the Three Kings, the Death, and the Resurrection. So very much to look at as the priest droned on and the choir behind us sang lugubriously in Latin. The singing never sounded like music to me, although of course it was, but always I see my father's handsome face, hymnal open in his workman's hands, his beautiful mouth, which my older sister inherited, shaping so carefully the Latin sounds. What could I then recognize as beauty?

Or, thinking of my grandfather, father, and our uncle in a small clearing cutting grass to feed the workhorses and milk cow with large hand scythes, that slow, steady swing—I knew nothing of Thomas Hardy then, I wasn't even in school—while we small children, warned firmly to stay far away from the men, all girls in our mother-made overalls, running shrieking and laughing through the emerald grass that reached above our heads, sunlight sparking waterdrops, nuggets of sun caught in our hair.

And, of course, how can I not think of, perhaps this country's greatest painter, Emily Carr's transcendent painting of a simple wooden, white-painted church, a few crooked, low white crosses flanking it, standing in the midst of a towering, even overwhelming, dark green jungle-forest, surely signifying the immense power of nature and nature's gods over the paltry buildings of civilization. Once called *Indian Church*, the painting's name has been changed to *Church at Yuquot Village*. I once saw another such church at Stanley Mission in Saskatchewan. The local First Nations people built it between 1854 and 1860, and it stood before the forest on the immediate shore of a wide, fast-flowing and life-giving Churchill River. I thought it unlikely that the local Woodland Cree people, so much of whose lives were spent on the river, had chosen that name, so I looked it up to find, from *The Canadian Encyclopedia*: "The name—for John Churchill, first duke of Marlborough and governor of the Hudson's Bay Company from 1685 to 1691—was applied to the river as early as 1686. The Cree called it *Missinipi*, meaning 'great waters' or 'big water.'"

You have to see it to feel how powerful and fully alive that river is, and how very appropriate the Cree name is with its echo of awe, while "Churchill" now sounds ridiculous, not just because it is a long-dead white man's name, but because it takes no account of the river as the highway it is and was among northern communities, to wildlife and other food sources and also, once the whites arrived, as a major fur-trading route.

But I have heard of no movement to have the name changed back to the original. There is another Churchill River in Labrador, this one named after Winston Churchill but formerly called by all Grand River, a translation of the Innu name.

When we approached in our boats, the Stanley Mission church, although more elaborate than the one at Yuquot Village – it even has a clerestory – was almost as moving to see as Carr's painting of the church in the northern BC forest. And yet, I wondered what our young male Cree guides saw when they looked at the church, or First Nations people looking at Carr's painting of the Yuquot Village church. What Carr caught in that painting is the slightness of the white belief trying to stand as a bulwark against the mysterious, overwhelming power that was the rainforest itself. The forces of nature that whites have taken a long time to recognize.

So, I mistook big round hay bales for cattle because I hardly saw them, all I wanted to see was the field: of my education, of my unending wonder, the source of my answer to a deep question: What's next? Is there more? What happens to the past? To the last one, I say, it is still here; sometimes you can walk into it, as happened to me in the field.



With the new widow's permission, I did walk through "my" house though, before we left, which is how I know some of the paint applied during my reign was still on the walls, although in other rooms my arrangements had been changed drastically. I should have felt something when I was wandering around in the corrals and along the river, or through the house, but I didn't allow myself. My feeling was like that when you drive for hours to the city, and finally it appears, a thin line gleaming across the miles of fields along the far, low horizon. Those were where my feelings were, out along the far horizon, and I didn't get near them. I would not forget that my first visit back years earlier had been an emotional nightmare. Nor did I let my sense of the futility of my pain touch me; wasn't it just how life is? Just how life is for most widows? I was thinking how hard it must be for this widow to manage such an enterprise all by herself despite her rural, agricultural upbringing, a graduate degree in range management, and years of experience. I thought how she must wonder, every day, as I do in Calgary, and most other widows do around the world, what will become of her; where she will go, if anywhere; how this difficult period of her life will end, as I also wondered still, most days in Calgary. I kept cheerful, but I was anxious to get back in the car and move on to Regina, where I would not be assailed by loss, where I could be cheerful, too, about my past on the hay farm in the valley.

I turned back to the kitchen where my friend, the newer widow, was sitting with Lucinda, both drinking from frosted glasses of ice water, the weather being far too hot for anything else. We stayed a half hour, and I know we should have stayed longer, but I was antsy, wanted to get out of there, I think now because I was afraid of being overwhelmed, of being unable to extract myself from that past, and anyway, as I said, we still had to get to Regina, and already it was mid-afternoon.



**IV**

We stopped in Shaunavon, forty kilometres from the hay farm, for gas. Ten kilometres north of Shaunavon, the Redcoat Trail turns east. We would have had a more enjoyable trip on that winding, scenic southern route, but because it was too slow, single-laned, and, as I remembered it, too often in bad repair, we kept going north to rejoin the Trans-Canada again at Gull Lake. Also, "Absolutely no Timmy's on that road," I warned Lucinda, who had already revealed herself as a Tim's coffee fan.

In fact, my knowledge of that road was out of date. I'd drive on it again in July 2022 with other friends, heading to a village south of Moose Jaw, and although the speed limit was still lower than on the Trans-Canada, and it was still single-laned, the road itself was now well maintained and easy to drive. Because the Redcoat Trail was more interesting and pleasant than the Trans-Canada route, I'd be sorry I hadn't known that in July 2021.

I don't remember much of the drive to Swift Current; I was still sunk in the mood brought on by visiting what had been my home for over thirty years but never would be again. I was determinedly fixing my eyes on the road ahead and not allowing myself to think about my life there, the good parts of it anyway. Even as I thought of staying right there on the hay farm with the widow (not that I asked her if I could), I knew that without Peter, the place no longer made sense. And anyway, I didn't want to go back to worrying about the bulls getting out, or about helping shovel manure out of the barn. Or going down at midnight to help pull a calf, or holding the instruments while my husband doctored a de-horned steer whose wound wouldn't stop bleeding, him cursing softly, "Goddamn de-horning. Wouldn't *never* do it if I could help it." And the other steers quietly standing in a circle a few feet back from us, and me saying, "Look," in puzzlement, anthropomorphizing them, thinking they stood in empathy and maybe a sympathetic fear, and he replying, his voice flat but with a hint of clarity at their way of being, "They smell the blood," and crying then, as I might have been in danger of doing, would do nobody any good. I could mourn the past now, as we rushed away from it, but that was a waste of time, not to mention the uselessness of carrying around the pain-weighted heart.

Hey! We were on a trip! Worries banished, we're going somewhere! Mmmm, ya. Regina.

## V

In 2022, a year after the trip Lucinda and I took following the Redcoat Trail and visiting Peter's grave, I flew to a big city to visit some of my remaining relatives. Most of my time with them was gratifyingly pleasant, and some of it, as tends to happen in families, was less so. I came home dazed, neither still in the larger city nor fully at home in my own place, suspended somewhere between the two. I was filled with wonderment over the odd, even dissociative state I was in. Weirdly, I found myself disliking an accomplished, lovely painting on the wall across from me that I'd always especially liked. Now I found my determinedly bright, non-"greyge" (grey-beige) home insipid, failing to satisfy what I needed although I had no idea what that might be. Maybe it was only that I felt lost the way most travellers do for a while after returning from a journey. But the city only took an hour to reach by air; I'd only been gone three days. Still, I was tired, and I sat in bafflement staring at the television, not seeing or hearing it.



It was as if I'd found out I'd missed a part of life, and being with close family brought back a sense of some huge mistake I'd made, of a place where I'd gone wrong and had never seen it or known it was there. I must have been in shock at recognizing this gaping hole, whatever it was, which now seemed more important than the life I'd lived. I sat there fighting to learn what it was, but couldn't, nor could I come back to what I'd been when I'd left to spend a few days with family. Eventually, I gave up and went to bed.

Beginning the night I arrived home, for three nights I dreamt the same dream. Or rather, the same somehow harrowing scene appeared to me that, on waking, left me steeped in desolation, a darkness encompassing me that even awake I couldn't overcome. I carried that feeling all the next day and into the next day and the next. On the third morning I woke to find the dream-mood less paralyzing. Until late that third day, I had not even thought of trying to understand the dream, something that for the last thirty or more years whenever I'd had a disturbing dream I had always done. It hadn't even occurred to me to try to study this one, this because I was drenched, absolutely in the thrall to the dream's force. When I saw my nearly three-day failure to step back even a little from the dream, I was further shaken.

Finally, I began to look up the dream's chief symbols, the main one being the cave-like appearance of the room I was in, its twilight, its musty oppressiveness, which smacked of my childhood, although in the dream I was an adult. The space seemed to be a bedroom with a number of single beds pushed haphazardly about at different angles but all touching each other so that it seemed a sea of beds, and on each bed under tangled bedclothes I could see the bumps that indicated sleepers, who seemed to be my sisters although I couldn't see their faces. The bedcoverings were different shades of a deadened light grey-blue tone: only one near the front was a dulled dark red, and I knew that was the place of my oldest sister.



Because of the rough curving walls and very low ceiling and the shape of the opening, I thought I was in a cave. I, the dreamer, was at the far back wall, half-sitting, gazing across the beds and beyond them to the opening that was shaped like a wide, partially opened mouth and through which, far beyond, I could see a patch of a softened pale-yellow light that I took as sky, but too pale and far away for any rays to reach the room. I remembered that yellow as the colour of the sky, although much brighter, in central Saskatchewan where I spent most of my childhood, at the end of the afternoon rainstorm that, in summer, came nearly every day.

I woke each morning at first not knowing where I was. The first morning I was so disoriented I had to force myself to ask: Where was the window in the room where I'd stayed on my visit? Was there a chair by the window? Are those my clothes on that chair? And then gradually understanding: I am not in the dream; I am not in the room of my visit; I am at home in my bedroom.

I began to distance myself. I knew the sleeping bodies were my siblings, each one of whom I love, have loved, will always love, although there was no sense of this intimacy among us in the dream. There *might* have been an old or a middle-aged woman, robed in dark red, even shrouded, her hair covered by the mantle, seated in shadow on the left of the opening, her face lost in shadows. I did not look at her but only at the beds and across them to the patch of distant, weak, pale-yellow light.

That was not a cave, I realized; it was a *womb*. Further, that I had wakened.

Easy to see that the dream was about clinging too hard and too long to my family's story, which was also my own story, easy to see that once awake, I could not go back to sleep, nor stay in the cave-womb. Or, perhaps it was a prophecy about what writing this book could, or would do for me, and to me.

# FIVE

# SOUL

## I

Just short of one hundred and fifty years after the NWMP trek across the southern prairies began, we were in our car speeding in the opposite direction through the same territory, two women, one middle-aged and one elderly, and the land through which we travelled no longer wilderness, but when not Crown land, all owned by somebody, fenced and seeded to crops or hay or left as grazing land. Almost none of it open any longer to the incursions of anyone but the owners. I wonder what William Francis Butler would say about it if he were to come back to life and try to cross the same territory he did a century and a half ago. Miles and miles of wild grasses gleaming gold and cream in the sun, at night silver, or at dawn or sunset pink or mauve or a deep bronze. He would probably think, *all of it gone*, and all the wildlife he'd seen gone, too, or extirpated: plains bison and bears, prairie wolves and swift foxes (the latter has been reintroduced), to name the larger species, all that space and distance and sense of pure wild freedom gone, too. But the loneliness of "the great lone land," as he called it, both so resoundingly deep as to bear no description, and yet so blessed to find in a steadily churning, noisy world he would find doggedly preserved in pockets here and there.

Too much information, I'm afraid, is what Lucinda would rightfully have said to me if I had given her all that data or told any more of the stories I knew. I had been in a rush to leave the hay farm, although I think Lucinda wasn't even remotely in a hurry, my anxiety with regard to meeting deadlines and sticking to plans always overwhelming any longing to take it easy, to follow chance and opportunity. Such behaviour leading to laziness, irresponsibility, bad manners; the unruly soul always needing to be held in with tight reins.

Or was it that the longer I stayed in the place I'd come from, the sooner my knowing would come that that life that I had both loved and hated was really over, that now it was as if it had never happened, the sooner things I didn't want to think about would come, and the long-feared ruin would ensue. Every year, it seems now, as I continued to refuse to look back at my own history, as I had become expert in holding my soul in check, I had also distanced myself from my own present life. Although I was proud to be no longer at the beck and call of desire, my heart had slowly frozen.



On we went to Regina, cool and comfortable in the air conditioning while the rabid sun snarled down on us. I'd been afraid that in the intense, unrelenting heat the AC would break down, the difference between being raised in my era, the early part of which did not contain automobile air conditioners, so that in summer we drove with all the windows open, the hot air flattening us against our seats, covering our faces with dirt, which got into our eyes and ears, up our nostrils and even into our teeth, and destroyed our hairdos, and being raised in Lucinda's era, the sixties when air conditioners first began to be commonplace in cars.

Just in case, though, mimicking our mother who had been a champion of preparedness, I had brought those two sun hats, one for each of us, imagining trying to survive in that scalding sun by the side of the road without even a head-covering for shade until we were rescued. I learned on day one on the treeless southern prairie that while riding a horse in summer you wear a hat. Period. At least, if you don't want to slide off your horse in a dead faint from sunstroke. But ever prepared also, Lucinda had brought her own hat, although the vision I had of dying of heat stroke wasn't her reason for bringing one along: Lucinda is a normal person, even though a poet.

Besides worrying about the air conditioning, I remembered how my first husband and I and our baby son, on our way from Vancouver and driving the original, although second-hand to us, Volkswagen Bug, stopped for a couple of hours on a hot day like this one, in Dinosaur Provincial Park to look at the hoodoos. Then our car wouldn't start, and not another soul was around and neither a town or village or hamlet that we could reach on  foot and especially not with a baby who wouldn't survive direct, extended exposure to the heat. My then-husband guessed that it was a vapour lock in the fuel line, when the gas vaporizes, blocking the flow of fuel, caused by the extreme heat. He said we could do nothing but wait for the car to cool sufficiently that the vapour lock would disperse on its own. We walked around for a while more; he turned the key again; and despite the fact that the heat was if anything greater than when the car had refused to start, it sputtered to life.

Thinking about that long-ago trip from Vancouver to Halifax, all the old worries came back to haunt me. This is what it is to be old—you worry about things that don't exist anymore. The air conditioner worked away, hour after hour cooling us without a hiccup, although it turns out that in gasoline-fuelled vehicles you can still get a vapour lock, although we didn't. I knew that my anxiety was at least due to having been married in total for nearly fifty years, I wasn't used to the absence of a competent male and his superior knowledge, in my experience, anyway, about how vehicles work and what to do when they don't. I also worried about flat tires, not that on the entire trip we came anywhere near to having one.

In Swift Current (population roughly sixteen thousand people), I directed Lucinda to the downtown Timmy's for her ritual coffee, not remembering that there was one just off the highway in the north, although on the other side of the divided highway we would pass down. Although she said nothing, I know she was unimpressed by Swift Current, a place as friendly as it can be to those who know it and its people, maybe a bit dismal for somebody raised in Vancouver, especially if you don't have time or don't know how to find its pretty spots that I'd been years finding myself, along Swift Current Creek, which runs through the city cutting it in two.



It is the market town for the agricultural people of the wide, sparsely peopled area surrounding it; the larger city of Medicine Hat is 224 kilometres away and in another province. Swift Current is the place that everybody, quite a few from the nearby Hutterite colonies, too, goes to on a day of heavy rain when the mall parking lot is full of mud-splashed trucks. Hard to get in and out of those trucks without getting mud on your going-to-town clothes. In richer Alberta, a lot of country roads are paved, but not in Saskatchewan. On really wet days, only four-wheel-drive trucks can get through from home to the highway and during the rare three-day rains when outdoor work is impossible, everybody takes time off and goes to "Swift" for the day. Later, your errands done, you wait around in a café usually, or maybe at a relative's or friend's house until your husband decrees that in the descending night's cold, the mud has "stiffened up" enough that the drive home, once you leave the hard-top roads, will be easier and you won't be so likely to get stuck or slide into a ditch and have to walk the rest of the way.

Lucinda and I didn't linger, but soon drove on east, the next significant marker after Swift Current being, at least in my opinion, Moose Jaw. I pointed out the Chaplin Nature Centre about an hour east of Swift Current, where it's not possible to miss the results of the salt mining, or "sodium sulfate collecting" from underground that goes on there, long high banks of something white well back from the highway and the earth scraped flat and nearly pale as the white clay deposits on the Ravenscrag buttes, so that when you see the area, even in July, at first you laugh in surprised bafflement, thinking you are seeing snow.

**II**

Further along, if we deviated south from the highway, a road leads to the ranch belonging to Colin Thatcher, the convicted murderer of his ex-wife, JoAnn Wilson. I'd heard that Colin still lived there with a new wife after serving twenty-two years in prison. I found it hard to believe that thirty-seven years had passed since the trial that gripped the province, even the country, because Thatcher had once been a provincial cabinet minister, powerful and hated by a few and disliked by far too many more people; his father had been Liberal Premier of the province from 1964 to 1971, years when I was still in my first marriage and had become a New Democrat, having come from, aside from my French-Canadian father who came from a long line of Liberals, a family of devoted CCF-ers whose respect and admiration for the Scottish-born former-preacher Tommy Douglas, Saskatchewan's premier from 1944 to 1961, remained profound.

Douglas's focus in government had always been on making life less arduous for the ordinary people of his province. He said that his proudest accomplishment was rural electrification by the act passed in 1949, the aims of which were achieved by the late fifties. But in 1946 he and his party passed the Saskatchewan Hospitalization Act that laid the groundwork for what would become, on July 1, 1968, Canada's comprehensive, universal health care system, inaugurated right there in the Swift Current region that we had just driven through. That, I did point out to Lucinda, and with a lot of pride.

In 1957, my younger sister who in 1947 when she was five had been severely disabled by polio, needed life-saving back surgery in a long and difficult operation, which my parents had been told she might not survive, although without it, doctors said, she would not survive long, either. When the surgery was over, and she came home after months in the hospital, the bill, which was already paid, arrived in the mail. I remember the look on our parents' faces as they stared at the size of it, a number that, if they had had to pay it, would have destroyed us. Sending it was either an error or else a finger-wagging reminder, maybe even from some disapproving civil service clerk, because when the act was instituted, the whole province had been in an uproar, even to the extent of an infamous doctor's strike. We guessed sending the bill of the true cost of my sister's treatment was meant to make us grateful that the government would pay, or else done out of anger that the taxpayer was forced to. I thought it might have been sent to us purely in disapproval of socialism, but now I'm told it was standard procedure. My mother walked around the rest of the day wearing a stunned expression.

Thinking also of my beloved grandparents, fallen on hard times then, and old, I still get tears in my eyes thinking of that courageous, life-altering government initiative that began in

1946, along with dismay that, today, the health care system has all come to complaint, disorder, and apparent malfunctioning. And yet, I keep reminding myself that in Addis Ababa in the mid-nineties, I saw men dying of AIDS lying silently on the ground, the Black Lion Hospital, we were told, being too full to accept more patients, and, it seemed, no other help to be had. North of Addis on our way to Lalibela, we came upon a major vehicle accident and a few miles from it, a group of villagers on foot carrying an unconscious man on a pallet to the nearest clinic, which we were told was thirty-five miles away.

In 2004, Canada's public broadcaster, CBC Radio and Television, held a contest to name the "Greatest Canadian." Tommy Douglas won it, hands down. In fairness, I note that no women were on the shortlist of ten, or First Nations people, and the contest wasn't broadcast in French.

Fifteen years had gone by the day Lucinda and I passed the road going south, since Thatcher's release from prison and return to his family's cattle ranch. I'd written a book, half memoir, half documentary about the murder of a girl with whom I'd gone to high school, Alexandra Wiwcharuk, murdered May 18, 1962, in Saskatoon, and had reported in it that a few people I interviewed insisted to me that Colin Thatcher was her killer, too, an accusation I couldn't see as logistically possible; nor, apparently, could the police who investigated this possibility. I don't know why so many people wanted Thatcher to be guilty of that murder, too, and were so angry about it, other than that both murders were vicious beyond understanding, clearly committed by a rage-filled killer, whoever he was in Alex's case, the rage probably caused by the refusal of each woman, although in different ways, to submit to him.

I was stunned to discover that I could drive by the road that would lead to his ranch, just like that, that he was down there somewhere, in his eighties now, riding his horse across the flower-dotted, sun-bright prairie, rounding up his cows and living his life as if nothing had happened. I wondered if people remembered, if his neighbours cared. Was he still enraged that he'd been caught? Despite the evidence and the guilty verdict, he has never stopped insisting that he didn't do it, the question arising then, who did it? And for heaven's sake, why? Who else could have held such irrational rage toward her?

Nearly thirty-nine years after the murder of Thatcher's former wife, my subject's murder fifty-nine years earlier still unsolved, and all the cruelty of Alex's and JoAnn's bloody, bludgeoning deaths, the fury of each attack: JoAnn's finger severed in the beating she endured before she died of a gunshot; Alex, much earlier in Saskatoon, had had her skull shattered, her face punched in, and been raped before she died of asphyxiation in the shallow grave her killer had made, covering her still breathing body and face with dirt. All of those events had thinned and faded as if they had been only a bad dream. And I couldn't understand how that could be.



A few years ago, quite a while after Peter's death, I had a relationship with a man who knew all the people involved in the JoAnn Wilson murder case. My moving to live with him was on both our minds then, but I was hesitant, and although it was what he said he wanted, because of his age he felt it wrong to try to persuade me. When he became seriously ill, it had been a year and some months since we had parted, although, as is the way with the old, occasionally we still talked on the phone without hostility and with mutual sympathy. We both believed we had something he called a Celtic connection, because I knew when he was in trouble, no one told me. I phoned him to find out what was wrong and to offer my emotional support, which he accepted, even welcomed, even though I couldn't help him in any practical way. Later, when he was in distress and in hospital, I told him I would come to see him, and he said he didn't want me to. After the night I got up from his sofa and in shock that left me unable to breathe normally, my throat too tight to speak in my own voice much less shout, I walked out of his house in a late November snowstorm, hard dry snow pellets pinging against my car and sweeping across my windshield all the way, and drove too fast toward home, I never saw him in person again.

It would take me almost ten more years before one ordinary day when what was for me a devastating scene from my first marriage thudded like a swung bat into my brain. I've lost the details, or refuse to think of them, remember only that I had been holding my newborn as I fed him, and that I was crying hard but silently, when our baby started to choke as new babies often do when feeding. We were young, and new parents, and with no one there to call on, my young husband who had been lost in some rant panicked, turned frantically to find a solution or help, grabbed the phone, tossed it down again, spun as if to think where to run for help, while I stopped the choking as I'd been taught to do simply by tilting the baby so the milk could run out.



I'd never told anyone what I can remember about this incident because it was too unbearable to speak of, so I had never come to terms with it, so that it lurked deep below – still – in all its wretchedness. Then, many years later, at my elderly boyfriend's house when something too close to the same happened, my reaction was beyond extreme, it was unwarranted, even inappropriate in its violence, in terms of the offence, which was an out-of-the-blue verbal assault over some crime he thought I'd committed but that made no sense to me and that – I thought and still do – was completely unprovoked. Instead of responding by arguing, yelling, name-calling, throwing things, or punching him (he was over six feet tall and burly), I dropped instantly into a voiceless darkness, could not even think, for a full hour I *literally* could not speak or move so much as a finger. I baffled even him.

I didn't understand then that what had happened was what is called today a trigger, that I was dealing with someone else, something else, which in my years of supressing the first instance so fully, I had not found a way to manage that old wounding, not a scintilla of relief had come to me in the nearly sixty years since it had happened. Until, eventually, in this new, repeat situation, it came to me: *I can leave.* Then I was all action, gathering my few things, throwing them into my vehicle, speeding away forever.

I recount this story concerning the two men and me, both of whom had to have had their own torments to deal with or neither event would have happened, because I know no better



way to describe the power of the psyche to hold one in thrall to it. That is what this storytelling is about, not about the facts of the two incidents. I think again of that relentless drip of water from the ceiling, which became a fast-flowing stream that threatened to drown me, that warned me that taking this trip with Lucinda, on the surface so innocent, pleasant and safe, would send me on a more perilous journey, one from which I might not return. Pooh, I must have replied; I'm only going to Winnipeg and on roads I've been driving on since I was thirteen years old.

But when I left my boyfriend's house that night, I wonder if the young husband from so many years earlier was the real man I was leaving, something I never did, and only indirectly the man sitting in the same room with me, who, when he saw me gathering my things, saw how serious I was, finally asked me not to go. But I was once again on the run, leaving behind what I couldn't deal with or allow, shutting it off, trying to forget it, all of it, everything, my whole past with which he had had nothing to do.

But then I remind myself plenty of women in the world are just as bad to the men close to them, sometimes even worse, and whose behaviour does every bit as much damage. I might have been thinking of my mother. I remembered, too, something I'd forgotten. In their last years our parents sat quietly together watching television, our mother knitting or crocheting. No more shouting, door-slamming or crying, and how she sat at his bedside for days as he died. But she had always repeated grimly, decisively to us, speaking of women she knew who were in miserable marriages, "In the world we come from, *you do not leave your husband*." Maybe I was running from that dictate, too.

I was also thinking then that it had taken me sixty years to take control of my life by walking away, but now I am also thinking that at some level I must have believed that this was the price I would have to pay, to put it simply and without histrionics or romanticism, to be half of a stable couple, and the day had finally come when I would not pay that price anymore.



I never thought that I was also probably reacting to all the childhood scenes when our parents fought, screaming accusations at each other, saying awful things, never mind that four or five of their children were standing right there, awash in anguish, desperate for them to stop. That my soul-deep despair following the first time was caused by what I had seen of my parents' marriage and up to that moment believed I had escaped. That escape was possible. I think I despaired then also because I thought that love meant there would be no such scenes. Maybe my excessive reaction to the second verbal assault so many years later was also caused by the lifelong damage done by the kind of marriage our parents had, where, in extremity, no words were too hurtful to say.

Now *there* is a thread in my life I never saw before, a weighty one, and it is one more likely to save me than to drown me. If the reader wonders at my boldness in writing this, from the mistakes of my parents, dead now for fifty and thirty-six years, to my ex-husband whom I haven't so much as seen in over thirty years, and then my last about-to-be-life-partner, dead now for years, I beg the privilege of age, by which I mean, now is the time to find and tell the truth, so that one doesn't go to one's grave in turmoil and unmitigated pain. I'm not trying to get even; I'm a writer, and the material of my life is what I choose to write about. This turns out to be a book about psyche and its immense power that holds an individual in its relentless grip until one day it erupts and after its spewed contents cool, there is finally some relief.

In quoting the great Carl Jung on the matter of the unrelenting, unyielding drive in some of us, I point out that I have been, always, driven; I am not by any means a "great" artist as Jung confines his remarks to addressing, and no one will ever choose to write my biography. Nevertheless, this quote applies to many of us artists who give our lives to our art but are not considered to be "great" by anyone. But, also, it's pretty much agreed that Jung never was that good on women, and he does point out that creativity lives, too often unknown and misunderstood, in all of us:



"The biographies of great artists make it abundantly clear that the creative urge is often so imperious that it battens on their humanity and yokes everything to the service of the work, even at the cost of health and ordinary human happiness. The unborn work in the psyche of the artist is a force of nature that achieves its end either with tyrannical might or with the subtle cunning of nature herself, quite regardless of the personal fate of the man [sic] who is its vehicle. The creative urge lives and grows in him like a tree in the earth from which it draws its nourishment. We would do well, therefore, to think of the creative process as a living thing implanted in the human psyche."

The lives of Western women have, up until recently, at least, been set: We marry, we have children, we have the primary responsibility for them, we do all the work of running the home. For most of us, at least up to now, the decisions to marry with those concomitant assumptions were made when we were too young to fully understand what we have signed onto, that we have given over our lives to our family. But there have always been women who could not subjugate themselves totally to these demands, especially that women as mothers are predominately in charge of raising and caring for the children, and when a woman (not for reasons of poverty or severe abuse of one kind or another) refuses in part or whole to do so, she is scorned in society, viewed as dissolute, uncaring, not fully human. It hardly needs pointing out that men are not subject to the same sanctions. Alice Munro, our greatest Canadian writer and only literary Nobelist, is a case in point. She began writing as a teenager, but married at twenty and had three children (a fourth, born in 1955, died the day she was born, the grief and long-lasting effects of this to Munro almost never mentioned). All the while continuing to write and growing more famous, more successful with every passing year, while also attending to the demands of such a career: being away from home to take part in literary festivals and conferences, give readings, speeches and to do interviews, accept awards and so on, while also responsible for her children and their care. Here is *one* way of understanding the title of this book, *How to Breathe Water* (or, better, in this one case of making art, most likely, *It Can't Be Done*).

When the scandal broke in July 2024, that in 1976 her new partner had sexually abused her youngest daughter, Andrea, who often called herself by her second name, Robin, when the child was nine years old, and that others knew of it but no one told Munro until Robin herself did in a letter, in 1992, and that when Munro was informed, she chose her partner over her child (who by then was twenty-five years old), I was at first as appalled as anyone by what we saw as Munro's motherly failure. Munro had died at ninety-two, in May of 2024, and the press seemed to believe they could now tell the public of our most treasured writer's dereliction of her (apparently) ages-old duty as a mother, never mind the fierce, instinctive love we also believe in, of the mother for her child.

Munro, however, had left her partner, Gerald Fremlin, for several months in 1992 after receiving Robin's letter (signifying deep thought about what she should do, for both of which she seems to have received little to no credit). In a December 23, 2024, article in *The New Yorker* ("Alice Munro's Passive Voice"), Rachel Aviv says that Fremlin later flew to Munro in Comox, and that together they saw a therapist. We do not know details of their communication during that time, and in the end, Munro returned to Fremlin. I had imagined Munro during this time as thinking deeply about the situation and what was expected of her and what she expected of herself, in much the same way she approached one of her stories with all their nuance, subtlety, weaving together of past, present and future, careful reckoning of details and hard truths; that is, with long serious thought and many abortive trial solutions.

I wondered, too, can pedophiles be cured? I don't know the answer, but my tendency is to doubt it. When caught and faced with sanctions, do they say they are sorry and promise never to do it again? (Fremlin wrote in letters that it was all the nine-year-old girl's fault.) But if this was, to Munro, an infidelity and not criminal harm to her child, how then might such conversations, if they did take place, have gone? If he couldn't accept responsibility, what would he have said to Munro to convince her to stay with him, if indeed, he did try to do that, or was some other bizarre reckoning going on: Munro trying to forge a way she could stay with him and not hate herself for it?

According to Robin, Munro did not respond to her child with motherly rage at her partner's assaults, and so, a few months after Munro's death, determined to be heard, Robin found an editor who published her essay about the abuse she suffered and Munro's lack of support for her once she found out about it. Robin described how Munro, in her decision to support her partner and not her child, blamed our misogynist culture, apparently for the unquestionable expectation that she must, as a woman, choose her child over her partner (that is, that her own life and needs did not matter, that she should sacrifice them to her child's need). She also said that she had been told too late, seeming to imply that if she'd known of the abuse when Robin was a defenceless child, then her daughter's needs would have taken priority over her own, and there would have to have been some reckoning between herself and her partner, in which Robin might even have participated. But Robin says she didn't tell her mother in 1976 because even then she expected that her mother would blame her. Many abused children believe this whether or not (I believe) there is clear reason to do so. When parents separate, frequently small children feel they are to blame, also an irrational but extremely damaging belief. Since we can't know whether Munro would have blamed Robin or not, we can't blame or defend her. It is hard to argue with the fact that Munro could not protect her child if she did not know what was happening. Robin seems to have been devastated by her mother's unfeelingness toward her pain, which included Munro's ultimate decision not to leave the man who had assaulted her child.

Being far from the Perfect Mother myself (I *truly* shudder to think of all the ways I failed – I am not being charmingly ingenuous here; I mean it), I certainly felt, at the same time, a nagging sympathy for Munro, or, if not exactly sympathy, a sense that the great mistake in this case was not hers. In 2024 it was reported that Robin told her stepbrother, Andrew, about the abuse, and he told her father and Munro's former husband, Jim Munro, who then "instructed the family to stay quiet." ("What Alice Munro Knew," Giles Harvey, *New York Times Magazine*, December 8, 2024). I was most appalled at Robin's father and stepmother, and the other adults who knew what Robin had endured and decided against telling her mother. These are, or were, well-meaning, highly thought of, intelligent adults who must have had much-discussed reasons for this decision. I can only think that they must not have understood the far-reaching reverberations of such childhood abuse in the lives of those who suffer it. If they had never suffered it themselves, nor paid much attention to adults with sexual abuse in their childhoods – and why would they, if this was far out on the periphery of their worldview as it mostly is or was for most middle-class adults, absolute silence being their usual way of dealing with abuse – they would have felt that the genuine love, sympathy, and other attempts at support for her by her father and stepmother would be sufficient to overcome her shame, sense of injustice, anger, and, perhaps at bottom, fear of being unloved, or, below the conscious level and worst of all, of being unlovable. Perhaps they would not have seen the details, the extent and far-reaching implications of the emotional harm done to the child. I write here in a general sense as I have no personal knowledge of any of this, having met, of these figures, only Robin's father and that only briefly when in his bookstore, he scolded me mildly for not having attended a party he had given the night before for writers. "I was very tired," I lied. The truth was I thought either my childhood positively pathological shyness would take over and I'd be miserably uncomfortable, or worse, I would go around saying stupid things out of my anxiety and forever alienate everybody there. Although once at a party, feeling the same way, but this time more drunk than sober, I had an incredibly interesting (to me anyway) long conversation with David Malouf.

Many of the friends and acquaintances, some writers, I have spoken with about this scandal mention the fact of Munro's celebrity and high reputation as being the obvious reason that Munro wasn't told immediately about the abuse. From the beginning I took the view that her high standing as a writer and her fame were background and would not strongly motivate, one way or another, the other principal actors in this quandary, that the *real* decision (to tell Munro or not) would be more likely to come out of individual roles, family histories, private sentiments, and inter-family experiences than it would be about the effect on Munro's public persona and her career. The *New York Magazine* article cited above reports that Jim Munro chose secrecy because he worried that the disclosure would wreck Munro's new relationship and that he would then be blamed. If Robin's two sisters and stepbrother had their own private reasons for not telling her, they haven't been reported that I have found.



After Robin told Munro herself, and Munro called her a liar, Robin took Fremlin's self-incriminating letters to lawyers and on to court, where he was found guilty of sexual assault. Later, after her mother had died, Robin seems not to have doubted that the world should know that their "idol," (let's not forget the "feet of clay" adage), was not the "Saint Alice" of some peoples' imagination. Munro herself, beside her fierce determination to hang onto her partner and her relationship, might also have been worried about what the revelation could do to her reputation and literary status, but about that, one can only guess. Her first consideration, at least out loud, appears to have been to protect and retain Fremlin. Nobody would know better than an Alice Munro what deeper, barely conscious reasons might have flashed through her mind.

A very odd thing about this, strictly from my point of view as a writer, was that in 1992 I was commissioned by 25th Street Theatre in Saskatoon to write a play for them. My play was called *Rodeo Life*, as in "he liked rodeo life," and was performed in '93 at their theatre. In it, the grown children have gathered on the family ranch to wait for the elderly domineering matriarch's imminent death, the revered rodeo-cowboy-hero father having died some years earlier. In the course of the play (it takes place over a day and a night as far as I can remember), the long-troubled daughter tells the remaining three siblings that when she was a child, and as a treat was allowed to stay briefly with their father in his trailer at a summer rodeo, he, drunk, sexually abused her. Instantly (how wonderfully the actors, Carol Greyeyes and Sharon Bakker performed this scene), the oldest sister, almost before the words are out, as if to drown out the accusation, shouts, "Liar!"



I see now that that instant shout was a cover for what the eldest sister knew or didn't know she knew until her sister said it out loud. It replaced the more appropriate astonishment of, for example, a stunned reaction to such a seemingly ridiculous, indeed, perceived as a nutty, even malicious accusation: an instant of shocked silence, and then, perhaps, "How can you say such a terrible thing about our dad?" Followed by gentle or angry questioning. But the shout, "Liar!" places the accuser on the outside of the family.

When I started that play, I had no idea that was what *Rodeo Life* would really be about, no idea about what had happened to me as an infant, no idea that at roughly the same time somewhere in Canada the revered (profoundly by me) Alice Munro was shouting the same word to her grown daughter's revelation. No idea, either, in writing my play, how I knew that that would be the response of the about-to-be new matriarch and self-assigned protector of the famous father's reputation. She, the eldest child, wants before all else to hold things together. As Yeats, in "The Second Coming," put it:

*Things fall apart; the centre cannot hold;*
*Mere anarchy is loosed upon the world,*
*The blood-dimmed tide is loosed, and everywhere*
*The ceremony of innocence is drowned;*

Munro's decision to return to her husband and to view (as nearly as I can tell from the reporting on the subject) her daughter as a rival and/or a liar – obviously she couldn't be both at the same time – rather than a helpless victim shocks us all. At first knowing, we give Munro no quarter. But it seems worthwhile to point out that when she died it was well known that Munro had been suffering from dementia for some years (first reported in 2012, I believe, when Munro was eighty-one). Most of us are also aware, if only colloquially, that it is often reported by relatives and friends that signs of the approaching dementia can sometimes be seen many years earlier, at least in retrospect, in the form of inexplicable, uncharacteristic, inappropriate behaviours. I also couldn't help but wonder what so many years of adulation must do, or have the capacity to do, to an individual's sense of responsibility toward others, how corrosive to the soul fame can be, and of the Faustian bargain high achievers too often make, I would even say, have to make, and that is made gladly, willingly, and for which the rest of us, in some cases, owe a tremendous gratitude. As retired professor, critic and writer Joan Givner said to me, "No one understands what it takes to be an Alice Munro." By "no one" she meant all the readers, and writers, too, who claim, post-revelation, to be unwilling ever again to read Munro, to want not to see her books again, to utterly devalue her work. Who clearly believe that one's personal behaviour outweighs any massive, long-lasting artistic achievement. This is an old story, of course. Coetzee wrote a small novel about it, called *Summertime*.

I thought, too, of Munro's brilliant, inimitable stories, their depth, power, and incisiveness as well as their ultimate mystery, and asked myself how a woman of such vision and penetrating, even goddess-like insight could not respond to her own child's suffering. I think in the sanctity of my own kitchen as I write at my table and without ever having even lain eyes on Munro in flesh, much less spoken with her (although she did once send me a postcard!) and having my own failures as a mother to deal with, that she was simply too far removed, and part of that removal, maybe the biggest part, was the cold clear vision of the great artist.



But, I also see in Alice Munro's work a kind of toughness that I don't see in the work of most others of her literary status – or perhaps it's only better disguised – and I wonder where that toughness came from that is really a shutting off from participation in another's pain, a distancing, but coming as I do from a working-class background in wilderness and small prairie towns from my birth to my early teens, and then again in later life for thirty-three years, I think I recognize it: Life is bitterly hard, it says, and nobody gives a damn about you, so you'd better suck it up, get tough, get real, and never forget that you're on your own. It is also saying, so you had a hard time of it, eh? Didn't we all? Quit your complaining. If you are as gifted as Munro was, and see a future full of the highest success possible, there is a part of you – there might be – that will do whatever you have to do to reach that goal. But here is also where Jung comes in.

Beyond explanations for her behaviour or possibilities as to what else might have caused it, I've ignored the biggest one in the artist's life: the powerful drive to create that can push aside, even disregard the needs of others around the artist. This, I suggest, while viewed as unforgivably cruel and a failure of a mother's duty, nonetheless, and because of the weakening of strong human ties in the artist's life (how very odd that insatiable clinging to the profoundly flawed Fremlin), a pitiless clarity regarding human relationships and human drives comes to the artist. I believe that it contributes to making the art greater. Again, not classifying myself by any means as one of Jung's "great" artists, I have seen that response in myself, have been horrified at myself, and have tried to fight against it. I think that mostly, I failed. It is indeed a kind of narcissism, but different in that it exists in the service of art, of that inexorable, driving creative force. That is the artist's struggle: every day, every minute of the day, every dust mote floating down light, every barely perceptible hint of emotion in a voice, every turn or tilt of the head is the material of art; awareness, attention, contemplation never shut off. To shut them off is to start to die. As Rudy Wiebe (twice Governor General's Literary Award winner for fiction and a man who understands what it is to be an artist) once chided me, "It is a sin not to write." I had told him I had to stop in order to move in with a family member to care for her for the ten months it took her to die. Rudy was old in 2024, as I was, older even, and I wondered what he would say now. At the time, I thought, but did not say, oh yeah? How many beloved (or not) dying family members have you felt it to be your duty and more, something greater than mere duty to look after? Meaning, he can say that and even mean it: He's a man. That work is left to women. But then, I'll never win a Nobel either.

In one of the three stories in the 1989 film *New York Stories*, this one directed by Martin Scorsese, starring Nick Nolte as an important, successful modern painter, there is a telling illustration of this point (although the story's principal theme is this male artist's need for a "muse," whom he seems incapable of seeing first as a living human being who needs his attention and love, and whom he discards at will, presumably in serial, for another, fresher one whose beauty and appearance of childlike innocence inspires him to make great art). Each young woman becomes mere collateral damage to the painter's art. It's worth reading Henry James's 1888 novella/short story, "The Lesson of the Master," on this subject, although of course, it is a misogynistic piece of work, and the artists in question are male. The female artist's need for her husband and children struggles powerfully against her need to make art, and sometimes – perhaps even often – her drive to make art wins. When Doris Lessing left South Africa for London to write, she left behind two children from her first marriage. On the other hand, when Margaret Laurence left Africa to go to England to write, she took her two children with her. I barely know what to make of the fact that Lessing became a Nobelist, while Laurence, although achieving high literary status, did not. No wonder that in the nineteenth century most literary art, especially that by women, came from the classes who could afford nannies and tutors, cooks, and maids, and not from the working class.

There is the question, too, of neglectful mothers, of mothers focused on themselves rather than on their children. This, we are not allowed to say about Alice Munro, or to question whether she was one of these or not: to do so seems disrespectful of her as a great artist, worse, heretical. It can only be implied. I have no trouble drawing yet another (narcissistic) parallel to my own life. Munro is quoted as having said she had children because, more or less, that was the expectation, one she didn't examine but simply took for granted. "Same thing happened to me," as singer-songwriter John Prine put it. I was in love; I got married; two years later, I was pregnant and had a son. Despite having three sisters younger than I am (and one older), I had no idea how to be a mother, having never thought of being one. Nor had I bargained on what being a mother would do to what I fondly thought of as my life. Of the possibilities of what I might become without that responsibility. So it must have been for many women of my generation (born in 1940) and Alice Munro's generation. This could never be spoken of, nor does it, for nearly all of us, preclude our deepest love for the children, who, for most of us, have changed and usually limited our lives. This is simply the great confusion, the great paradox for many of us who in those days became mothers. (Don't forget that there was then no pill to prevent conception.) Besides that, there has never been a rule as to who can become pregnant and deliver a child. If you were a woman, that was your role. Period. If you didn't want children, you didn't marry, that being the only way (in average, everyday lives) not to have them.



So you married, you gave birth, usually more than once, and if all the while you really wanted something else, you either stifled that desire with all your might, or you tried valiantly to squeeze out a little room for whatever it was. If you were successful at that desire, you would not give it up. If you were successful enough, your family wouldn't force you to give it up. But inevitably your family would feel you had not given your whole soul to them, that you cared more about that desire than about them. But that is an old story, one we all know and mostly tsk-tsk about it, even if we then go into the kitchen and cry a few tears over our own lost desire. And we severely castigate the one who appears to have managed to have both. "I don't know how she does it," we say with mixed emotion, and in some puzzlement, or with fake admiration, probably because we know you can't have both (unless you are wealthy, we tell each other) and not pay a price one way or another, usually in being the object of scorn, often in marriage breakdown and all the kids deciding to live with their father (and his new partner/wife) at least for a while, since the mother is so clearly at fault for not putting them first.

For a long time, Munro held onto both whether she really wanted to or not. She is quoted in Robert Thacker's 2005 biography, *Alice Munro: Writing Her Lives*, as having said "that these were the twin choices of my life . . . marriage and motherhood or the black life of the artist." She tried to do both, but after twenty-two years, her marriage ended in divorce. Robin was then about seven years old, and in the divorce agreement, according to one report but otherwise in another, she lived with her father and his second wife in Victoria and spent summers with her mother and her new partner in Ontario.



Fremlin, author of all this suffering, found guilty of one count of indecent assault, received a suspended sentence. It is reported that when he was arrested, Munro, who had known of Robin's accusation and denied it for thirteen years, was "furious," not with Fremlin, whom she defended, but with Robin (who was not present). According to the Ontario Provincial Police detective who was present, Munro once again accused her daughter of lying (*Canadian Press*, July 16, 2024). But Fremlin's own letters proved to the court that Robin was telling the truth. As we know from many other cases, the mother blaming the child for "seducing" the spouse and/or accusing the child of lying are familiar stories and suggest to me a mind that denies unbearable truths, that cannot face the discomfort, loss, dislocation, and many other difficulties of the ensuing probable marriage breakdown. (I remember once telling a friend that I didn't want to leave my husband because I didn't want to leave my new sofa, the sofa, of course, being a stand-in for my home and my way of life.) Munro stayed with Fremlin until his death in 2013. Her attachment to him strikes me as not rational, and possibly, despite her saying it was, not entirely about love.

The *New Yorker* article is very long and very detailed, so much so that I left it feeling that it is hard as a lover of Munro's work to pull oneself above the family quagmire to see the story in its simple facts. A woman acknowledged to be a great writer is now also thought to be a failed mother and the two are intertwined because, out of this story – her own, that was for her untellable – she made art. By this act, Munro became, finally, one of her own stories.



Despite all of this, she remains a great artist, alone in her particular genius in the literary world, but unfortunately hardly alone as a Nobelist with scandal behind the genius. Saul Bellow married five times, Pablo Picasso frequently changed partners and had many children by them, Knut Hamsun was part of a Hitler scandal, etc., those being only the ones I can think of without looking anything up. Or do we just more easily forgive men as serial relationships and bad fathering being their nature and while not exactly celebrated, pretty much only to be expected? Munro was right to blame our misogynistic culture for demanding she be the mother few of us actually are, and right also that she was told too late.

I wrote that I had taken Munro's celebrity and near-celestial artistic reputation as merely background and of small importance in the ongoing family drama; I think now that I was wrong. Even when family members were thinking of how they themselves should feel about what happened and how they should act toward those who were or were not a part of it, I think that the implacable, barely recognized or not recognized at all, aura of celebrity enveloped them like a fog or perhaps a miasma through which they moved, that they were affected by it though not knowing in what way, nor how to stop it. It was who Munro was as long as she lived – inescapably her celebrity, the effects of which were perhaps loved and perhaps hated by every one of them; that, although celebrity and talent are not the same thing, they are inevitably linked in this story, that Munro could not turn off her drive, that she was entirely her talent, the way she spent days and nights thinking of the story she was working on, then thinking of words, the right words, and how best to place them, and their sound and weight in the heart or the soul, at every moment sunk into the work of unravelling the mystery in human lives and endlessly probing to find it. Great art is not free, not for anybody, not for the artist nor those around them. Saint Alice and a genius in one world, a monster in another.



We are like meteorites trailing our fiery histories behind us as we hurtle mindlessly through space, powerless to stop ourselves as we carom violently off other hurtling meteorites before spinning off on different tangents. Surely, despite protestations to the contrary, we are all in some ways, large or small, personally damaged, struggling to find the source of the damage and to understand its effects. Yet, as for Robin's unassuaged pain, with her mother gone never having apologized to her nor shown that she believed that her child's needs should have come first whether a grown-up or not, I can only say that I know something about that pain, and that there is little relief to be had from it beyond the long passage of time. At eighty-four years, and knowing that the person in pain can never believe this, I have learned that—at least in my experience—childhood horrors, though always profoundly regrettable and unjustifiable and whose scars always remain, at last begin to seem less rawly terrible, less unmanageable, the rage weakens, the horrors' ramifications come clearer and more directly understandable. And then they fade, finally, into the long, always surprising narrative of one's life.

So do I really believe that an honest life comes only out of our pain and then out of facing directly, clearly, the pain of others, both now and that of the long past? Susan Sontag saw that, and Sebald, who could not lift from himself the weight of recognition of terrible historical facts, so much greater and more important than my own tiny personal one.

And yet, the puny and personal is, in the end, what moves the world.

## III



I didn't mention any of that to Lucinda either, just as she, mulling over her own memories in silence, said nothing to me. We smiled, we laughed over this and that, we pointed out things along the way that one of us noticed and the other didn't. We noticed birds and animals, the few we saw, we enjoyed each other's company. We didn't need to fill the silence by turning on the car radio. It was a wonderfully relaxing time, at least for me. I wait for Lucinda's writing to tell me what the trip was for her, although recently she said, in company, addressing me and smiling warmly, openly, something like, "I can't believe now that we took that trip together," and I replied, laughing, "It was an epic journey!" Laughing because it was so comically un-epic, and yet carried, surprisingly, so much weight in the hearts of both of us, the simplicity and friendliness of it, the easy days of peaceful driving, the uncomplicated vistas we passed through, the steady, unconflicted routine of our days together. We had both been ambitious, hardworking, even driven, life hadn't been easy on either of us, and now we were alone, our children gone, our husbands dead, and all that committed, complicated, unremittingly stressful part of our lives was over. (Or so we thought.) What a contrast this road trip book is to the Kerouacs, the dozens of other mostly (but not all) male writers heading off to the ends of the earth to "make their bones," to prove their courage and hardiness. Lucinda and I had proven something different. Or, better, we had no need to prove anything.

After I'd finished writing that section about the breaking of the last romantic relationship I'll ever have, I shut off my laptop, left my desk, got in my car and drove to the park beside the city reservoir to go for a walk among the trees, below the birds pumping across the sky, or those – chickadees, flickers, crows higher up – hopping from branch to branch beside me.  I was hoping to shake off the way I no longer seemed to fit properly into my own skin, and I tried to, but in the end, the emotion aroused by my writing had drained me of energy for walking. I found a bench among the trees and sat listening to the birds, mostly seagulls, going crazy. The city was draining the reservoir below where I sat to make room for the melting snowpack that would soon come down from the mountains. The wheeling, squawking birds must have been excited because of all the treasures the bottom of the now nearly waterless reservoir revealed to them. Or could their agitation have been that they feared disaster in the sudden disappearance of so large a body of water? Or, like humans, were they merely excited at so drastic a change?

Squinting against the sun, I made out high above a couple of eagles floating in wide, serene circles, black specks disappearing behind feathery clouds, appearing, then disappearing once more as they advanced slowly in hunting circles across the sky. I thought about my life from the time I was thirteen on, about the dream before we left on our trip of water dripping down from the ceiling, threatening to become a stream and then a deluge that would drown me.

After I finished writing Chapter Two, I'd had an absurd but upsetting dream. I had discovered that a couple of people whom, in real life, I haven't seen in years and who would never have done such things, had been revealed as running a scam that involved stealing from all their friends. They hadn't been caught before, nor had the extent of their fraud, part of a nefarious larger network, been exposed before.

I woke up with my heart thudding in my ears, the hissing of my old-age tinnitus amped up to a sizzling roar, my muscles tensed, my skin sticky with sweat. All this not because of their betrayal—that was silly—but because of how angry I was in the dream, so that I couldn't say a sentence that didn't have at least three f-words in it. Awake, that enraged, cursing person upset me far more than the deceit, which was merely dream-absurdity. I use the f-word occasionally, sometimes as a joke, sometimes an inadvertent curse, but not very often, and my dream stream of cursing I believed was entirely unlike the real me. I spent the rest of the day worried and disgusted, and yet, also baffled. *I am not that person*, I kept reassuring myself.

It took me a while to see that whether I understood that dream or not, it was part of the fulfillment of the warning of the Ur-dream about the stream of water that could drown me. My fury, unlike anything I could remember feeling in waking life, which seemed purposeless and futile, I would in time come to see as part of me. Could I complete the writing of a whole book this way? Waking each morning after a nightmare, the certainty of a placid old age destroyed? Was it wise to keep on writing if this was going to happen and then get worse, and then worse again?

I didn't know the answer except that if I am not writing, I flounder; in the absence at that time of nearly all loved ones, all my lost homes, the deeply familiar sites that formed me, I was sometimes no longer sure I was alive, or that being alive was worth the trouble. This subject was, perhaps, the journey of one human soul, a subject that seems meaningful enough to write about. It seemed I had been – I still was – willing to pay the price. I said goodbye to the squawking seagulls, got up off the bench, and went back home to my typing.

I was reminded then that this was a travel book of sorts, and although short on details, it was about the history and geography of the land we passed through. It was hemmed in on all sides by my own laziness after too many years of doing little else, to do now more than sketchy research, also by my polite restraint in talking about my travelling companion, or our interaction that was so amiably commonplace, and also, even especially, by the imperative not to reveal too much about other peoples' lives. All of these constraints of the classic memoir form.



But nonetheless, because we rode no donkeys or camels, hitched no rides with truckers, sailed no schooners, failed to surf, cross deserts, climb mountains, go caving nor fall through any ice, or took rockets to the moon or submarines to the sea bottom, and in other books I've already written nearly all of what I know about the Palliser Triangle and its people, the travel aspect here gets short shrift.

This book is a memoir; it is about memory. And in my case, it is about forgetting and then, in horror and sometimes a redemptive reclaiming, remembering again.

# SIX

# HEAT

## I

We were nearing Saskatchewan's provincial capital, named in 1883 as the territorial capital, and the place where in 1885, after a trial shameful for the atmosphere of racism surrounding it, protested by some even at the time, the verdict pretty much decided by all before the trial began, Louis Riel was hanged for the crime of high treason having to do with his leadership in the 1885 rebellion, now called by scholars a resistance. He was the first Canadian of two in our history to be convicted of this crime, but only he was executed in Canada. Today there is a movement in Manitoba to make Louis Riel the Honorary Premier of the province.

The Métis community refused a proffered government pardon on the grounds that Canada was the one who committed the crime, not Riel. The work he did is no longer treated or even thought of as criminal throughout most of the country, and he is revered as a Canadian hero by the Métis Nation, the large French-Canadian community, as well as by many other Canadians.

Worse, although not nearly as well known, was the trial in Battleford, Saskatchewan, even shoddier in its cursoriness than

Louis Riel's trial. Eleven days after Riel's hanging in Regina, eight First Nations men were simultaneously hanged on a carefully designed, freshly built eight-person gallows. It is reported that with impressive courage the men sang their death songs as the trap was sprung. As a further deterrent to any resistance to the law of the government, First Nations people from surrounding reserves were gathered and forced to watch the men die, including the Indigenous students of the Battleford Industrial School. The bodies were then placed in coffins and buried in a mass grave on the bank of the North Saskatchewan River behind the fort at Battleford, where today there is an interpretive plaque and a headstone with their eight names on it: Kah-Paypamahchukways, Wandering Spirit; Pah Pah-Me-Kee-Sick, Walking the Sky or Round the Sky; Manchoose, Bad Arrow; Kit-Ahwah-Ke-Ni, Miserable Man; Nahpase, Iron Body; A-Pis-Chas-Koos, Little Bear; Itka, Crooked Leg; Waywahnitch, Man Without Blood.



Each of the eight had killed someone, six at the Frog Lake Massacre during the uprising, and two in the "looting at Battleford," but a newspaper clipping of December 14, 1885, from the *Saskatchewan Herald* says this:

"It was reported to-day (Nov. 24) that representations have been made to the Government respecting the conduct of Stipendiary Magistrate [Charles] Rouleau which may cause the postponement of the execution of the eight Indians sentenced to be hanged at Battleford on Friday next. He is reported to have threatened that every Indian and Half-breed and rebel brought before him after the insurrection was supressed, would be sent to the gallows if possible. . . . Judge Rouleau was a heavy loser pecuniarily by the Indian outbreak at Battleford, it is contended that he should not have been allowed to preside at the trial of the prisoners. . . ."

Rouleau's house had been burned to the ground. He himself had fled to Swift Current. Other extenuating circumstances concerned the harsh treatment of the Indigenous people, especially the enforced near-starvation when whites refused to give them available food supplies. The trial itself was held in a climate rife with racism, little actual evidence, no legal counsel for the defendants, and virtually no translation. Rouleau acted as both judge and jury. After this hands-cleansing, this desecration of justice, the federal government under the first Prime Minister, John A. Macdonald, conspired to further punish the "Indians" as a group and to tighten the bonds of their imprisonment, readily using even forced starvation. In this he was aided by, among other officials, Edgar Dewdney, Lieutenant-Governor and Indian Commissioner, and Hayter Reed, then promoted to Indian Commissioner and so hated by the "Indians" that their name for him was Iron Heart.

Pile of Bones, otherwise known as Regina, has risen into view.



## II

Over and over again I had spoken to Lucinda of the many years from about 1975 to 2008 I'd spent in the area running from Lethbridge or Medicine Hat in Alberta east to Regina, occasionally as far as Winnipeg, and from the Montana border north through Swift Current to Saskatoon. I had mentioned people I'd known along the route, and had now introduced two of them to Lucinda. So far, only two, and I had made arrangements ahead of time to visit them. I didn't recognize one person we ran into along the way, nor had one stopped me and said, "Sharon! It's you! How nice to see you." Although it's true we had spent nearly all our time driving, sitting in restaurants or sleeping, and saw very few people. I was beginning to wonder if Lucinda thought I'd been lying and had never lived in southwestern Saskatchewan, or been to Cypress Hills Interprovincial Park before, or been in and out of Maple Creek the dozens of times I claimed.

The hotel in Regina that Lucinda had suggested we book rooms in, whose name I hadn't recognized, although I knew by the address where to find it, turned out to be the very place that, under its old name, I stayed in many times when I lived in the country and came into Regina on literary business. "Oh, for heaven's sake," I said, beaming with pleasure. "I know this place." I think I showed her the hotel's back door in from the parking lot, smug when I did it as proof of my claim.

But Lucinda was not there when the desk clerk, who told me he had worked at the hotel there for twenty-seven years, actually remembered me by my first name: "Hello, Sharon!" I felt restored to grace: I did not materialize newly created on the day I drove by myself into Calgary excited to shake off the tentacles of the horrendous immediate past, if also full of trepidation for what the next day would bring, and refusing to think about my history, if I could ever in my life avoid it.



I had always thought, should anything happen to Peter, which I was sure it wouldn't, that I would return to Saskatoon. But when that enormous "something" did happen, my son and his family were living in Calgary, and so, without a lot of thought, that is where I decided to go to live. I even thought then that maybe changing my mind and going to Calgary instead was actually a good thing, not a bad thing. Calgary, the biggest city on the prairies, youthful, alive, constantly, rapidly growing, the perfect place to start a new life. In Calgary life would go well; I would make friends; I would go to the places that *I* wanted to go to, eat in flashy restaurants, buy fashionable clothes, and have places to wear them. Plays! Art Galleries! Concerts! Opera!

Films! This list naming all that I'd left behind when, thirty-three years earlier, I'd married Peter. I would be alive again, a different kind of alive, an attitude that had lasted about a year before it started to dissipate as real life intruded.

We dropped off the books we were carrying with us at an antiquarian bookstore, then found a fast-food place for dinner. After, we drove down Albert Street to the Legislative Buildings and parked there so that we could look at the well-tended, bright flower gardens and maybe walk around Wascana Lake. The lake is a repair of an older lake made as early as 1883 by damming a creek, then during the Depression, as a make-work project, was deepened and widened by over a thousand men using horses and wagons. *Wascana* comes from the Cree *Oscana* meaning "pile of bones," which was the original name for the settlement. In 1882 the government changed the name to *Regina*, in Queen Victoria's honour.

On our way north to the legislature, I pointed out among the many fine old houses, the homes of Regina's reputedly finest, the one that in its garage, as far as I could remember, in January 1983, JoAnn Wilson had been bludgeoned and shot to death. I didn't think Lucinda remembered the whole terrible business, one of the biggest scandals in the province's history, but of course, I had to remind myself, Lucinda never lived in Saskatchewan.

I was thinking, also, about the summer of 1961, when I was twenty, about to turn twenty-one, and had been lucky enough as a full-time university student to be one of the two-dozen students hired each summer by the Department of Education to prepare the thousands of paper copies of the Grade 12 final exams for all the graduating high school students in the province. It was a huge job, and doing everything manually took us all summer long. I think we were paid well, although we were nearly all females in a period when females were routinely paid less than males for the same job. Female university students found it hard to find a summer job that paid more than minimum wage, at that time around seventy-five cents an hour, so that earning the money to pay for a university education was very hard. In 1956 and 1957, I had had a summer job for which boys were paid a dollar an hour and we girls received only seventy-five cents. Boys could also get good-paying jobs in construction, especially on roads, that we girls couldn't. I had had to resort to doing two jobs my first summer to raise enough money for tuition, fees, and books.

That summer of '61, my dad drove me and my belongings to Regina from Saskatoon, and helped me find that tiny two-room upstairs apartment in a house somewhere along Wascana Creek. A few days later, I advertised and found a roommate. But I knew I'd never be able to locate the right house the day Lucinda and I drove into Regina, so I didn't even try, although gazing at the Legislative Building with her and remembering that same summer, I found I could still point out the window of the room where sixty years earlier I had occasionally been sent to shuffle paper for a few hours or a day.



My boyfriend had left for the then-obligatory Jack Kerouac-ish trip bumming around Europe with his best friend. That was the then-obligatory adventure that I never had, because I was too determined to get to university, and that meant having two summer jobs and saving every penny I could. My older sister did, though, having worked for a year first to save the money. She and her best friend travelled, romantically, on one of the last crossings of a sailing ship, about which she said what fun she and her friend had shipboard, much in demand among the young men and dancing every night away. I was so naïve about – well, practically everything – that I didn't even think about using the proper stamps for Europe, and it was about six weeks or maybe more before my boyfriend picked up the packet of letters that I'd been faithfully writing at least once a week and certainly each time I received one from him. He was upset with me, although laughingly, and I heard a lot about it before it faded into the past and before my more general incompetence became a well-worn theme. Writing this at eighty-three, I realized that he must have actually been in love with me to be that upset about not receiving my letters that summer we were apart.

One very early morning, alone in the rented apartment, I was wakened by pebbles hitting my window and a male voice softly calling my name. When I peered groggily out the upstairs window, he was standing on the lawn gazing up at me, duffle bag dumped on the dewy grass beside him, containing the two novels by Henry Miller, *Tropic of Cancer* and *Tropic of Capricorn* (that would appall and disgust me then, although as was my habit, I kept my mouth shut about how I felt), which had been published in France in 1939, but were banned, so that you couldn't buy them in the U.S. until 1961. We must have been truly in love, because we were married, I think three weeks later, on my twenty-first birthday, in the chapel of a Protestant church in Saskatoon. My Catholic father had the requisite fit over that, but he attended the wedding nonetheless, maybe because when he and our mother had married in 1935, no parents attended the ceremony, although my father's family were at the reception.

I remembered that at the pre-nuptial interview with us, the minister, misunderstanding a hesitation in the conversation, thought that I was trying to tell him I was pregnant, which I definitely wasn't, but in 1961 there was no question then but that he would marry us. I didn't realize until after the interview what had happened, when my husband-to-be told me. The minister had been dubious up until then because neither of us were members of his congregation, I wasn't of his faith, and, also, we were so young and obviously had no clue what we were doing. Or maybe he mistook my fiancé's barely hidden hostility toward him for his reluctance to be married, at least to me. I knew my fiancé's general refusal to accept convention the way I did, I even loved that about him then, though it often shocked me if in a delighted way and occasionally even frightened me. I remember wishing he would be more polite, but in those days, at twenty-one, I missed most nuance.

I remember feeling that day that the interview didn't matter much, that this was a step none of us wanted to be going through, and that it was supremely difficult for all of us: my guilt as a fallen-away Catholic and my betrayal of my father's beliefs; my fiancé's bitter relationship with his father and resulting difficulty with authority; the minister knowing he could, but shouldn't, refuse us, although he wanted to. I think now that the minister saw that very day the inevitable marriage breakdown lying ahead of us.



Maybe, it occurs to me now, the minister would have been right about my fiancé's attitude, that that was how he really felt about getting married despite our being in love, but because of my shocked refusal to live with him without being married, he had felt forced into doing.

That same summer of 1961 was one of the hottest on record, and it caused the worst of the province's too-frequent droughts. I still carry the picture in my mind of driving each weekend in the appalling heat, which barely bothered me when I was young, down the then-single-laned highway between the wide yellow fields, their crops baking in the unrelenting, rainless heat so that the air smelled, I thought, of roasting wheat. Sixty years later, here I was, back in Regina, where I'd spent one of the most significant summers of my youth, the first time I left home, staring at the windows of the Legislative Building with its fat black dome where we student-workers that summer had climbed, with trepidation and exhilaration, too, up the rickety wooden stairs built against the inside walls of the dome and without any proper railing, the stairs that were later closed in, to the fenced walkway around the bottom edge of the dome. There we gazed out over the small city, virtually high-rise-free then, spread out on its flat plain, Wascana Creek trickling through it.

Here, I'd worked with the other university students, and when not at work, wandered around the streets, bored, in our crisp cotton sundresses and freshly polished white sandals or, some of us, spending hours in the public library. I remember some of those girls: one who was busy planning her wedding to a man of whom her parents disapproved; one who was my roommate and strongly disapproved when she found out I'd slept with my boyfriend; one who was from Japan, quiet and proper, with whom I sometimes walked downtown, and never forgot because she was one of my first longed-for brushes with the wider world.



In fact, not so many years ago, I was riding on a bus somewhere in Ontario while reading a paperback of *The Lake* by Yasunari Kawabata, when I noticed that the translator was Reiko Tsukimura, and thought, wasn't that the name of the Japanese girl I worked with long ago in Regina, sometimes walking downtown with her and another girl at lunchtime, once when we were all eating ripe cherries from a small box of them? And one of us got cherry juice on her dress? "That'll never come out," we said, although I don't remember whose dress it was.

Now into our eighties, who knew what had happened to each of us in the long years since we had strolled down a city street in the heat, and a young, good-looking man called out to us from the open window of a beer parlour, also for the benefit of his unseen friends inside the pub, "I just saw spring walk by!" By this, we knew he was an immigrant; the boys we grew up with would never have *thought* of saying such a thing. I think some of us blushed, although we said nothing to each other. I was thrilled enough that sixty years later I still remembered that tiny incident.

Sixty years later, the weather was once again scorching hot, the heat I'd once barely noticed now a trial to me, the prairie once again in the midst of another hair-raising, heartbreaking, farmer-ruining drought. The 1961 drought, when precipitation fell by sixty percent, is considered to be the worst of all Saskatchewan droughts, with crop production forty-nine percent of 1960's. The summer of Lucinda's and my road trip, crop production would be reported as falling by forty-seven percent. As I wrote this in 2023, the CBC had reported farmers as saying that 2023 was worse even than 1961, but by late November, it seemed unclear which year was the worst, and a few sources blamed the widespread lack of rainfall on climate change.



As we stood looking at the Legislative Building and grounds, the day had drawn down to early evening, the sweltering heat was being replaced by a pleasant, cradling softness. Every Saskatchewan summer I'd ever lived, nearly eighty of them, hung in the air, as if it were all of a piece, the feel of the air, the warm stillness, the memories floating gently past me blending sweetly from one into the next: boys, kisses, dresses, lilacs, the delicate, spicy smell of the prairie, my sisters, my aunts and uncles and cousins at picnics on grass in the shade of trees, swimming with girlfriends in public pools or at rivers or in lakes. The unbroken sun was everything to us then, its heat on our skin, the soft swish of lawn sprinklers accompanying us as we sauntered down sidewalks, the safeness of it, that the world was proceeding the way it was supposed to, and was waiting for us to announce ourselves.

Lucinda and I were strolling from the main Legislative Building across an expanse of carefully watered and mowed green grass, then the long, narrow parking lot, then the ornamental gardens full of flowers we admired and talked about as we moved down the narrow paths around them. After a while, we strolled closer to the lakeside to listen to a musician playing jazz on his saxophone, considering whether we should attempt the walk around the lake, which I knew my Regina friends often did, even daily, and that a few of the clusters of people at the lake's edge were doing. But I declined regretfully, and I'm sure Lucinda, an athletic woman, was disappointed, but I knew it was too far for me to manage after that long day in the car and our visits in and near Eastend. It was her turn to give no sign that she felt otherwise.

We turned away from the lake to watch as car after car drove up and parked beside each other along the grassy edge of the flower gardens, and young people, all of whom seemed to know each other, climbed out, hugged, high-fived or back slapped, and then hung around by their cars chatting. They were all males, the few young women who eventually arrived seemed to hang back from the young men, not leaving the vicinity of their cars, and the men didn't seem to think this was strange, nor did they seem to feel much need to welcome or talk to the young women, although they seemed to us an accepted part of the gathering.

We couldn't hear their voices so didn't know what language they were speaking, although if it wasn't English, French, Ukrainian, German, Italian, or Spanish, I wouldn't have been able to name it anyway. I've learned in Calgary the names of Asian languages: Gujarati, Punjabi, Hindi, etc., not that I can tell one from another when I hear one spoken at an LRT stop or passing by on the sidewalk. But most likely they had been born in Canada and were all speaking fluent, colloquial, accentless English, and their gathering here had nothing to do with the colonial past.

We speculated. Maybe there was a big family wedding going on, and the young people had come here to escape for a while from the aunties and uncles, moms, dads, small children, and grandparents. Although it didn't seem to be a special occasion: no balloons or firecrackers, no shouting or cheering or celebrating with a picnic, or barely hidden alcohol, no mock fighting, or perhaps they were too old for that, maybe in their twenties, probably were either university students or had jobs, all of them well dressed, well mannered, good natured, never loud, and seemingly greatly enjoying being together.

That it wasn't a racially mixed crowd of young people puzzled us. Who had rebuffed whom, we wondered? And if a response to racism was the reason for this gathering, and not something far more natural as we had thought, what did that say about Saskatchewan? So, in our motherly pleasure watching them, we felt an uneasiness that had nothing to do with their gathering or their behaviour or anything else, but only of the awareness of the seemingly unremitting background of racism. But then, I thought, why almost no females? If racism is a scourge, and it is, the same is true of sexism.



The many writers I used to know who lived in Regina might have crossed my mind, but I don't think I even considered calling one for a glass of wine and a conversation. We had only that evening, Lucinda wanted to see a little of Regina, and I did, too. Anyway, I didn't know who was left, except for Dianne Warren, winner of most of the literary prizes and author of one of my all-time favourite books, *Cool Water*, and Connie Gault, who wrote *The Beauty*. Bonnie Burnard, author of the internationally bestselling, prize-winning *A Good House*, had moved back to southwestern Ontario some years before, and in 2017 had died at only seventy-two. Or perhaps I could have called Gail Bowen, for a long time the queen of Canadian mystery writers and still going strong, but, although I knew and liked her, I'd never hung out with her. Nor did I call my one non-literary friend, nor the few Nature Conservancy people I knew.

Now, in 2021, in the midst of another drought, I might have mentioned them as Lucinda and I made our slow way out of the city. But I was lost in the past, as if we'd been there in Regina the whole of the sixty years my mind had been travelling through, while outwardly, we wandered, talking, through the legislature grounds, and eventually, the next morning, began travelling further and further east through Saskatchewan, as the devastation of the drought grew worse and worse. "Look how short and thin that grain is; there's just nothing there!" I must have declared more than once.

Lucinda always politely declined the much-used paper road-and-city maps I'd brought along, preferring to use her cell phone's GPS. I recognized this from my son who, to my astonishment and admiration, had been doing the same thing for years. But I've never even downloaded a GPS app onto my phone: My days of world-beating are over, I like familiar things, and anyway, it's probably already there on my phone. As well, my eyes aren't good, and I can't catch the images at a single glance the way younger people can. As I never go anywhere anymore anyway, that I'm not technologically adept doesn't matter much to me. I know I must sound annoyingly smug to the young, and a good reason for them to think that old people have become too incompetent even to know how out of touch with the world they are. If the GPS on an iPhone is the world.

I suspect there is no way past this generational impasse; we elderly loved the world once, too, and thought everything new was wonderfully exciting, nearing miraculous: DDT, a synthetic insecticide first used as such in 1939 and everywhere, mostly in places it should never have been in my forties' childhood, leaking ballpoint pens, the introduction of margarine in plastic bags, plastic bags themselves, aerosol sprays in general. I even remember the day in 1956, in our Grade 11 science class in Saskatoon, when we were told to take out our texts and pens and change the number of chromosomes, given there as 48, to 46, which, with slightly bewildered headiness, we did. But with Sputnik in late 1957, we were entering the era of awed worship of scientists and their work, to the detriment of other fields of learning and a deeper wisdom such as to be found in the arts and philosophy. Even when I was just a kid, I laughed out loud when someone remarked that science would solve all our problems. I couldn't believe anybody could think that.

Later, I noticed Lucinda studying one of my paper maps and was sneakily pleased.



When I was young, I wanted to know the answers to questions I couldn't articulate, which already ran around in my brain but that had no firm shape, no outlines. The world then seemed to me immense and at the edges sinking into dark, un-plumb-able shadow. I think for many years as a child and maybe even in my young adulthood, I read books and studied what they had to say because, as with so many others, I wanted to clear that darkness; I wanted to put light on my world; I wanted to dispel that shadow. Books were, for most of my life, the only place where people who know more about the world than I did, and do, actually explain things about life to me.

I suppose that is why I read for thirty-plus years when I was Peter's wife and lived inside the landscape with him. The fourteen or so years of my first marriage were hectic and also chaotic: I became a mother, tried to start a career, and we bought a car and a house, and then everything fell apart, and for a while there I lost my mind, but in my second marriage I had found a semblance of peace, although hectored, I felt, on all sides by some of Peter's family and by members of the community, and mostly unsupported by him, who, in matters of psychology and sociology, saw only what he wanted to see. He didn't speak up when anyone said something nasty to me in his presence, although he might put his arm around me, and we might together walk away. Or for instance, once when the provincial government gave a grant to a local committee to be divided among the local organizations, the arts council I'd started and supported was, as far as I knew, the only one that didn't receive a penny. I could go on, but every insult went undefended and unrectified. I never protested officially, but I had slowly lost trust in the community. Year after year, I withdrew more and more from efforts to contribute to it or to become a part of it and eventually viewed it only with bitterness.

I thought I was reading four to six hours a day to learn how to write, and then to learn how to write so well that I would become a famous writer, travel all over the world and meet other famous writers and artists and the statesmen and women and otherwise interesting people from many countries. But now, in old age, I realize that all that reading and walking across the prairie thinking and studying the rocks and the grass and watching wild animals was really, still, only to clear away the darkness I saw all around me, not to let it cover me, too, as it covered so many of the people I met and talked to. Everywhere, every day, I sought light, I sought clarity, I sought—I was seeking—wisdom. And the search for wisdom seldom, or only accidentally, leads to power and riches, but leads instead to death. This, I hope my readers will understand, is a poetic truth. Another outcome is possible: the refusal, then, of riches and fame, and the return to innocence. To simplicity. The guru on the mountaintop, my sense of humour suggests, who is laughed at by most of the world as a symbol of idiocy and futility. Innocence and simplicity as the place where truth lies.

Weirdly, another novel I once read comes to mind and will not be chased away, although I can't remember who wrote it or what its title is. A small part of it concerned an attempt to rescue a very famous elderly man, a Jew living in Germany, and either a great painter or a scientist, from the Nazis. When after much danger and subterfuge, one rescuer finally reaches him, he finds the old man running with a butterfly net in a wide, flower-dotted green meadow trying to catch butterflies so as to study them, and he doesn't even appear to hear what his rescuer is telling him about the danger he is in and how he must flee at once. The great man is so absorbed in his endeavour that the would-be rescuer eventually forgets his mission, and begins to chase the butterflies too. Such is, I guess, the wisdom of the great. But I've only learned it when life has already thrust it on me.



Do Not Write Dreams is one of the first rules of the writer's craft – readers don't like to read dreams, the dreams of others bore them to death, they skip them in order to get back to the narrative thread, the plot, the characters and their quandaries. But in some lives, as most readers know, the dreams are themselves an encapsulation of the narrative thread, that is, of the dreamer's life. All books are life, or begin as life.

Another bizarre dream: I was back in the Frenchman River Valley; it was summer and some kind of festival was taking place. I needed a toilet, and I went looking for one, climbing hills and even small sandy cliffs, going down prairie trails in the grass, from house to house, including one that had five toilets in it, trying to find a toilet that was free that I might use. Through all this, Peter was waiting for me in shadow at the edge of the dream, far back on my left.

One house, whose male owner sat in a lawn chair some feet back facing it to guard it, I thought was built of logs as settlers' homes were, but old dark-stained ones, that I soon realized were not logs but were instead railroad ties, the wood nearly black from being soaked in creosote and other toxic chemicals to preserve it. On the only wall I could see, which towered above me as I stood below in the ankle-deep, intensely green grass, leaning toward me as if it might topple on anybody standing under it, was a long row, just under the roof, of identical small, wider than tall, rectangular windows. They gazed like eyes, blank and somehow haughty, making it clear that I would never be able to see what was inside. And all the while, the guard, bearded and wearing the countryman's plaid jacket and a hat with turned-up ear flaps, sat in his chair watching me with a steady, non-threatening expression. I knew he was there to keep me from going closer.



I walked away to Peter waiting for me, and where, strangely, it was winter, both of us wearing the thick sheepskin coats of the Slav immigrant-settlers of the late nineteenth and early twentieth centuries, which caused others to call them "the sheepskins." We walked off together, through the ice and snow, until we disappeared in the darkness.

As I wrote this, it dawned on me that this dream was a settler-dream of history, of my family's and Peter's and of thousands of other Palliser Triangle settlers of whom, history shows, at least half failed. It was a foundation story of the West. It was the Canadian Pacific Railway whose imperative was to tie the new country together; who named the villages along their railways – in places you can still see how they named them alphabetically, for example, Fenwood, Goodlove, Hubbard,

Ituna, Keliher, and Leross. Towns lived or disappeared according to the will of the CPR, that alphabetical naming a symbol of the power of wealthy white men far away in eastern Canada and the cold-bloodedness of the commercial and political decisions they made that turned so many people into slaves on the promised free land on which, for most of three generations, they could never do much more than survive. All the while congratulating themselves on how, by building their transcontinental railroad, they had forged Canada.

I learned that in school; I guess children still do, it's the Bible of the mostly, but not all, Euro-Canadians with roots in the West's settler generation. There were also Black families and settlements, many Chinese-Canadian people, a few Jewish farming settlements, and eventually Japanese-Canadians, twenty-two thousand of them, whom in 1942 the government displaced and interned, while confiscating all their property. During both World Wars the Canadian government interned a large number of white settlers, chiefly Slavs, but also Germans and others, as enemy aliens. "Canada is a good country," a well-educated African told me in sincerity in the nineties when I visited the continent, but Canada in reality has a long history of racism as despicable as anywhere else on the planet.



That part of the dream, that dark, log house with the row of high windows through which nobody could ever see, I know is the crucial life-scene, the place of the original wounding that for me made all this thinking and dreaming necessary, all the books, the search into the meaning of the journey we are all on, so that I began as soon as I could to read and to think. And the visceral memory, the body memory is nearly all that I have, and all that I ever will have, of what happened in that wood cabin when I was perhaps a year old. My despairing screaming at what can only have been something that had just been done to me, although what it was was never a part of my memory, that, and the way the world had lost all colour, had turned grey, I will not forget. Searching back, trying to think of my earliest memory in life, that scene came back to me. I had never forgotten it, although I had never had any idea what I was screaming so hard about; I did not understand how or why everything I saw had become grey, all colour having been leached from the world. When I asked them, my writing students' first memories were about sunlight, of being saturated with love, or of little incidents that thrilled and puzzled them when they were very young, all of these from before they had language. Mine was, I think, about horror, about the discovery of cruelty, but I did not know from what, and had no names such as "horror" or "cruelty." When I was in my teens and remembered that scene and puzzled again over it, I believe I thought everybody's first memory would be something like that.

I was sixty when the first hint of its meaning was given to me, and more years, after much question-asking and putting together of bits of information, that I became convinced that I had just been sexually assaulted.



That fortress-like building representing more broadly the pioneer West, which we Westerners so valorize, but that keeps hidden what we also know: the bloody violence, the body-ruining overwork and frequent maiming and crippling accidents, the lack of birth control and subsequent often deliberate use of children for labour, the hunger, the poorly or never treated disease and birth defects, the familial trauma running from abuse to rape to incest to even murder, the despair of many of the settlers, the stories of someone's hair turning white overnight—all of it locked firmly away forever behind the relentlessly repeated story of courage of those first settlers in the face of such enormous difficulties that had made possible their present middle-class lives.

But worse is the now slowly revealed desolation they struggle to overcome, the deepest sorrow and profound anger of the First Nations people who were constantly betrayed, reduced to hunger, had their children stolen from them, their women violated, who had to hide their spirituality, lost their languages, were taught to feel worthless, learned shame, were murdered, and became prisoners on the land given them by the Creator.

Lucinda and I kept travelling east toward Winnipeg, while in my dream of the forbidding house built of railway ties, I was returned to the Saskatchewan I came from, far to the north of the highway we were driving on, north of Saskatoon; Prince Albert, too, to the place of my beginnings. The place that, no matter how many ways I changed my life, would prevent me from ever being anything else, the place that had fixed for me my destiny in the world.

Then, the warning dream of the dripping water came back, and for the first time I thought that I was strong enough to survive this other journey, haphazard as it was, looping back over and over again to redefine things, or shooting off on a new trajectory. This journey that I hadn't planned for nor wanted to make, yet found myself a captive of, driven on helplessly, tumultuously through. My own struggle to find myself, inside the dream of the West.

# SEVEN

# WATER

## I

Another hot day was promised us, the sky clear and high, the Trans-Canada smooth but crowded as, on our third morning of travelling—only our third day!—we headed east out of Regina. After a half hour, the traffic thinned, many cars turning north-east toward the resort areas in the valley along the Qu'Appelle River, the section that runs from Echo Valley Provincial Park on the west to Katepwa Provincial Park on the east, an area where the river swells to make a series of lakes called The Fishing Lakes. Or perhaps they were going to the several towns along the Qu'Appelle River: Fort San, Fort Qu'Appelle, B-Say-Tah, Lebret, Balcarres a bit north of the others, and the resort village of Katepwa. But mostly, they were heading toward the road that branches off to lead to the many family cottages along the lakeshores.

I travelled there at least once, the summer of 1964, with my first husband, whose mother had insisted he present his wife and their great-grandchild, our baby boy, to her elderly parents, who had a prosperous grain farm above Katepwa Beach near Balcarres. I found them to be good people, and even my husband, their grandson, seemed to think that. His grandmother had been the first white baby in the area, or was it the first red-headed baby in the area? I don't think I got it straight even then. I remember the frame farmhouse, because its size was unusual for the prairies, I think two-and-a-half or three storeys, one floor having five or six bedrooms, which were mostly shut off by then, holdovers from days of the large threshing crews, and also being shown in the high heat and dust the empty sheds and small corrals where cattle, horses, chickens, turkeys, ducks, pigs, and who knows what else had once been kept. Their emptiness gave me a sad but also uncertain feeling, but I trailed valiantly along trying to think of appropriate things to say while our baby slept in a cool room in the house, watched over by his great-grandmother.

Both my parents had come from farms, and to them, "the farm" was Paradise Lost forever, as it was then for all the many farming people who had been driven out by drought and debt in the years after the settlement era. In the fifties, the Saskatchewan countryside was dotted with deserted, falling-down farmsteads, evidence then of the failed dreams of hundreds, if not thousands, of settlers. So, I was a bit quizzical, too, about how my husband's grandparents had managed to be both still on their farm and seemingly still prosperous. I suppose by coming so very early, and to good land not in the Palliser Triangle.



When I was a university student in Saskatoon, I had a part-time job at the provincial archives, then located in the basement of the university library, as one of the students hired to convert the pertinent data from the province's thousands of Homestead files, some thick and some not, to filing cards. The statement on the internet is a bit indecisive as to how many actual files, the ones I and the other student-employees held in our hands actually were: "The Saskatchewan Homestead Index database contains 360,000 references to the men and women who, under the . . .

Dominion Lands Act, took part in the homestead process in the area now known as Saskatchewan from 1872–1930" (Wikipedia). Now the data must be digital, and the actual paper files containing handwritten letters as well as signed documents that we held in our hands must be stored somewhere, or not. The archivists to whom we reported cherished the files, as did I, as evidence of the struggles and accomplishments of the homesteading era. One day, at work there, I came across my father's name. In the thirties, before he met my mother, he and one of his brothers had registered jointly on land in the North Battleford area. My mother was surprised when I told her, having known nothing of it. A clerk had scrawled across the file, "Surrendered. Too rocky, too swampy." From my research on who had once owned the land that was consolidated by the Butalas into their ranch, I know that sometimes one quarter section (160 acres) had been filed on and abandoned as many as a half-dozen times, where others were never filed on, and I think only one quarter was filed on only once and the owners had stayed over twenty years.



I remember, too, that one of those hot afternoons, on that first visit, my husband and I and our baby drove down to Katepwa Beach for a cooling-off swim in the lake. I also have a vague memory of making the trip from Regina to Fort San, slightly west of Fort Qu'Appelle, in a Regina writer's car, I don't remember whose, but it could have been Bonnie Burnard's, along with another writer or two, in the late eighties or early nineties. Our destination was Fort San, the first of three tuberculosis sanatoriums built in Saskatchewan; the other two were in Prince Albert and Saskatoon, on the North Saskatchewan River and the other on the South Saskatchewan.

Fort San was built around 1917 and closed as a sanatorium around 1971, a collection of large buildings, some administrative and some dormitories, which the Saskatchewan Writers'

Guild, among other arts organizations, had begun using for their summer programs, and where I was to teach in its writing stream, or be a guest resident, I can't remember which. I never went there as a student to study writing because I didn't think then that I could leave my husband and the hay farm during the busy haying and irrigating season. Later, as I became better known, that compunction weakened and almost vanished until the day of his diagnosis, when I cancelled a summer's worth of engagements to stay with and care for him.

On that first trip to the arts summer school, I'd been anxious that I might have to stay overnight in a particular dormitory. Before TB was virtually eradicated in Canada, the death rate was about fifty percent; the disease was so prevalent that in 1949 our whole school was tested for it. It was well known that people who stayed in that dorm were often accosted by ghosts who, it was agreed, had to be those of the many tuberculosis patients who had died there. A few writers had told me their stories of frightening encounters with apparitions. One man who was around sixty told me that in the night his mother had appeared to him, ghostly and pale, bending over him, not once, but twice.



"Were you scared?" I asked. He looked at me as if I were a moron or perhaps insane, and spluttered about just how frightened he'd been.

I said, "I asked because I thought maybe your mother wouldn't frighten you." But he was done with me, walking away shaking his head. I hadn't posed my question because I didn't believe him, as he seemed to think. We were standing on firm ground in sunshine half a province away from the San when I'd asked him, easy to be fearless then. I began to imagine a world in which we strut around like the kings and queens of the earth but all the time, we are strutting through crowds of the dead. Or they are floating around, between and through us.

But on the way to the San the first time, I was in a sweat of dread, afraid of being assigned to that dorm. In the end, I wasn't, and I have a vague memory of, on another occasion, as I sat on the lawn with other writers one hot summer day gazing up at it, being told that it wasn't used anymore, at least not by our Writers' Guild.

As a young woman, our mother had worked for two years at the Prince Albert Sanatorium as a practical nurse, a job she often told us about and seemed to have loved and found endlessly interesting and moving. She told us that the first task she was given there was to handwash bloody sheets left soaking in a bathtub of a patient who had hemorrhaged to death in the night. Sometimes she would muse with a tender half smile, not looking at us, about a young male patient she had looked after; it was clear to us that they had fallen for each other, were perhaps in love, but who sadly had died during her sojourn there. And how the staff at the San got only a half a day off a week, and they got so tired that they couldn't sleep, and "the nurses would take [drugs] from the drug cabinet so that they could rest."



In 1935, she and our father married over all their parents' disapproval, so that as I've written more than once, none of the four parents attended the wedding, although my father's sisters told me that all of their family attended the reception. But in late December 1937, my grandmother recorded in her memoir, our grandparents, our parents, and our mother's brother, Uncle Don, all answered the call for free land newly opened to settlers in the Garrick area. One result of the move was that four of the five of us were born in Nipawin in what had been a Red Cross Outpost Hospital but was by then called the Lady Grey. We first knew life up in the black fly, mosquito-riddled "bush," as everybody called it, and I suppose I will never be able to call it anything else. I think though, that my older sister and I were the only ones of us who retained direct memories of the place and of life there, and I suspect that all were coloured by our mother's pained memories of how hard life there had been. Like me, my mother said more than once, "I try never to think of it."

But as we drove east that morning, I remembered being in the Qu'Appelle Valley a few miles north of us when I was still a university student in the late fifties and early sixties, and had swum and sunbathed at Katepwa Beach. I can't remember how that came about, but I must have known people whose families owned cottages there. I also remember wondering how my friends wound up in families with lakeside cottages and I didn't, but I was careful to hide my envy. It wasn't serious envy anyway, rather like wanting to know a movie star, or be one. Maybe I had hoped that one day I too would own a cottage there, but of course I never did, nor anywhere else.

Much as I yearned for that lakeside summer cottage at various times in my life, it never rated as a life-goal as I know it did for some prairie people. I was too ambitious to waste time on such a triviality, but I think that the desire must have remained floating in the background of my life, even when I lived for four years next to the daunting dark blue Atlantic, or my year a few miles from the warm Pacific. When three of my four sisters went to live in coastal towns in BC, and two stayed there, by then I was living on the ranch with Peter. We already lived in the perfect place, the Saskatchewan prairie.



I couldn't understand how people who lived by it could stand the ocean's steady racket, until after dark one night, a guest at a house on the BC coast set in a placid bay, I was standing alone on its rail-less deck that was built low, out over the water. The late evening was dark and perfectly still and silent, when slowly, as I listened, the sound came to me: a steady, unceasing soft exhalation, a *shhhhhhhhh*. Then I understood.

Still, in these last years, I dream about a cabin by water, the place always the same, the colours always the same: pale beige, fine sand spread out in low hills, rough, bright green grass growing in patches up from it, the paler green body of warm water, itself half sea and half lake, rolling softly, white foam along its diminishing waves, which lapped gently onto the sand, we slipping on the sand as we move toward the sunbathed pale water and plunge in. All of us swimming fearlessly even in the patches we knew to be very deep and ocean-like, cutting across those spots feeling only a little afraid, I feeling braver even than the other swimmers, arms and legs moving in easy synchrony, bodies rising and falling with the water, the water alive, a thing in itself with presence and determination. I have almost never in life experienced such joy. I always wake wanting never to leave the sand and water.

I think that dream begins with the North Saskatchewan River on the banks of which we lived for some years when I was a child. That opaque, pale sea-green was the colour of the river near its shore so long ago, before the dams were built on it; the smell was the North Saskatchewan, the white foam that of the small waves that sometimes came up onto the sandy shore.



There was a large family there who went to the river at a shallow spot where it swirled, hidden by willows on three sides and, bringing soap and towels, would bathe there once a week, and there was a lot of whooping and splashing by the males of the family. My mother would stop whatever she was doing and listen, her expression bemused. She saw this way of getting clean as barbaric, I've no doubt, but at the same time, I think she yearned toward it, and an eminently sensible person herself, saw the wisdom of it, all of us with bathroom-less houses, at the same time as she also hated having come so close to the edge of survival.

We were taken home, then four of us, water heated on the wood-burning cookstove, in winter, melted snow, poured into a tub and one by one washed, fresh nightgowns pulled on, tucked into bed, all of us in one room. I remember how precious that time was, before our mother's anger and pain had overtaken her, as if I were someone else then, or now, watching it as someone else, not me. Whoever "me" might be.

**II**

I couldn't find a date anywhere on my aged paper road map, but I thought it was produced in the mid-to-late seventies, forty-five or more years earlier, my point being that, evidence to me of the disdain some people felt toward the occupants, it didn't have the First Nations Reserves marked on it. I told Lucinda that, a few miles north of the Trans-Canada we were passing along so easily in the high summer heat, there was a fairly large concentration of reserves. It was beyond me to name more than one or two of them, and, later, checking the second *Atlas of Saskatchewan*, I counted fifteen in the Qu'Appelle region, eight of which were along or in the near vicinity of the Qu'Appelle River near where for many years summer vacationers had congregated to swim, bask in the sun, boat, waterski, barbecue, and fall asleep to the sound of water lapping along the shoreline. Oh, I thought, with a touch of sourness, lucky them. I would hardly be the only one in the vicinity to imagine this, and not all the imagining, despite a century of justification, would be benign.

When I pointed out there were all those reserves a few kilometres north of where we were passing, after a second Lucinda let out an abrupt, "O-hhh," softly expelling air, and then, "the unmarked graves!" Remembering at the same time, I too drew in a quick, gasping breath. She was referring to the announcement of May 23, 2021, just a month and a half earlier, of the

215 unmarked graves found in the grounds surrounding the Kamloops Indian Residential School in Kamloops, BC, and that, as far as we knew at that point, they, or at least the greatest number of them, were the graves of children believed to have died at the school. No one knew now who they were, or when they died, or how they died, or who their mothers and fathers were, their siblings and grandparents. Worse, that First Nations families of the missing children had not been told what happened to their children; they had simply vanished. Whole nations of people living with that pain, and not believed or given help when they tried to tell the whites that their children had never come home, that they needed to know what had happened to their babies.

We were stunned into silence by our inability to comprehend that anyone could be so cruel, our shame that we belonged to the tribe that had committed this crime, sorrow for suffering children, pity for their mothers and fathers.

I knew only that since the Kamloops announcement by the chief of the Tk'emlúps te Secwépemc First Nation, other unmarked graves had been found using ground-penetrating radar by other First Nations near their former residential schools. I knew without asking her that Lucinda, a mother as I am, and a responsible, productive Canadian citizen, was trying to process this information, too.



We were then driving along the Trans-Canada through the white farming town (population about five hundred and fifty) of Broadview, Saskatchewan. A mere twenty-four kilometres north of us was the Cowessess Reserve in close vicinity to the Qu'Appelle and the most easterly of those along the river. Cowessess translates as "Little Boy." The reserve was named after Chief Cowessess who signed Treaty 4 in 1874.

Here the Marieval Indian Residential School had been since 1898. The school was Catholic-built and in its first seventy years was run by the church. From 1969 to 1987 the Canadian government had taken it over, and finally, in 1987 the Cowessess people had begun to run it themselves until it was demolished in 1997. I should have known that only the previous month, June, the Cowessess people reported finding an appalling seven hundred and fifty-one unmarked graves in the grounds near the school. They did not then report how many of these appeared to be the graves of children.

There was plenty of shame to go around: not just the Catholic Church – some of the schools were run by the Anglican Church, the Presbyterians, and the United Church and, of course, the governments. And what about all the whites who must have known, but chose not to say anything (or did and were silenced at once) about the malnutrition, disease, violence, and sexual abuse being perpetrated on the children of the powerless in such schools?

This was a well-known fact to First Nations people, but I cannot recall anybody ever mentioning to me the children who died and were buried there, although, stuck in my brain from the late fifties or early sixties, I recall a distant relative of my mother's, a teacher, coming to stay with us while she attended summer school at the University of Saskatchewan. A mother herself of grown children and now a widow, she was supporting herself by teaching in one of these schools, I suppose until she could elevate her credentials sufficiently to work in a public school. I remember her telling my mother in a low, deeply sober voice, not looking at her as she stood at the ironing board in our kitchen, "They don't treat them very well," referring to the children in the school. If she said more about it, I have forgotten.

And yet, I don't think I forgot; I think she had a lot more to say, but didn't, because she needed her job, and probably because she was ashamed that even as a non-abusing teacher, by working there she was tacitly supporting the abuse. And who was "they"? The school administrators, I guess, the other teachers, many of them clergy. I wonder what she had seen that she wouldn't speak of, even to her relative, even in the safety of our kitchen.

"We need to know who died, we need to know how they died, we need to know who was responsible for their deaths or for their care at the time that they died," Murray Sinclair, former head of the country's Truth and Reconciliation Commission, told England's *The Guardian* newspaper in June 2021. "We need to know why the families weren't informed. And we need to know where the children are buried."

I'd been researching dates, places, numbers, and suddenly I noticed that it was the first anniversary of the original report released by the Tk'emlúps te Secwépemc First Nation in Kamloops, BC, of the two hundred and fifteen unmarked graves. Today, First Nations people all over at least the plains would have ceremonies to commemorate the many children who died, and there I sat, typing, thinking of the children, some, I've read, as young as four. As an adult, I knew that the whole mission of the schools was frankly genocidal in nature, its purpose to "take the Indian out of the child," as declared calmly by Sir John A. Macdonald, our first Prime Minister, and that our former Chief Justice of Canada, Beverley McLachlin, has since called what happened at the residential schools "cultural genocide."

After we'd completed our drive to Winnipeg and returned to Calgary, the Archbishop of Canterbury arrived in Prince Albert, Saskatchewan, and apologized to First Nations of Saskatchewan for its role in the shame: his heart was "full of darkness," he told the gathering; Pope Francis apologized from the Vatican: "I am very sorry," and said he would come to Canada to apologize to Indigenous Peoples in person, which he did in July 2022. After listening to the survivors tell their stories and expressing his shame and dismay, he told the press on his flight back to Rome that what happened was "genocide." In August 2022, The National Centre for Truth and Reconciliation in Winnipeg announced that it had so far collected and documented the cases of four thousand one hundred and eighteen children. (By 2024 records of another two hundred and twenty had been found.)

Prime Minister Trudeau apologized in November 2017 for the residential schools, but before the unmarked graves were announced. After his official apology for the unmarked graves on June 25, 2021, he travelled to a number of reserves and apologized again at each one, and his government made funds available so the search for graves could be completed. I wondered, would the Vatican release not only its records of the schools it ran but provide money to help find and name the dead children? Would it pay reparations?



Lucinda and I were driving across the southern Canadian Great Plains, passing a few miles south of the many reserves east of Regina, Saskatchewan. Why so many reserves there was a question we didn't ask: I knew the answer, or at least part of it, but I didn't say it. Or maybe I did, or maybe Lucinda already knew about how, in the late 1800s, up to five thousand First Nations people had gathered at Fort Walsh in the Cypress Hills in Saskatchewan. They were there because, with the demise of the bison, they were starving. They went to the North-West Mounted Police to ask for food and were told that to be given food they must first "take treaty." One of the conditions of "taking treaty" was that they and their people had to move either into the Fort Carleton area on the north side of the Saskatchewan River, or else go to reserves east of Regina. That is why to this day the only reserve anywhere near Fort Walsh is the Nekaneet First Nation in the Cypress Hills south of Maple Creek, Saskatchewan, there because Chief Nekaneet refused to sign, or perhaps he did sign, but refused to leave, and he and about one hundred of his followers stayed behind to make their own way in a world that was no longer theirs. Eventually, around 1913, the government gave them a few acres for a reserve there, which later was expanded.

First Nations had asked for contiguous reserves all across the southern prairies. That was farm or grazing land, needed for settlement to ensure that part of Canada wouldn't fall to the Americans; as well, such a massive presence of Indigenous people was seen as dangerous to white people. To this day, the thousands of acres south of there, both east and west, do not have a single reserve on them. The one exception is a reserve at Wood Mountain for the descendants of Sitting Bull's Lakota people. Otherwise, only in Maple Creek will you often see First Nations people, while east of Regina along the Qu'Appelle River, there are fifteen reserves.



When Lucinda and I passed south of the burial grounds where the Marieval Indian Residential School once stood, we didn't even *think* of turning north to visit it in sympathy and shame, partly because we couldn't yet face it, partly because we thought we wouldn't be welcome, might be seen as atrocity-tourists, might even be subjected to rage and abuse. At the least, we would look like the worst kind of hypocrites.

### III

Instead, we went on our way into Manitoba, aiming for Winnipeg and the search for Lucinda's paternal grandmother's house where, as a five-year-old, she spent a wonderfully happy week one summer more than fifty years earlier. A street photographer had caught her youthful parents; she showed me the photo.

Awed, I told her, "They look like movie stars." She smiled to herself as she put the picture away.

At the town of Broadview, we were only about one hundred and fifty kilometres out of Regina, and Winnipeg was another four hundred-plus kilometres away. We drove through Broadview, not speaking, and, in silence, on to Moosomin, where we would make our ritual stop, before we headed out again into Manitoba.

Here's a strange thing: After my dream about the pool of water dripping on me, threatening to become a deluge that would drown me, and the other dreams I've mentioned, I have begun having ordinary dreams again. All night long, it seems to me, I am racing around the new house at the hay farm busily getting things done, or one sister is going to New York City with "mom and . . ." one of our other sisters, or my son is a small boy again, and I'm zipping up his little red parka, making sure the fur-trimmed hood is tucked tight around his face, and watching him lovingly as he walks away. Busy scurrying dreams reflecting my life as it was for so many years.



The dream-sister who is gathering her things to prepare for her trip to New York actually resides in a care home in Vancouver because she is semi-lost in dementia brought on, we believe, by a lack of oxygen to her brain when she had repeated cardiac arrests some years ago and her heart had to be restarted nine times until the physician refused to start it again if it stopped.

Our joy when our sister finally seemed back to herself after her massive heart attack, and then, slowly, the forgetfulness creeping in, bit by bit, always growing worse. Only a few days ago, on her birthday, telling me over the phone, with her daughter's help, that she was in a hotel in ". . . I'm not sure where," and couldn't tell me what the weather was like in Vancouver, because she wasn't in Vancouver.

The barriers were down again, I could admit it: the ones to my feelings that I had resolutely closed off, thinking it would be easier to live out my last days if I didn't remember the past, since I couldn't change any of it, anyway. By reliving all that pain, I told myself, I gained nothing, but it always remained, indelible and as powerful as ever if I dared to look at it, while the so-fleeting joy that was there too, I could almost never find.

All of this caused me to say to myself, "My four sisters have been almost the *most* important thing in my life, most of my life," even when I thought I'd cast off that world of childhood and young womanhood when I married my first husband on my twenty-first birthday, sixty years before the summer when Lucinda and I set off on our journey. The power of this realization startled and shook me. It was as if I'd always known this but had not once consciously thought it.

Although, not so long ago I was invited to stay with friends who live in a small, pretty town in southern Saskatchewan. The  first morning I got up, went to the kitchen and began to pour myself a cup of coffee, as my hosts each in separate corners were busily preparing their own breakfasts, when suddenly, in one of those flashes of emotion that come out of nowhere, tears formed in my eyes and threatened to spill onto my cheeks. I had to struggle to keep them from pouring out. In that instant, I had felt through my whole body how much I missed my mother and my four sisters, how I had missed them all of the many years since we'd grown up and moved in different directions, my mother dead for thirty-five years, my father for fifty years, my sisters for twenty-four and nine years, the third sister in care for two years, the fourth and eldest unable to travel without people to push her wheelchair although her mind was sharp as ever, and we could still talk on the phone. How terribly I missed *home*, the one that no longer existed, perhaps never existed, and *family* despite all our difficulties.

Gone from my daily life, every one of them, and I remembered the five of us in the kitchen in Saskatoon, on a Saturday morning with the radio on, and as we did the housework our mother demanded of us, putting down our mops, brooms, and dust cloths to dance to Elvis and then later, I guess when my older sister and I were gone, the younger ones danced to the Beatles. Talking, laughing, telling stories, admitting to crushes or denying them, gossiping and quarrelling. I wonder, could I be imagining the dancing-in-the-kitchen scene from *The Big Chill*?

But no, we did dance to the radio in the kitchen, we oldest jiving or teaching a younger one to jive, singing along with the radio and arguing, too, of course. I remember telling my youngest sister, nine years younger than I, that I couldn't understand what the Beatles were about as "they just sound like everybody else," and my little sister, dead at sixty-four in 2014, shouting,



"*They do not*!" almost in tears, as if I had mortally wounded her. She was right, and I, forever of the Elvis generation, wasn't. Although, Billy Joel said last night in an interview on CNN that if the Beatles hadn't written lyrics to go with their music, nobody would have noticed them. How surprised I was at my little sister's reaction to what I thought was a perfectly innocuous remark. Or was I? Or was I just being sibling-cruel?

And yet, examining that memory, I realize that our oldest sister probably had a job then and wasn't there, she might even have been off at her first year teaching school; the sister next to me was disabled, dead since 1998, and certainly wasn't dancing, so maybe it was only me and the two youngest sisters. But if I was seventeen or older, the youngest would have been only eight and surely she would have been older than that when the Beatles came on the scene. In fact, my son was born in late

February 1964 when his father and I were still listening to jazz and rhythm and blues and never gave the Beatles a thought beyond wondering if their fans had all lost their minds. Did that dancing scene, indelible in my memory for more than sixty years, ever happen, and if so, when, and who was there? Yet I can still see the look on our mother's face as she walked by the room on an errand, the small, inward, *real* smile, at us, her daughters, having fun together.

Somewhere in there, though, possibly 1965, my first husband, our little boy, and I drove from near Vancouver where we'd been living, on our way to Halifax, staying for a week or two in Saskatoon, then travelling on through Ontario where we stopped to see the couple who'd once been our best friends, who had stood up for us at our wedding, and who had now joined the middle class with a house in the suburbs and two small children and a nice car. In the evening, the kids in bed, we went downstairs to their rumpus room where they got out an album so we could listen to music. It was the Beatles: *Sgt. Pepper's Lonely Hearts Club Band.*



My husband the jazz lover looked dubious although too polite to challenge our hosts, but it was a revelatory moment for me having nothing to do with the music itself. In that second, I saw my childhood, my teenage years that I had put so relentlessly behind me, opening up to me again, a kind of liberation, and I did not know how I should feel, besides very surprised and faintly excited. And yet, to tell the truth, that is the only time I can remember deliberately listening to the Beatles. We'd always gone to concerts of classical music, and I still do when I can get to one, but music for my then-husband and me was Mingus, Miles Davis, John Coltrane, etc., etc., etc., until we slid sideways for a while into rhythm and blues, and then it was Aretha, and before too long, we were divorced. After that, for me and my women friends it was Stevie Wonder, the Pointer Sisters, Melissa Manchester, Helen Reddy, Carole King. That terrifically good film *The Wanderers*, released in 1979 but set in 1963, in which a member of my generation living in what he thought was still his own era follows a girl into a packed club and sees Bob Dylan at the microphone singing "The Times They Are a-Changing." The signal of the shift, right there, and me, still stuck like the movie's hero in the wrong generation. Much as I am today.

I only listen to classical music now, not because I am indifferent to other forms, but for the opposite reason: they raise so much emotion in me that I mostly can't bear it. In the evenings, I work at my books, watch a little television, and then I'm tired and go to bed.

**IV**

Broadview, Saskatchewan, was a prosperous-appearing little

town that day we drove through it in bright sunshine, the white storefronts gleaming as brightly as the clay cliffs at Ravenscrag as we passed slowly by. The further east we travelled the greener the land and trees became, despite the historic drought we were driving through. And how the sun expanded to fill the cloudless sky, shimmering and scintillating as it poured heat and light down on us. Broadview, in my memory as we passed through it without stopping, seemed to shine brightly white, even while close by, the repercussions of a great historical wrong were being felt anew; evidence of the worst crimes now revealed as shadows on glowing screens. A mere fifteen miles north of our pleasant trip, unassuageable grief reigned.

I couldn't remember if we had stopped in Broadview or not; it had left a blank spot in my mind, and I thought of the things we had done in other towns and villages we passed by or through. I remembered only the bright white of a store we passed, the wideness of the main street that was also the highway, the fact that I seemed to have no personal connection to the town and for a long time couldn't even remember having passed through it.

I stopped typing, and although I tried several times to come back to my work, each time I failed. Three weeks went by during which I travelled a bit, did a reading, went to a party, then another gathering, read several books, and still the question bedevilled me: What had I to say about Broadview? And why could I not say whatever it was? Even my bafflement baffled me. It began to seem easier to dodge the issue by going historical.

Broadview, eighty kilometrers east of the Manitoba–Saskatchewan border and about one hundred and twenty-eight north of the American border, began in 1882 when the Trans-Canada railway was built and the CPR decided it would be "the divisional point" (*The Encyclopedia of Saskatchewan*) between Brandon, Manitoba, and Moose Jaw, Saskatchewan. *Saskatchewan* is Cree for something like "swiftly flowing."



So, Broadview's early prosperity was built on the railroad. As with most Saskatchewan towns, its population increased in good times and decreased in poor times, settling in at around half of what it had been at its peak. This fact about the prairie West, including the western United States, reminds me of a visit I made to Rutgers University in New Jersey to meet Dr. Frank Popper, a geographer with interests in climate change and policy, who, with his scholar-wife Deborah, were briefly famous beyond the academic community for suggesting that the American West, parts of it doing very badly at the time, should be shut down to farming and ranching and become a "Buffalo Commons." This suggestion outraged American Westerners, who, in rebuttal, suggested that New Jersey should be razed to become an enormous parking lot. This, at the same time Peter and I said that parts of the Palliser Triangle should become a great national grasslands park, not just the few thousand acres the government had managed to buy a hundred miles east of our ranch named the Grasslands National Park, but an area much larger.

I had rejected Broadview, Saskatchewan, and unconsciously must have felt that the discovery of the unmarked graves by the now-vanished residential school to the north wiped out any meaning Broadview might have had. I knew then that we hadn't stopped in Broadview, and that for a long time afterwards, we had remembered Cowessess and what happened there, and didn't speak.

We drove on, and at Moosomin we stopped for our usual break. We were then only about nineteen kilometrers from the Saskatchewan–Manitoba border. That was where we noticed that we had forgotten to put our watches ahead an hour as we should have done at Broadview. That hour seemed then, in that high sun and heat, on the sparsely occupied highway, and in the face of the desolation of the First Nations people, meaningless.



## V

My sisters and I have all always reminded ourselves, as a way of explaining how she was, that our mother had had to deal with her own firm and demanding mother, and instead of rejecting that kind of parenting, she couldn't release herself from it and was the same with not all of us, but I think she was that demanding of only me. Our older sister, the firstborn, was exceptionally bright and also unusually pretty and was adored by all the adults in the family, and I could never measure up against her. The third child was developmentally delayed from anoxia at birth and left physically disabled when she was five.

Naturally, during those years, she took up the greatest part of our mother's energy; the next child was too young during most of our childhoods to do much housework, and the last child, five years younger, lived in a family so changed that our childhoods were different. Looking back, I saw that most of that work fell on me. As the years of her mothering went on from 1938 into the sixties, our mother, understandably, grew less and less focused on parenting, so that in adulthood, our youngest sister remarked, she didn't really notice what she, our sister, got up to, nor worry about her outside certain loose parameters. But for me, the rules were firm and there was no dodging them; I was always under her watchful eye.

I am telling my own truth here, and know very well that my sisters, both the living and the dead, would be unlikely to agree wholly with me, and some maybe even partially. This, however, doesn't make me wrong, because this is my story as I understand it; it is the reality in which I have lived my life.

But, if I felt unloved, was in fact unloved and as a child was mistreated by my mother, I think now that our mother had had the heaviest burden to bear in her own family when she was growing up, and might frequently have also felt unloved. In my memory, when we were children, whenever she and her mother were in a room together, they spoke softly to each other, briefly, leaning side by side against the kitchen counter, sitting beside each other on a sofa or at a lunch table. They showed little emotion, only that soft, ladylike near whispering, sometimes laughing lightly, none of this a normal mode of behaviour for our mother. I was struck by how quiet she became, how – if she'd been a child I would have said – well behaved, and reticent, without a hint of the assertive, brisk parent we knew. She spoke of her mother always as "Mother," never "Mom," nor "Momma," as we all did of her, and although she was never, even as an old woman, at all disrespectful of her mother's memory, she was instead fixated on memories of her father, often smiling or laughing as she told us stories of his wonderful sense of humour and his loving behaviour. I suspect that this was because she received so little direct affection from her own mother, which was at least partly the result of the stern culture in which our grandmother had been raised.

Our mother's younger brother, born in 1912, at nine years old suffered from a fever of 106 degrees that no interventions of the young parents could bring down, and when after three days it finally passed, the fever had taken the bright edge off his thinking process. Our grandmother called it rheumatic fever, it had also damaged one leg pretty severely, and after the fever passed, he dragged that leg. Our grandmother said in her memoirs something none of us knew, that he had vision only in one eye and was rejected when he tried to enlist to fight in World War II. I remember him, my grandfather, and my father as extremely hardworking, trying to make a living in bush country that in winter was frigid and buried under mountains of snow and in summer hot, wet, and so insect-ridden that life was nearly impossible, a place where you wouldn't survive if you didn't work steadily, relentlessly all day, every day. Our uncle had a sore on his lower lip caused by constantly holding a cigarette there. Later, the sore would turn to cancer and kill him when finally it reached his jugular vein and he hemorrhaged to death, falling out of his hospital bed as he reached for the bell to call a nurse. This was in 1949, when he was thirty-seven. That same year our youngest sister was born. I'm surprised by the unexpected but clear nexus of the old settler world he was part of, and the new modern one belonging to our baby sister. Our mother hanging up the phone, sitting on the living room couch, her face held steady, her eyes large, not seeing us.

Our mother, born in 1910, was the eldest child and the one given all the household responsibility. The next child, a girl, was born in 1917 and, as nearly as I can determine, became the favourite child, apparently because she was viewed as having poor health and in need of extra attention. A third girl was born in 1919 and had what seemed to us, as little as we knew her, to have a different personality than her sisters, a sort of willful recklessness, but that in the end served her well, as she was the only one who escaped Saskatchewan history, and who, after the war, lived in Florida with her husband and children, eventually dying there. It was there, visiting her sister, that our mother found the lump in her breast that four years later would kill her.

Being the focus of a stern mother's ideas about childrearing is very hard on a child. But not feeling loved tends to dampen all the normal emotions, especially care for others, having failed to receive care oneself: A coldness sets in; the heart freezes; one's judgment is destroyed, along with all self-esteem. I know because this is how I have been. But now, at last, I see that our mother must have suffered from the same malady, and passed it on to me. I would ask now, of the five of us, why me, but I believe the answer lies in the specific sexual violence that happened only to me and that I feel sure she never knew about. But I believe now that she had a chunk of ice impaled at the centre of her heart, too.



I was in my mid-to-late-seventies when, on a vacation in Maui, I woke one morning so disturbed by a dream that I couldn't come back to my daily self and had to be comforted by my companion, who thankfully was an empathic, generous, and also patient person. Our disabled sister for whom I'd been given a lot of responsibility when we were children, whom I had moved in with in 1997 to care for while she died of breast and lung cancer, was the focus of the dream. I loved her wholly, unreservedly in a way I've never loved anyone else, so much so that during that year, during her worst times, I found it hard to separate what was her and what was me. In the dream, she was wrapped in a thick down parka, its fur-edged hood pulled up, a woollen toque under it, heavy mitts, snowpants, and winter boots. All her clothing was stark white, but it was also entirely covered in thick frost leaving her at the edge of freezing to death. I was trying to help her climb a ladder, in life an impossible task for her. Waking, I realized that the frozen person in the dream who was near death, was me.

### VI

Moosomin, the next town after Broadview, once had a population of about three thousand people, a big town for Saskatchewan and a prosperous one in the days of the railroad coming through. *Moosomin,* a Cree word that refers to the mooseberry, or high bush cranberry, is named after Chief Moosomin from Treaty 6 days (1876), whom Lieutenant-Governor Dewdney appointed as chief around 1880. According to the Canadian Plains Research Centre's *Encyclopedia of Saskatchewan,* once the railway arrived, settlers looked with acquisitive eyes on the many hectares of good land that had been allotted to the reserve, and by 1909, seven years after powerful Chief Moosomin's death, the reserve had surrendered its land. Professor Bill Waiser, in his wonderful *Saskatchewan: A New History,* puts quotes around "surrendered," suggesting that it might not be quite the right word. In return, this Cree nation was given less and poorer land at Cochin on Jackfish Lake, north of North Battleford, the very Jackfish Lake where my first in-laws owned a lakeside cottage when my son was a baby, and where my youngest sister, brother-in-law, and their children spent many happy summers at theirs.

But what I am really thinking about is a friend who came from the Peguis Reserve in Manitoba. In 1907 his reserve was moved from its original home near Selkirk, Manitoba, 170 kilometres up the shore of Lake Winnipeg to its present location near Fisher Bay, I'm told, an illegal move. But mostly, I am remembering my friend telling me about how the government moved all the people to their new reserve standing in a boxcar. His grandmother was one of those people. It's clear that whoever made those decisions at that time did not think "Indians" were fully human, knew that they had no rights and therefore that a boxcar was good enough for them, good enough for my friend's grandmother. This thought made his voice go funny; he looked away, a cloud of emotion settled over him and wafted to me.

By then, both Lucinda and I were losing track of the ordinary markers of daily life: times, purpose, deadlines. We recognized: the need for coffee; the need for a bathroom; the need for gas. We might have been driving for weeks; we might have been dreaming we were driving. And yet, every once in a while we reached somewhere and remembered our almost forgotten purpose.



From the moment we began to head southeast on the Trans-Canada south of Calgary, the countryside was less and less green, drier and drier looking, not appetizing and, I suppose to many, not even intriguing. The smell of dust hung in the air; the sun growing more and more intense until no one could look up, paling as the day wore on, gold to yellow to hazy cream to white, at the same time as it seemed to swell to fill the entire enormous sky. Years ago I wrote a novel called *The Gates of the Sun* about a rancher in southwest Saskatchewan starting from the settlement period up to the eighties of the twentieth century, the only time up to then that I wrote an entire novel from a male point of view. I based it on stories I'd heard from an old rancher-cowboy, long dead now, who'd been brought west, unusually, by his mother, as a five-year-old child in the early twenties and never left, and also from my husband's stories and those I overheard of his ranching-cowboy friends. It was a fascinating and as heroic a world as any. And a nearly waterless world, ruled purely by the sun as it burned down on the barely peopled miles of native grass, the animals and birds, the great sweep of land itself.

And yet, in poetry and folklore and living experience, it is the cold that kills.

# EIGHT

# GREEN

## I

We chatted as the landscape sailed past us, trees, grass, ponds, a river that we crossed several times. My mother's move as a child from Manitoba and my father's from Quebec meant that I had close relatives I didn't know only a few miles from the highway we were driving on, and others in Winnipeg. I had that familiar sense of the impermanence of every arrangement in this world and the feeling that all I could do was wait with fast dwindling hope or else imagine us all together someday in the same city.

After, when I tried to remember that part of the trip with Lucinda, I recalled mostly a blur of rich green, unrolling on both sides, a loveliness of green, even in the middle of a drought, and I must have thought first of my father's family who came to Saskatchewan around 1912 or so, but to a better farming area not far from Prince Albert, and then of my mother's parents who, having lost their land in green Manitoba, instead of waiting out the drought as farmers usually do, around 1924 headed further west to the "good land" they had heard about in Saskatchewan, eventually trying to settle on free homestead land on the edge of a forest, where all but one of my sisters and I were born.

Maybe it was the reassuring green and abundance of the trees there that attracted them, even though all of them, with Herculean labour, had to be cut down, their branches sawed off, and their roots dragged out of the ground in order to start a farm.

But it was not rich black land under the trees, and soon my mother's people moved on, arriving in Prince Albert in 1938, and farmed in that area after that. I say this because I remember clearly, as does my older sister, staying with them in a log house on the farm where they lived, playing together at least once along with our cousin Gayle, three weeks younger than I am (sadly, dead in 2024), in our grandmother's flower garden. And also, in our makeshift beds, possibly on the floor, waking and seeing light shining on a smooth leather boot of a kind none of the men of the family wore, at the Christmas tree, and insisting the next morning to the smiles of the adults that I had seen Santa Claus.



And yet, our grandmother's memoir of those days does not mention a further move to a farm, and she is wrong about a date or two, even getting the birthdate of her husband wrong by one year. I have seen the government census that specifies the date of his birth, which confounded our aunt, his daughter, and that throws into uncertainty the rest of the memoir's dates. The Prince Albert newspaper in printing her obituary gets the date of her death wrong by one year, too, all of which is a good lesson in the instability of memory and the general speciousness of family legends that are not provable by any firm means and that destabilize one's ability to establish with certainty the events of one's own life, let alone that of one's family.

Nothing amazes me more than to read our mother's mother's cheery account of their lives after they left Manitoba, year after year after year of genuine, crippling privation and bad luck, and yet to think that neither of our grandparents died until they were older than I am now, all my suffering having been mostly psychological, though just as real as hunger and illness, and yet not killing me, either. All of our family hardship being only minimally unusual because we lived pioneering lives for the most part later than other pioneering Canadians. Recently at a literary festival I listened to older First Nations women who were presenting ridiculing the idea of the mostly Euro-Canadian newcomers as "pioneering." I assume they meant you can't pioneer in a land that is already settled, in this case by them.

Lucinda and I must have noticed that we'd travelled across two-thirds of Canada's southern prairie, that we were about to cross another invisible line between provinces, or to sail through an imaginary one, such boundaries, in contact days, in my opinion more accurately seen by First Nations as having a magical quality, "the medicine line," into a usually much wetter and greener Manitoba. I sometimes think that Manitoba is the most neglected in the popular Canadian mind of all the provinces so that I didn't know what the name means or where it came from and had to look it up.



". . . possibly derives from either Cree *manitou-wapow* or Ojibwe *manidoobaa*, both meaning 'straits of Manitou, the Great Spirit.' Alternatively, it may be from the Assiniboine 'minnetoba' meaning 'Lake of the Prairie' (the lake was known to French explorers as Lac des Prairies)" (Wikipedia).

It's impossible on the Canadian prairies, wherever the original First Nations' place names have been allowed to remain in some form, not to notice that they refer mostly to where Indigenous Peoples met and rested or prayed or were in battle and held ceremonies, and to the speed of rivers or mysterious enormity of certain lakes or to incidents in particular places: Old Wives Lake, Cut Knife, Yellowknife, Whitehorse, White Fox, and so on. Colourful, meaningful names rather than the names of dead men or replications of names from the British Isles, Germany, France, Russia, or Ukraine.

White settlers in southwest Saskatchewan named their farming communities Enterprise, Climax, Success, and so on, the names tending to express the opposite of what happened to most settlers there, but no defunct villages are called Despair, Desolation, Loss, Misery, or Sorrow. The Butalas, however, were one of the settler families that survived and even expanded their property, although getting rich, despite some of the neighbours' certainty that we had, remained a pipe dream.

I heard a Blackfoot Elder use the Blackfoot name for Calgary on the radio only the other day: *Moh-kíns-tsis,* the Blackfoot word for elbow. The Stoney word for elbow is *Wincheesh-pah, Otos-kwunee* is the Cree word for elbow, and *Kootsisáw* is the T'suu T'ina word for elbow. The elbow referred to is the place where one of the two rivers in Calgary, the other is the Bow, makes an elbow-like right-angle turn and thus is called the Elbow River. The settlement briefly became Fort Brisebois; next, at the behest of James Macleod, eventually Commissioner of the North-West Mounted Police, who was born on the Isle of Skye, it became Fort Calgary, after the Scottish Calgary on the island of Mull, finally becoming Calgary, about which name Wikipedia says:

"The name comes from the Gaelic, *Cala ghearraidh*, meaning Beach of the meadow (pasture)... 'Cala' is the word specifically used for a hard, sandy beach suitable for landing a boat, which relates plausibly to the location. However, the museum on the Isle of Mull explains that *kald* and *gart* are similar Old Norse words, meaning 'cold' and 'garden,' that were likely used when named by the Vikings who inhabited the Inner Hebrides."

Apparently, Macleod had once visited an estate at Calgary on the Isle of Mull. It would be hard to find a more inappropriate name for a city looking west onto the heart-stirring Rocky

Mountains and east to Canada's Great Plains and situated a thousand miles from the nearest sea. Unless at the confluence of the Bow and Elbow Rivers in the heart of the city, there might then have been something resembling a stony Isle of Mull beach.

**II**

Manitoba fascinated me and my sisters when we were children, because our mother mentioned it so often as the Elysian Fields from which she had come. She was part of a large farming clan, the Grahams and the Elders, nineteenth-century settlers south of Brandon. Her father, born at Portage la Prairie in 1880, was one of the Irish Grahams still called in Ireland "the Ulster Scots," that is, Scots who settled in Northern Ireland in the seventeenth century as a result of wars between Bonnie Prince Charlie and the Jacobins, a complicated and bloody history ending with the British triumphing at the Battle of Culloden in April 1746, which caused our ancestors to flee to Northern Ireland, where their descendants still live.



My mother's mother, Jane Taylor Elder, was a pure Scot whose Lowland ancestors arrived in Quebec in 1817, and as did my mother's father's family, a branch of the Elders slowly moved west, stopping for some years in Ontario and a branch staying to settle there. Her memoir says this:

"I was born in the municipality of Cornwallace 18 miles southeast of Brandon. My father, James Tully Elder, homesteaded on the land where I was born in 1883. He came from a place called Elder's Mills, [Ontario], which was not a town, but just a post office, and was named after my father because he had a flour mill there and served quite a large portion of that farming country with flour. The mill was powered by damning the Humber River to drive the large stone crushers that ground the wheat to make first class flour, I am told. The nearest town was Woodbridge, about ten miles from the mill. My father was a fairly young man when he decided to come west. He was born in 1834 in Quebec . . ."

My grandmother explained further that her father married Jane Alexis Taylor, and they lived at Elder's Mill for ten years during which she gave birth to five children, two of whom, girls, died very young, and as tuberculosis was rampant in the family, her father decided they should go west to a drier climate. Jane Alexis Taylor did not join her husband until 1883, when she already had tuberculosis and was pregnant with my grandmother, who writes, "I was born on August 17, 1883, and was just one year and eleven months when my mother died." On June 24, 1908, she and our grandfather, Francis Graham, from the nearby Irish-Canadian farming clan who before 1746 had been Scots, were married.

All our childhoods, as our parents' fortunes fell and then fell again, and their marriage grew more unhappy, our mother constantly remembered to us her happy, prosperous childhood in the midst of countless relatives, also all farming people. After her family's departure in 1924 for Saskatchewan, she went back to the Manitoba area she had come from only once, long after 1973, when she had been widowed, and it seemed to us, her daughters, that she found it a satisfactory visit, but she mused on it for a long time and in silence, and my sisters and I never knew what she had found of her childhood there, other than in some way I've forgotten, and perhaps some of her memories had been wrong. Or that other things had happened after she was gone, about which she knew nothing and that seemed to have shaken her.

On the eighty-eighth anniversary of my parents' marriage in 1935, I recalled her daintiness, and her femininity, which she never lost, a kind of innocent, gentle loveliness she sometimes moved in, and in this picture of her, it is early morning and she is wearing a nightgown and a light, pretty dressing gown over it, and gazes at us as we eat our porridge, with a distant half smile, as if she sees us, but not quite as her children. And then, I'm guessing, she would waken to our lives and the clamorous needs of her five children.

We were in Manitoba, passing town after town with their familiar names, which I pointed out to Lucinda, who was kind enough to ask me if I wanted to turn south and find Rounthwaite. There had once been a village there, and a school that may still be there that my mother and her siblings had attended. Did I want once again to see the church where she was christened, and which was also near the farms of all her relatives? But I was wondering about things that merely passing through would never tell me. I had no land descriptions anyway and could have been sitting in the middle of an Elder-owned or Graham-owned field of grain and not know it, nor be any the wiser if I did know, about what was in her heart from 1910 to 1924.



Many years earlier, when Peter and I travelled to southern Manitoba for some occasion that I can't remember, we had found that tiny church. The door was wide open, bird droppings covered the tall, iron parlour-stove. Back home, I wrote to the appropriate Manitoba government department to express my dismay at the approaching loss of such an historic and beautiful building and the urgency of putting some money into saving it. Whether that happened or not, I didn't know, as I'd never been back, and that day in July 2021, as we drove along the highway not far from the church, I refused to go to see it as if such a visit belonged in a different enterprise than the one we were on.

In 2010 I stayed for two weeks at the Tyrone Guthrie Centre in County Monaghan, Ireland. I had taken it for granted then that I was in the Republic; I was bemused to find on the

Monaghan County Council's website that "County Monaghan is one of the three Ulster counties in the Republic of Ireland. . . . some ninety percent of the county is located within ten miles of the border with Northern Ireland." I still can't figure out how it's possible to be in Ulster at the same time as in the Republic.

To be honest, I went to the Tyrone Guthrie Centre because it was only about fifty miles from Enniskillen, in Ireland's lake district, and the market town of Lisnaskea (also spelled Lisneskea and sometimes Lisniskea) in County Fermanagh from which my paternal great-grandfather, John Graham, had departed for Canada around 1864, followed in 1865 by my great-grandmother Margaret Grady or O'Grady, the inconsistent spelling a story in itself that I did not unravel until I asked our tour-van driver, who seemed to find it mystifying that I didn't know that in Ireland then, he said, an 'O' before a name identified the person as a Catholic, which in Northern Ireland in those days was an unfortunate thing to be. The Graham family were Anglicans.



Margaret O'Grady disembarked from her ship in Canada carrying in her arms their year-old son, Robert. What a scandal that must have been back in Lisnaskea, as they were not married in Ireland, despite a Manitoba newspaper clipping from the 1960s where a descendant declared that Margaret and John Senior had been married in Ireland. But I have a copy of their marriage certificate, which clearly states they were married in 1865 in Montreal. Their descendants had cleaned up the disreputable history or else they simply didn't know it, or maybe their elders had lied to them. I went to the retreat centre in order to have a headquarters from which to travel, hoping in some vague way to see the original home of our Irish family, the name of which, Drummach, I'd known since childhood.

By sheer coincidence, not long before I left for Ireland, a friend in Calgary introduced me to a friend of hers who had emigrated from that very district, whose market town had been Lisnaskea, who had the same surname although was not related to my family, she said, and who then put me in touch with excellent friends of hers in Lisnaskea. Sometimes the ancestral spirits really are taking a hand in your affairs if it also concerns theirs, because in the Irish Republic, those wonderful Irish friends of a friend's friend drove to the centre, picked me up, and spent the day driving me around. "This is the road where *things* happened," they told me, as we drove down the winding, narrow road between what was the Republic and Ulster, and meaning, bombings, abductions, and murders, hard to imagine that day in that beautiful Irish countryside. They found for me the churchyard full of my mother's father's line of ancestors, the house from which a great-great-grandmother had come to the house where my great-grandfather had been born and raised and from which he departed for Canada, and the current owners jokingly asked through my escorts if I wanted to buy it. Amused, I thought how that little joke sounded just like the jokes of my long-dead grandfather.



My escorts pointed out the long green field stretching out from the front of the house to the road, a few acres, a lot less than a quarter section, and remarked, "You can see why the Grahams were well off," and I nodded sagely although I was perplexed. Still, such rich grass would support a fair number of cows – what? Five? Ten? More? And also, I reminded myself, here there is year-round grazing which there certainly isn't in Saskatchewan. Then we went to Enniskillen to see the school that Samuel Beckett and Oscar Wilde had attended, Portora Royal School, founded in 1608 and still in service.

One of the stories about our Irish great-grandfather had been that he was sent away to school because of the disgrace of getting a Catholic servant pregnant (but all the servants in

Ulster then were Catholics). I finally got up the courage to write to the elegant school on the hill above the lake in Enniskillen and ask if they had a record of him attending there. When I received the reply, as I unfolded the letter, I could sniff the amusement coming off the page, no matter how graciously worded, at the very idea. It is certainly true, even allowing the vicissitude of memory, that settlers often glorified their old-country backgrounds, because who would ever know the real story?

Then my escorts took me to their beautiful new house in the town, introduced me to their children, such gorgeous young people, served me a wonderful Sunday dinner, and then took everyone on another drive as dusk was falling, to the loveliest old dark grey stone church dwarfed under ancient green trees and in front of which a brook slipped softly by. There their daughter had recently been married. Only Emily Carr's *Church at Yuquot* moved me as much as that Irish church in the Irish countryside, even though it hadn't anything I knew of to do with my ancestors. Although it was old enough, it could have, I mused, thinking of the Irish poets as I gazed in an unsettled way at the church, the magnificent trees, and the gentle stream, murmuring as it slipped by.



After that, they drove me back to the centre, where I finished the book I'd been working on, although right now I can't remember which book it was. Thinking of that day later, tears briefly threatened, for what I was not sure: the contrast between the rough Canadian world I was born into and that ancient, peaceful beauty. Peaceful now, I reminded myself, as Irish history is full of trouble.

In the early nineties, Peter and I drove through that farming country in southern Manitoba, had gone to visit relatives and, later, the local cemeteries where we found the headstone of my great-grandparents, the storied John and Margaret of Lisnaskea, County Fermanagh. We met cousins my mother had spoken of, gracious elderly women, who mentioned my mother affectionately to me, among whom I could imagine my mother sitting, ghostly, but in all other ways just like them: a graciousness, I thought, with a disposition for kindness, and living out their lives in a community in which they were intimately entwined, the latter that my mother lost when her family uprooted themselves and went to wild Saskatchewan.

On we went toward Winnipeg, noticing as we drove how the landscape changed, despite the drought, grew richer-looking than southern Alberta and Saskatchewan, the highway taking us across rivers flowing under low bridges only to discover later that we had crossed the same river each time: the Assiniboine. *Assiniboine* refers to a First Nations people also called *Nakoda*, that translates as "stone people," probably meaning "people who cook with hot stones."

I remember about that long afternoon of driving only trivial things: that I drove for over an hour on the high-speed divided highway, and when we stopped for a break, I asked Lucinda to take over because, although I'd done more than thirty years of highway driving, it was rarely on such busy roads; I was out of practice, and getting more and more anxious that I'd have an accident.



A passenger again, I focused on the green highway signs as we passed them. At Portage la Prairie, I told Lucinda that my Irish grandfather was born there in 1880, when John, Margaret, and their children stopped for two years on their move from Ontario to Manitoba, before settling, finally, near Rounthwaite.

We stopped next in Brandon, the small city that in my mother's childhood was her mythical New York or Toronto. It was also where our grandmother, a fine young lady from a prosperous farm, in photos from around the turn of that century wearing glorious hats, had been sent to Brandon College and also to dressmaking school between 1900 and 1908, when she married. Winnipeg must have been my mother's Paris or London, only to be dreamt of, never once seen.

Onward, ho! Or, Wagons, ho! Or whatever it was American movies say the settlers' wagon masters shouted as they moved out on their trek west. There were covered wagons in Canada, too; my Graham grandfather claimed to have been born under his family's in 1880 at Portage la Prairie, but the-under-the-wagon box detail turned out to be only his little joke, to the dismay of all his gullible descendants, including me, who never thought to question the story and who loved having a grandfather who was that Western, that "first." In the long string of much-admired white Western "firsts," it was a hard one to beat. Come to think of it, maybe that was what he was making fun of.

And, of course, arriving on the edge of Winnipeg (population just under eight hundred thousand) and the home of most of my remaining relatives on my dad's side, both of us were daunted by the need to find our way through the city neither of us were familiar with, to the hotel on the fork of the two rivers that run through Winnipeg, the Assiniboia, and the Red, and where Fort Rouge once was. Ever-modern Lucinda pulled out her phone, found maps, and in no time we were in the parking lot, still alive, if winded. I was thinking how none of it would have happened without her. If I was sometimes the Sancho Panza to her Don Quixote, she was a good deal less hapless than the wonderful Don. I seem to have been the one with a head full of myths.

Now, thinking about our arrival in Winnipeg, a place I rarely visited even though we had relatives on both sides of our family there, I find myself thinking of our parents' marriage and what a muddle it was, and remained. How that so-wrong marriage, it was hinted at by older relatives, was done by our mother, apparently, out of the need to punish her parents for chasing away the man she truly loved as unsuitable for their eldest daughter. But I know she loved our father, at least in the first years. This, after her parents had insisted that she, who loved school and books above all, must leave school at the end of Grade 10, something she was ashamed of all her life and never told us until the day she and one of her friends, as sixty-year-olds, took the Grade 12 Equivalency Certificate course and got their Grade 12 graduation certificates at last.

And our father? We don't know; he must have loved her. He was a warm man and often loving. Our grandparents didn't speak to our mother for a full three years after their wedding, until she gave birth to their first grandchild. Yet in her memoir, our grandmother resolutely does not mention one word about this. Both parents seem to have had a rigidity bred of believing yourself better than the common run of mankind. My grandfather, although we all truly loved him because he was always kind to us, was also an Orangeman and a bigot, as his younger daughter, our aunt Helen, once said to me. Marrying a Roman Catholic francophone, the very person our grandfather would never be able to accept, had to have been deliberate.



I sent my saliva to a DNA profiling company, which confirmed that my sisters and I, despite our mother's insistence that we were Irish, and allowing for the generalities of the profiling companies' results, were forty-one percent French, thirty-nine percent Scottish, and only ten percent Irish. It's possible, I suppose, that because our Irish family was originally Scottish and, despite living in Ireland for nearly three hundred years and considering themselves Irish, the original Scottish genes somehow hung on. I don't know, but I know that our father's family had been French, then French-Canadian, as far back as records went, and despite everything, my sisters and I had always been very proud of that.

My mother once said, after her parents and our father were dead, "You couldn't have my father and my husband in the same room." She said it more stoically than angrily, and none of us knew what to say, so we said nothing. Then I remembered a scene in my aunt and uncle's living room one summer when my mother's family was gathered. Her parents were sitting side by side on the sofa, the other chairs in the room occupied mostly by us children, when our father came in and sat in a chair across from our grandparents. He spoke softly, briefly. There was a long silence, I remember that because I found it strange. Even stranger, abruptly, our father got up and walked out of the room. Nobody blinked or moved or spoke. I got up and followed him into the kitchen where my mother and aunt were making lunch.

And yet, when I was seventeen or so, I recall all of them sitting side by side, on the sofa on Christmas Eve, smiling and laughing and sipping from glasses of liquor. No wonder, as my older sister and I have sometimes said to each other over the phone, she from her home in another province, me from my condo in Calgary, both of us widows now, and dreaming jointly of our pasts, agreeing at least that we were raised in the middle of a war.



One day while writing of these times, completely unlike me, in a Zoom meeting I lost my temper with a perfectly harmless, kind woman and then had to spend a good deal of time apologizing and trying to explain, without revealing too much, why I had behaved so badly. I was trying not to sink under the weight of what these memories were doing to me, as predicted by that initial dream of the water dripping onto me from the deep pool that was my past and perhaps my families' past and my ancestors' past, and instead of being wise and backing away, keeping that door to the past firmly locked, I'd taken up the challenge anyway, praying that what I found out about who I was would be worth the pain.

More, I was hopelessly curious; I wanted to know what the big deal was, what memories would surface, what dreams would come. I suppose, less dramatically, I hoped for more placid, satisfying last years, ones in which I wouldn't keep doggedly turning away from the memories of my own life. As W.G. Sebald has his character Jacques Austerlitz put it, "All my life had been a constant process of obliteration, a turning away from myself [and the world]." I thought that by daring at last to look backward I might, slowly, carefully, grow strong and wise, that I would achieve at last a degree of clarity.

### III

I remembered then two scenes from my childhood: In one I was six or seven years old and a boy had climbed on the roof of a shed in our yard and had thrown a small stone that hit me hard on my forehead at the hairline, and that because of the wound's location bled copiously so that I couldn't see for the blood streaming down my face and covering my eyes, and I began to scream outrageously and somehow, probably the other children guided me, I found myself, still screaming, in the kitchen, where my mother and my aunt, not knowing what had happened, stretched me out on a table and began to sponge away the blood so as to see what was wrong. During this procedure, I screamed as if I were being killed until my mother shouted at me to stop, so angrily, her expression so grim, that my aunt was shocked enough to scold her, to which my mother paid no attention, and I gasped and swallowed, my chest convulsing with the effort, and finally managed to choke down my screams.

Remembering how hard it was to stop myself, I think I was ominously close to convulsions.

The second memory occurred when I was a teenager; it was summer, and a girlfriend and I were sleeping in a ground-floor bedroom that looked out over trees, full-grown shrubs, and lawn. The windows were open, and we were both sound asleep when I was wakened by something brushing my face that I kept trying to push away until I was fully awake. Frightened because I didn't know what it was, I closed the window and eventually must have gone back to sleep. But the next morning, trying to tell my mother what had happened, she said, flatly, dismissively, "It was a bat."

To my own amazement as well as everyone else's, my friend and whatever sisters were present, I began to cry and in seconds had escalated to hysterical sobbing. Again, she said to me harshly, loudly, to stop at once, I struggled to obey, and eventually, chest shuddering, gasping, hiccupping and wheezing, succeeded.



In both instances, her instinct was not to comfort me, nor did she ask me of what I was so irrationally afraid. That there was a deeper cause should have been obvious to a woman as smart as my mother was. (And I wonder now, what did she know? What caused her anger at me whenever I was in crisis?) And of course, now, when it is much too late, I know that indeed there was a monster who had attacked me when I was a baby, because it had to have been before I had language or I would have told her about it then. It had to have been the reason why the perpetrator chose to attack me and not my sister, who, two years older and very bright, was highly verbal, which would explain in part why my mother never knew. There must have been physical damage to my genital area, which my father would have found when he changed my diaper, and therefore he knew. He also would have known who was responsible, but by the time our mother returned – I'm guessing she was giving birth to our next sister and would have been gone ten days or more – I had healed. She would have had no reason to suspect such a thing. Our father wouldn't have said a word, because he was so horrified, and that it had happened on his watch, among other things, must have shamed him. Probably the disregard in which his in-laws – our mother's parents – held him then was part of the reason he would never have told our mother, sure that she would tell them; he did not know what would happen then. He might have been afraid she would take their children and go to her parents' house. Perhaps he even feared that the police might become involved. (Given how I understand my grandmother's nature and upbringing, passed on in many ways to our mother, not a chance. For both of them, I think, the matter would have been too shameful for anyone to know about.)

I had some trouble recreating the series of events that happened between when I was nearing fifty years and when at sixty, I put the pieces together and felt I knew for certain, knowing full well that nobody would believe me, that I'd been assaulted sexually as a small child, a toddler, almost certainly before my ability to speak coherently had developed. I even remember now, one day at least eighty years ago standing up in the truck cab between my mother and my father, who was driving. I think it was raining and the road was a rough muddy trail. My siblings were not there, a puzzle in itself. I had been singing away and chattering blithely and continuously to myself – I must have been very happy at that moment – and my mother, laughing, said to my father, "Sharon came late to talking but once she started, she hasn't stopped since!" Readers will know that one of the reasons for "late-talking" children is, or can be, emotionally traumatic injury or injuries. When I was at the peak of my intellectual ability in my sixties and early seventies, I was very articulate, so it wasn't a lack of mental acuity nor a medical problem or injury that stopped me from talking. (I lost the best of that articulacy with old age, which loss I mourn.)

I was fifty when, steeped in the research for my next novel, which among other things concerned the history of French Canadians in the district where we had lived when I was just starting school, I dropped onto the cot in my small office strewn with paper maps of the area where Gabriel Dumont's Petite Village had been and copies of old newspaper articles from that period, mostly in French which language I read badly, threw my arm over my eyes, and tried to clear my head to rest. Then, I heard my father's voice speaking to me: He said four things to me, his voice crackling as if it was hard for him to break through the ether so that I could hear him. He said a first name, then repeated it. Then he said the name of a village, then repeated it. That was all. I will be forever grateful to him to reach out to me from the other side, as if it were a debt he owed me; as if he understood how important it was that I know, and now with a concrete name and a concrete location, I would search out what I did not consciously know had happened to me when I was little more than a baby. Nor did I know that this thing, whatever it was, would explain how I had lived my life, how my failures, mistakes, and weaknesses were rooted in the crime done to me, that, and his failure to tell my mother, meant that she never knew why I was not ordinary in my reactions, not receptive to her efforts to be a loving mother to me, which very soon resulted in her rejection of me that lasted all through my childhood and teen years.



Years later, not long before she died and our father had been dead for close to fourteen years, still mulling over my father's message and also, again and again and again, that appalling first conscious memory in my life where I was screaming and could not stop and the world had been leached of all colour, understanding then that this was not a normal first memory, I felt sure I had to make a serious effort to understand clearly — as clearly as I could after so many years and so many people dead — what my father's message meant. I was suspicious about a certain man who had been around when I believe I was assaulted. I asked my mother as casually as I could who he was and if she knew anything about him. She replied with a bit of information and after a moment, gazing into the distance, remarked that our father hated him, but she never knew why, and had found his extreme dislike of the man an odd, inexplicable thing. But then she more or less shrugged at the memory. Both men were dead; their relationship was something out of the hard past, and best forgotten. When she asked me why I wanted to know, I was the one to shrug as if it were nothing. "I just remembered hearing his name," I said, "and wondered who he was."

The best of current psychology says that if never recognized, the trauma of such events is never mitigated nor released, and was triggered, as we say today, by the stone striking me and the blood pouring down my face and by the invader in the night. When our mother was diagnosed with cancer but still at home, my sisters and I had gathered to visit her. The six of us were sitting around the living room talking quietly together. Our mother had fallen silent, although we hadn't noticed this; she had fallen into a reverie, not seeing us, nor hearing our conversation. Suddenly, into the silence, staring into some void, she said as angrily as if it had just happened instead of many years earlier, "When Sharon was a baby, she was one of those babies who, when you picked her up and tried to hug her, would scream and stiffen and turn her head away."

My sisters, a group of very smart, very sensitive women, stared in startled silence with troubled expressions at her and at me. I suddenly couldn't breathe. I jumped to my feet, further startling everyone, and in such a rage that shocked even myself, in lieu of whatever it was I couldn't say, said chiefly to my sisters and very angrily, "Isn't that something you should know about yourself!" I'd never ever spoken to our mother in such a violent way, and my mother came back to herself as if surprised at where she was, and at all of us as we sat, me standing, looking stunned and furious – or something I can't even name. She must have said something – an apology, an attempt to mitigate or explain. I don't remember: after a few seconds during which I can't remember anyone speaking, although somebody must have, I went into the bedroom and, even though I wasn't supposed to leave for a couple of days, repacked my suitcase and walked out to the truck to drive the five hours back home.

One sister, who had a sore foot, hobbled out behind me. Another had once remarked that I suffered from terminal depression, a remark perhaps meant as a joke, which she immediately took back in a kind of apology. When my mother spoke, I felt I might burst, such turmoil inside me, yet I hadn't known what to say, my mind was a vibrating blank white screen; my blood pressure had to have been high, I was still short of breath, my body was in the grip of some feeling of high unreleaseable tension, my heart wouldn't slow down, I felt as if I might implode, or explode, it seems now a wonder I could walk. I had to have consciously known how important this revelation was, how vital to my understanding of my life, and somewhere below that, how angry I was, or would be in time, or had been all along, that nobody dealt with this, that nobody even told me, that I was about to discover that my life was not what I thought it had been.

Or, did I say that to the sister who had followed me out – about needing to know that about yourself – and not to my mother? If that is what happened, then what did I say to my mother? Or she to me? Or my sisters? I have no idea, and only one sister is left to ask, and I can't bear to. I suspect that now she might say she doesn't remember anymore, and anyway, I know now that she had her own traumas to deal with. She said then, as we reached the truck, astonishingly, as if this would help, "Did you know I tried to drown you when you were a baby?" I said I had a vague memory of hearing about it, not of the incident itself. I threw my suitcase into the cab of the truck, got in, and drove away. On the run once again, when I should have stayed and asked question after question, but our mother was dying, so how could I harass her? And it was evident to me that she didn't know why I was that kind of baby. As a trained special educator and sometimes school psychologist, I knew all about that kind of baby and child, the way they jerked their heads away if you tried to touch them in a kindly way – usually that was the result of constantly being hit on the head, or having had their hair pulled – in other words, of the steady physical abuse of small children, which I did not suffer from, but an action that would or might occur in any abused, traumatized child. Contact meant suffering. How gentle you had to be with such children. I never once guessed that as a baby, I had been one, too.



So, our mother never knew why I stiffened and cried when she tried to hold me, or why in later years I became hysterical over nothing. My father had to come back from the dead to tell me, or I would go to my grave thinking I was simply ineffectual, trivial, an idiotic human being, a crazed person, when I was merely suffering the results of being a traumatized child too small to say what I had been subjected to.

I know how very sorry my mother was in her last years for the way she had treated me when I was a child. She gave me explicit permission, when I began to be published, to tell the story of our relationship and her conduct toward me, the cause of which she seemed not to understand herself but profoundly regretted. And yet, although nobody has ever noticed, in my fiction almost none of my female protagonists have mothers. I think I simply don't know how to write a good mother-daughter relationship, or I can't face trying, because it seems so false to me. Or perhaps I would then have to face my own sorrow about having lacked motherly love and, having survived without it, I felt describing that absence would be merely whining.

I wonder, too, if as an adult I had known I'd been sexually assaulted, could name my abuser and had proof, if I would have done as Alice Munro's daughter did, and gone to the police. There was a moment when I first knew when I might have, but that moment passed quickly. The daughter of my mother would have felt too shamed if everybody had known about it. More than eighty years later, with both of my parents dead and probably my abuser, too, what can that kind of justice matter?

I realize now, too, that suppressing my natural impulse to cry, which came from fear of my mother's displeasure, from the second incident on, grew so strong that today I can barely cry at all no matter what disaster strikes. At the worst, tears fill my eyes, I sob once, maybe twice, and then it's over, and even if I crave to sob, even drown in my own tears, I cannot. That pool of water in the dream, the one above my head that dripped faster and faster onto me may well have been a dream of the pool made up of those years of unshed tears.

I realize that some readers will view this personal history as nonsense or flagrant self-pity, but if I'd written of being constantly beaten, starved, or locked in dark corners, they would not. Only in these last years has the hidden, constant sexual abuse and rape of girls and women of every walk of life, every caste, every race and nationality come into the open. How many generations will it take before it stops?

A part of me, on rereading what I have written, wants to beg forgiveness of my mother for writing about this for anyone to read. I am old now, and my love for her far outweighs my anger. The same is absolutely true for my father.

After our return from our weekend honeymoon at a lake in northern Saskatchewan, my first husband and I had been living in our new basement apartment for about two weeks when my mother phoned me and said, “Why don’t you phone me? Why don’t you visit?” And how surprised I was, never for a second thinking I would be missed, and nor it occurring to me that she would want to see me. And yet, she did. And in wonderment, I complied.

# NINE

# HOME

## I

We had been driving for three long days and had finally arrived in Winnipeg, and would soon fulfill Lucinda's goal, the main inspiration for this trip. We'd registered in our hotel, met my Winnipeg writer-scholar-teacher-counsellor friend Joyce Clouston, PhD, Social Worker and Cultural Carrier, and were eating a late supper together in the courtyard of a nearby café. She had given up three working days to be our guide through the city she'd lived in since she was seventeen. But by then, nearly ten o'clock, uncomfortably hot as it had been all day, at lower latitudes the prairies cool, sometimes drastically at night, and in the chilly near-darkness I soon began to be too cold, and also in that way when you come back into yourself from excitement and suddenly realize you are in pain and hadn't noticed or, as in this case, I found myself drained of energy. Both women, younger than I am, leaped up in concern, and in no time, I was back at the hotel and in bed.

I have a variety of bright but confused memories of our first evening and the following two full days in COVID-restricted Winnipeg: sitting in courtyards under trees eating, talking, or waiting, one evening having dinner in a café in a converted two-storey house with a newly met, accomplished, and wonderfully *sympatico* friend of Joyce, and where again, as it grew dark, I asked to move inside from the table under the trees – me, cold as always after dark and aggravated by the ever-hovering mosquitoes. I felt guilty then and still do for spoiling my friends' pleasure, not that I can't appreciate that urban people with inside jobs would brave a lot, including clouds of mosquitoes and too-chilly temperatures to spend an entire evening outdoors, and I should have been sensitive to that.

But I also think, out of my own experience of my failure to understand the exhaustion of the elders in my own life, I know younger people cannot understand what the quality of exhaustion of the elderly feels like: not the even delicious tiredness of youth and middle age, but something closer to mild illness. Still, I beg their pardons; I really do.

The Winnipeg Art Gallery and the Museum for Human Rights, which Lucinda had particularly wanted to tour, the St. Boniface Museum, the Riel House National Historic Site, and various other places we had planned to visit remained closed. Instead, we spent more time walking through the beautiful, very large Assiniboine Park, including the sculpture garden devoted to the work of Leo Mol, who, before his death, had lived next door to friends of mine, over and over passing by car the provincial legislature with its "Golden Boy" on the dome, perched like Hermes on one foot as if about to take flight.



There was a gathering of First Nations people in front of the legislature, there to raise awareness of the newly located but never before acknowledged graves of Indigenous children in residential-school grounds. Participants were wearing orange shirts and flying orange flags, the colour chosen to symbolize the suffering of First Nations children in those schools.

A collection of children's shoes rested, pair by small pair, on the steps leading up to the entrance. As we drove by in the heavy downtown Winnipeg traffic, we were silent, there being, for us, no words to express the weight of the inherited shame.

I had especially wanted Lucinda to see the magnificent pair of life-sized bronze buffalo flanking the Grand Staircase that rises above the Carrara marble floor inside the legislature, but in the light of the demonstration and those pitiable shoes, it was then an impossible thing even to think of doing. And, doubtless COVID had closed that building to visitors, too.

It seems more than a bit strange that the government commemorates the sixty-or-so million buffalo, which on contact roamed the plains, when to a large extent it was the arrival of the Europeans that caused their extinction and, mostly due to the resulting starvation, brought down the many proud Indigenous nations. The two bronze buffalo are one of the outwardly visible remaining signs of the fur trade Winnipeg was founded upon. Nowadays the bronze bison are best thought of as magnificent art, while viewers gaze at them in awe and with ancient memories of the great herds thundering across the prairies, so many that those who were there have said it sometimes took three days for a single herd to pass, that too crossing palely before viewers' eyes, who try to ignore the irony.



Joyce herself is walking Manitoba history: She identifies as Métis, having at least one Scottish stonemason in her family who came to help build Lower Fort Garry in 1830, where, in August 1871, the government, the Anishinabek, and the Swampy Cree signed Treaty 1. Another, her paternal grandfather, was a blacksmith at Lower Fort Garry and also helped run the grist mill there, one of the first in Manitoba. Frequently, intermarriage occurred between the Scottish men and Swampy Cree women, with their children referred to as Métis.

The Métis, including Joyce's family members, negotiated to join Confederation on the condition that they receive recognition of their ancestral lands. Instead, the government granted most of these lands promised to the Métis to European settlers. Her family members worked hard until they could buy back the land to become farmers, but the anger at this injustice remains to this day. As the years pass, the story grows complicated and infuriating with further injustices, but Joyce informed me that in 2013, the Supreme Court of Canada officially recognized the treatment of the Métis as unjust, and further, in 2021, the Crown's Department of Indigenous Affairs announced that it is working with the Manitoba Métis Federation to "advance reconciliation."

Joyce's mother's father was a Métis leader of Swampy Cree and Scottish heritage; the men of this family line had worked for the Hudson Bay Company during the fur trade era. Joyce and her siblings were raised on a farm in the stunningly beautiful, lush Interlake Region that lies between Lake Winnipeg and Lake Manitoba north of Winnipeg.

The Interlake area is also where my Cree-Ojibway friend from Peguis Reserve was born and had lived, the man who, with his wife, bought our hay farm from me after Peter's death. Back in about 1940, my grandparents on my father's side moved from St. Isidore-de-Bellevue in Saskatchewan to Ste. Rose du lac, Manitoba, in the Interlake area, to raise cattle, before moving on to St. Boniface, a historic French neighbourhood in Winnipeg. Nobody is more surprised than I am at all these interconnections of people and places in my life. If you'd asked, I would have said, but what have I to do with the Interlake? I notice that W.G. Sebald was fond of coincidences, too. Literary critics, who traditionally have despised coincidences, must lead very dull lives. This is one place where I concur with the postmodernists even if I think they rather overdo it.

The principal goal of our trip – to find Lucinda's grandparents' house (there were other relatives' addresses she might have searched out had we more time), where she had spent a gloriously happy week when she was five years old – might well have floundered and failed. I saw finding that house as the initial reason for our trip and had drawn us on through several months of planning it. Lucinda had the address, and Joyce, who said the street name had been changed since Lucinda was five, knew the new name, and said it was on one of the more, if not the most, choice, prestigious locations in central Winnipeg. A few yards from it, across a narrow street and down a grassy bank, the omnipresent Assiniboine River raced by.

There the house was, two-and-a-half-storey red brick with white-painted wood trim and white pillars at the corners of the back verandah, although I can't remember what the front of the house facing the neighbourhood looked like. It was set in a large yard longer than it was wide, surrounded by abundantly leafy green hedges – no hardy but un-beautiful caraganas here –  the neatly mowed green lawn replete with flowerbeds and the occasional now out-of-bloom fruit tree. It was one of those rare occasions when, it seemed to us, anyway, that the past actually lived up to the memory of it. But as the owners weren't home, only Lucinda went through the long yard and up to the very house. We were too far away and could see only her smile, not any nuance, as Joyce snapped pictures of her standing in front of the house that was once her grandparents'. I wondered if she had also been thinking of her own losses and the changes in her own and her family's history since so many years earlier, when she had lived out one of the most joyous weeks of her childhood.

When I was about to turn sixty, Peter asked me what I wanted for my birthday, and I asked to be taken back to the place of my beginnings in the forest north of Garrick, which we had left in around 1944, then roughly fifty-six years earlier. I wanted to see it, that was all. I did not expect joy; my memories, though etched in my brain as pictures, not words, were indelible, but not as precisely physically locatable as Lucinda's grandparents' house had been. The log shack in which we'd lived and where the assault on me must have taken place had been torn down, as had our grandparents' log house, although the site where theirs had been, named Fern Creek by our grandmother, was as beautiful as it must always have been. I thought of my grandparents, then already in their fifties, arriving maybe with a team and wagon, or maybe even on foot for the last few yards and gazing up at the spot where they would build their house, far from other people or the presence of urban civilization. Knowing where they had been driven from, I thought of how they must have swallowed hard, our grandmother refusing tears, smiled at each other, gone forward and did what they had to do for survival and for the secure future they dreamt of.

And yet, before too long, like so many settlers before them, in a few years they had left, only the firs our grandfather planted as each of us, their grandchildren, were born and which were evidence of a mindset that said, *we are here to stay,* were still there now tall and strong, although, as I've said, the house was gone. We stared across the trickle of water that was Fern Creek, although only in our family's memory. And Peter, I suppose, was considering how a settler might make a living there, evaluating the soil, thinking about wind and rainfall and the short growing season, while my mind was a confusion of memories – the terrible winters, the nightly howling of wolves, the constant presence and fear of bears, all imprinted on my small child's mind so that I didn't know for sure what I saw and heard myself and what I heard our parents say years later that I had inadvertently taken as my own memories.

This was, I saw more clearly now, the place of my origin, more truly than Saskatoon, my home: the mountains of snow, especially the men in their layers of heavy winter clothes shouting to each other, laughing, motors starting with a sudden roar, the snowmobile machines the anglophones called "bommadeers," but which our francophone father knew were Bombardiers, the name of the Quebec company that built them, First Nations women in their long cotton skirts at the door, frightening me, which annoyed and embarrassed our mother, the two of them unable to speak each other's languages, but comparing their newest babies, in my mother's case, my new sister Sheila, dead in 1998 of lung cancer that had begun in her breast.

My memory takes me further, through the childhood with the mostly poverty-stricken First Nations people, poorer even than we were – if you think in terms only of money and belongings – always present as background to what we saw as real life. How, in a bigger town we'd moved to, as a group of them passed by our yard, one of the women separated herself from her people, came close so that we stopped playing and stared, and handed my polio-disabled sister, then about six or seven years, a five-dollar bill.



Is that why I have sometimes given people begging on the street not change, but a twenty-dollar bill, and not cared about their sly grin or their delight or even anger and refused to guess to what end the money would be put, my friends thinking I'd lost my mind? I have been following a thread, without knowing why, know only that it is the act of giving that matters. Can you give without conditions? If so, I ask myself, then why not a hundred dollars, which might cost me what the five dollars might have cost that First Nations woman?

I am not trying to cure anything, but to acknowledge the earlier gift, to pay homage to it. I remember our mother's puzzlement and some other emotion, which as a child I couldn't read when she heard of the first gift and we gave her the five-dollar bill, knowing the woman who had given it to us was poorer even than we were. And yet surely the First Nations woman and her group knew we were poor, too, or she would not have done that. Or maybe she thought that the only thing whites understood was cash. Or maybe, as with all of us, in the face of a child's affliction, she knew no other way to express her sorrow.

Later, my older sister said she had no memory of the tree-planting story (that our grandfather had planted one tree for each of his grandchildren as they were born). I guessed that I had heard it from our mother, but in her memoir our grandmother says only that they planted spruces all the way across the front and down one side of their log house. When I was there at sixty in 2000, I think I saw at most only a half-dozen old spruces, and I realized that most of us weren't even born when they left that homestead. During this search for facts I had to face the biggest one: that our grandmother's memoir that she had written at her daughters' request and that one of them had then typed and copied and had given to each of us grandchildren, and that was up to this moment the family Bible, was full of inaccuracies and omissions, so much of her narrative failing to fit with the memories on which my sister and I were in agreement and could, occasionally, prove.



But watching Lucinda in front of the ancestral home that had brought her such happiness was for me more like watching a movie, one of those slightly sentimental ones, where the present is as good as the wonderful past, families are united in their love for one another, and all ends well. I knew very well, too, that I would be unfair in thinking of sentimental films in which everything ends happily. But that day when we stood at the edge of the property in the sunshine and heat as Lucinda walked around gazing up at her grandparents' house and thinking her own thoughts, Joyce and I, both children of a harder past, or so we judged, watched her without envy, with something close to motherly pleasure. The next morning, Lucinda and I would leave Winnipeg and turn back west again; I thought then that finding the house was the highlight of the trip. Would it have been for Lucinda?

Joyce took us back to our hotel and then went home, while Lucinda and I went to dinner at the house of friends of mine, people I'd known since my grad school days at University of Saskatchewan in the early seventies, before I walked away from academia to become a rancher's wife and live on land in the middle of nowhere and learned to ride horses and chase cows. Although the hostess and I were once very close friends, these days the only time I see her and her partner is when I'm in Winnipeg for a few days and call them. I tried to bring a bottle of good wine with me in a failing attempt to thank her for all the dinners she, a gourmet cook, had made for me.



As the years passed, nearly fifty of them, she and her partner had kept up with the group of old Saskatoon friends, of which I was a part, while I hadn't, being absorbed in my new life, working hard and living five hours away, and losing two friends during that time and not even hearing about either until their funerals were over. When I first wrote this passage, I was wondering if such visits and dinners to my once-dear friends in Winnipeg, and the gifts offered in full awareness of their insufficiency, aren't almost over too, as with everything else good in my life as I grow older and then older again, and all too soon wouldn't be able to travel at all, I was thinking—wrongly, it would turn out.

Barely a year before writing these words, I learned that even older friends of mine had both died, and it was as if someone had hit me in the chest with a heavy book, even though I hadn't seen one of them for five or ten years and the other for at least twenty. At moments like that one, you truly understand how other people can become an ineradicable part of you, and staying close to them geographically has not much to do with your feeling for them.

Here I went again, resolutely refusing to remember those years when my Winnipeg friend and I were close, without partners, and more or less, in my memory anyway, breaking rules, and, again in my case as we had different histories, feeling free for the first time in my life. But that was an illusion, which in subsequent years I would look back on in muddled half-delighted half-pained horror. Or else simply turn away from the memory.

I thought of Peter's mother, who in her last years was given to a loud, mirthless laugh at bad news, while we younger people stared at her in puzzlement thinking, dementia? Her poor hearing causing her to misinterpret? Her frequent eccentricity? It took me all the years since her death in 1984 to finally understand what her laughter was designed to mean. I used that laugh for my elderly woman character, Rhea, in my novel *Luna*.



Some days, now that I was older than Peter's mother was when she laughed in what we thought were wildly inappropriate places, I find an inclination to do the same. There was something goddess-like in that laugh, and something even mythic about her: her physical stature, her refusal to "fix herself up" so that she presented as a proudly old woman, her searing intelligence, which caused her to announce ideas ahead of her time that later would be confirmed as accurate, but that at the time served only to contribute to her reputation as an eccentric, her rage, all transmuted into that humourless, distanced laugh that I now hear, old myself, echoing hollowly around the planet.

The next morning, we began what would be our two-day drive back to Calgary, and I wonder now why we thought of our days in Winnipeg as such a success, when we had seen mostly only the outdoors. I'd said to my friends as we dined in their backyard that if we did not know how very many social problems the city of Winnipeg had, we would have come away thinking it was a veritable Eden with its beautiful parks, its greenery everywhere, The Forks by our hotel where the Assiniboine River flowed into the Red River, and where people had gathered as early as six thousand years ago, the magnificent old buildings from the fur trade and then the wheat-growing era still standing in the downtown core, still in use.

And at the same time, we saw little evidence of what we recognized in our few days there, the shockingly high crime rate, in particular the homicide rate thought to have been exacerbated by COVID, and historically, the unacknowledged and unexplained deaths of First Nations children at the residential schools, the unsolved disappearances and murders of First Nations women, the theft of land from the original inhabitants, the hanging in Regina of Louis Riel, buried in St. Boniface – so painful a history, whose ramifications and consequences echo to this day. The latter, despite reparations, promises, money, and serious attempts to listen that echo all across the West. We now have a new national statutory holiday: the National Day for Truth and Reconciliation.

Our Winnipeg friends replied, not smiling, that a previous visitor had said the same thing, and we were silent for a long moment thinking about this, a mix of enchantment and sorrow, also the title of Gabrielle Roy's memoir of her early life in francophone St. Boniface where my aunts and uncles, cousins, and grandparents had also all lived. Granted, the principal purpose of our trip had been fulfilled, and maybe that was all it took to turn the visit into a success. And Joyce, of course, who knew everything there was to know about what we saw and a good deal more, and from a viewpoint different than ours, who was, nevertheless, generous without limits to us.

Writing this I find myself thinking that Sebald-like I might insert photos in this text, which would have to be borrowed from Lucinda and Joyce, although Sebald searched European archives with great diligence to find the right photos, and most of those used in his books are not photos of his own family or their lives, although some are. And I think about all the things I've done to fill the unfillable pit where my mother's love should have been, and then of my now absent or dead significant others. Silly but commonplace things: travelled to distant places alone, on occasion stayed in hotels that were too luxurious for me, tried out buying expensive clothes, when younger, kept rejecting men for their adequacy unless they found me inadequate first, determined at any cost, which for me was endless hard work in place of a social life or other kinds of duties short of skullduggery to get to the top in my chosen occupation, and howled mightily when I failed. I see as clearly as my husband's mother must once have seen and my own now that I think of it, that none of them gained me a thing, other than books, which help me now that I'm nearing my end.



So now, do I substitute death; do I use it to fill that pit? Unknowable death, despite the teachings of every religion in the world? Now I understand my mother-in-law's ridiculous laughter that wasn't laughter at all. And the look my mother, once she was old and facing her death, would sometimes get in her dark green eyes that would turn liquid and pale, of a depthless sadness, which must have also been regret for her mistakes.

Before we left Winnipeg, we had a discussion with Joyce about which was the best way to go west to reach Saskatoon: on the same road we had come in on, at Regina turning north up to Saskatoon? Or heading northeast out of Winnipeg? But the latter trip, even though more desirable, would be two hours longer, and since the more common way of going between Winnipeg and Saskatoon is via Regina and is already too long at 836 kilometrers, we didn't feel we had much choice. Joyce, ever the lover of Manitoba history and raised in its natural beauty, was keen for us to travel down a lesser, more northerly road from Winnipeg to Portage la Prairie to enjoy its beauty and its history about which she knew a great deal and wanted to be our guide as we travelled. But we simply did not have time. Reluctantly, late in the morning, we set out back to Regina, regrettably once again on the Trans-Canada instead of an interesting new, more beautiful road.

Soon we had picked up our established travelling habits, stopping for coffee for Lucinda, gas and bathroom breaks, and occasionally, not often, switching drivers so that I held the wheel for an hour or two. Hours later we crossed the Saskatchewan border. This was where Lucinda asked me if I'd mind if we took a short detour south, passing through a few small towns, and then, a few miles west, curving back up to rejoin the main highway. No problem, I said, although my instinct said, what? We've got about eight hours of driving left and you want to take a detour? But I wanted to take the detour, too, and was delighted that she had suggested it. And Lucinda had proved herself to be, I thought, tireless.



I'm not sure where we turned to go south, but it might have been at Whitewood, only a few miles into Saskatchewan. The writer Mark Abley, on his 1986 epic trip, turned south at Whitewood in order to visit Forget. I'm pretty sure we passed through the village of Manor, and to do that, we'd have had to turn south at Moosomin.

As we passed through Manor, I think I told Lucinda that there had once been a British colony in the area, then called Cannington Manor, established in 1882, the same year as Saskatoon and Regina (Winnipeg was founded in 1812, Edmonton in 1795) by upper-class Brits whose members built big houses like nothing seen on the prairie outside of our cities, but few if any had been lived in for years and they were decaying. Their owners had played cricket, kept polo ponies, fox hunted, had a drama group and a poetry group, and gave teas, dinner parties and balls. *People Places: The Dictionary of Saskatchewan Place Names* (Bill Barry, People Places Publishing Ltd, 1998) says that there was a close connection between Cannington Manor and La Rolanderie, a "French/Belgian settlement (1886–90) south of Whitewood," the town at which I think Lucinda and I had left the Trans-Canada. The entry goes on, "After the estate in Belgium of Rudolph Meyer, the patron of the French Counts' colony . . . originally 10,000 acres . . . achieved a peak population of about 150. Led by titled French and Belgium noblemen, the colony was an attempt to transfer upper-class Europe to the prairies. Ventures (all failed) included cheesemaking, chicory, brush manufacture, sugar beets, sheep and thoroughbred breeding." Further, "Rudolph Armand Meyer (d.1899) was . . . an archconservative Roman Catholic and ultramontanist. La Rolanderie represented his conservative vision of Utopia." But I didn't see a sign for the original site, had forgotten all about La Rolanderie anyway, and so we didn't dip further south to see if there were any remaining historical sites.

These two settlements mostly confuse Saskatchewanians. It's not that they laugh at them, but that they stare in confoundment, wondering what could those crazy SOBs have been thinking? Then we wander off, shaking our heads.

The Cannington Manor project didn't last long, though,

prairie winters being enough to discourage the bravest, especially in those days when houses lacked adequate insulation and weren't properly sealed, and everything for miles in every direction froze solid, and, in that part of the province, snow piled up to the rooflines. As well, they knew little about farming, and in about fifteen years, around 1900, most of them had become bankrupt and then gone. I had toured the area with a writer-friend also raised in the country, both of us always longing for the landscapes we'd left behind, so that small journeys outside cities to places where both of us felt at home were our favourite entertainment. This even though both of us had come from non-farming homes.

Lucinda and I drove west on the secondary road and stopped in Arcola about an hour north of the U.S. border. Walking by windows of a main street building, I stopped dead at some memory I couldn't at first locate. Then I realized that we were standing in front of what had been the South Saskatchewan Photographic Museum of Adrian Paton (1934–2021). I had been there, probably on the same trip to see the two colonies, with the writer-friend who was a friend of Paton's and who revered Paton's collection of photos, which documented as far back as early contact days in Saskatchewan, and was keen that I should see them, too. We spent a few hours there being shown some striking photographs that I'd never seen in any of my books.



But the museum, as had happened frequently on our trip, was closed; Paton, although I didn't know it as we stood there looking through the window to the dark interior, had been dead about six months. When later I found out he had died, I made a cursory effort to discover what had happened to his collection, but with no luck, as I didn't want to call his family. Our stop in Arcola was short, we had only wanted to stretch our legs, and soon we were in the car and again heading west.

At the sign pointing a few miles south to Forget (named after Amédée Emmanuel Forget, 1847–1923, one of the earliest Lieutenant-Governors of the North-West Territories), I pointed out that the town's name was a French surname, pronounced "for-jay," not the English word *forget*, and that in 1987 prize-winning Canadian prose writer, journalist and poet Mark Abley had published a travel memoir, called *Beyond Forget: Rediscovering the Prairies*, about a tour he made of Alberta, Saskatchewan, and Manitoba. I realized that we were doing the same thing in 2021 as he had done thirty-five years earlier.

Abley was born in England and came to Canada as a small child, returning to England for his years as a Rhodes Scholar at Oxford. He had lived in each prairie province, ending in central Saskatchewan before moving to Ontario and finally to Montreal, where, besides writing books, he wrote for the *Montreal Gazette*, and where at the time of this writing he continues to live with his wife and family. My then-mentor,

Caroline Heath in Saskatoon, knew him personally and as an excellent poet, and had offered him contacts to help him along his way as he drove across the prairies trying to get a feel for our contemporary province. This was how he visited Peter and me briefly on the ranch. I had a photo of the two of us leaning against a weather-beaten corral and smiling lazily, agreeably at the photographer who must have been Peter. This would have been around 1985 or 1986, when I'd been writing only since 1978 and had published my first book in 1984.

That Mark had visited us to help fill in his knowledge about the prairies and was writing a book about it didn't particularly register with me; most literary people cannot seem to imagine how far I was, at least physically, from the world of literature, and for the most part had no clue what was going on in Toronto or Montreal. I think his intended book fell from my mind in the daily round of ranch work, so that I was surprised later when I heard that it was published.

He was not many years returned from Oxford when he made his trip across the prairies, which probably explains a few of his choices about whom he would visit and his opinions, or attitudes toward those people and the provinces in it that wounded Western readers who felt he hadn't been fair to them. I reviewed the book for the Saskatchewan Writers' Guild's newsletter, *Freelance*, and I was in places scathing, being new at review writing and having gotten the idea, long since corrected, that that is what reviewers do. As a lifelong Westerner and Saskatchewan native, I was insulted by his attitude. But it was his first prose book; he was only thirty-five, and hadn't yet learned to watch what he wrote, because, once published, there is no place to hide, a lesson that I, too, had very quickly learned.

I remember telling Lucinda about this long-ago literary brouhaha, which caused Mark to later admit to having made mistakes in his attitude and sometimes in his choice of subjects to interview. I doubt he ever read my review, as *Freelance* had a tiny circulation. I have since found him to be a fine man, without airs or pretension, and a valued and important Canadian writer. I think Lucinda was surprised by the story: we were on a road trip through what most Canadians think of as nowhere, and I was telling her stories about literary books and authors in a place where surely books and authors would be non-existent.



I couldn't even remember what we had all been so incensed about; all I remember was making fun – I lived on a cattle ranch for heaven's sake – of his reliance on raisins-and-nut snacks and his often-stated abhorrence of hamburgers. When I downsized to leave the hay farm, I gave away *Beyond Forget*, never dreaming I would regret it, and now, wanting to reread it,

I had to order it from the library. But beating up a writer whose book is thirty-five years old, and a first book, is not very sportswoman-like. In his later books he has redeemed himself, and more.

On Lucinda and I drove, the road soon curving north again to rejoin the Trans-Canada. Of the rest of the way to Regina (and maybe it wasn't even on that road), I recall only trying to get lunch in a small-town café and having to leave without it because the café's only two employees, both young males, were sitting on the back step having a smoke and weren't interested in new customers, starving or not. I had a moment's sympathy with Mark then. But we were just a pair of women, not local, worse, city ones, which meant that in true small-town fashion, they could afford to offend us.

Around that time, we must have begun speeding up from our more leisurely pace, recognizing that it was getting late, and we still had a long way to go if we expected to be back in Calgary by the following evening. At Regina, we barely slowed down at the turnoff leading northwest. Once again, I found myself on the 259-kilometre road leading from Regina up to Saskatoon and later that same blank white sheet trundled its way across my memories so I didn't remember a thing. Translation: I remembered everything, but resolutely refused to allow myself to think about any of it. I'd already written about driving up that road that long-ago August day on my way to be married on my twenty-first birthday, and sixty years later on another hot August day, driving my dying second husband up it, not guessing that in fewer than two weeks he would be gone forever.

Thinking again about the drives I'd made north between Regina and Saskatoon through the dried-out fields of wheat that stupendously hot, dry summer of 1961, I remembered that, quitting my job a week early, I went back to Saskatoon and was married. I remembered always the beauty of the wide fields of grain, the steady blue burn of the immense, unmarred sky that surrounded us right down to the ground we stood on, how it was like driving through the sky. It was the same at the end of July 2007, when I drove my husband from a hospital in Regina to one in Saskatoon where the doctors would do a pre-surgery evaluation. Each moment was all I could manage then, and I wouldn't have believed he was dying if anybody had told me. I don't know if Peter knew how close to death he was, but I think now that his knowledge of it was in every line of his body, in the skin of his face, and his pale blue eyes that were now without light.

How often in those last few weeks I would glance at him and see that he had fastened his eyes on me, and I felt, sometimes, that in those moments he was at last *seeing* me. But I could not say it, death, and he chose not to either. And, now, I was driving past the same glowing, pale-yellow fields under the same intense blue sky, but my former sense of wonder at the heat, my breathlessness at this huge beauty through which I drove in 1961 and 2007, were mostly gone for me. I drove, he pushed his seat back and stretched out his long legs, turned his head so he could gaze out his side window, and went silent. I don't think he spoke once during that three-hour trip, but looked steadily, silently, out his side window at the fields of grain.

Sometimes I think that up to his last months he was as I had long been myself: not really believing in the reality of others, nor in the damage my own actions did to them, thinking that I wasn't real enough myself that my actions could be *real*, living always in a detached narcissism. Maybe that's what I meant when I said I'd always wanted to be alive. Maybe "grounded" would have been the better word. To come back to earth; to believe fully in my own and the existence of other people.

On our way to Winnipeg I told Lucinda how a farmer can look at a field as he drives by it doing what is called a "windshield survey" and name what a particular crop needs – nitrogen, maybe – what is wrong, or right with it, at the right time estimate the crop yield per acre without pulling off a head, crushing the chaff in his palm, blowing it away, and counting the grains that are left: "There's nothing in those heads; won't go two bushels," and tell me how the farmer would try to remedy the problem, if it was remediable. Although, by the time the wheat would not pass the two-bushels-to-the-acre test, it wouldn't be.

During our trip back to Calgary, the temperature remained in the high twenties and low thirties, but the car's air conditioning had not faltered, so we barely noticed how hot it was, so intent were we on getting to Saskatoon on time to meet another of my long-time friends for dinner. Possibly Lucinda was merely tired of driving, and having achieved her most important goal and with responsibilities awaiting her in Calgary, was beginning eagerly to await the end of the trip. I didn't ask, and not wanting to offend me, she didn't say.



On our way north, we paused at Craik, one of the traditional places to stop on that highway, where we had and did the usual and about which I don't remember much except pointing out to Lucinda the shortcut that led south back to Moose Jaw. We returned to the car and back onto the highway with, once again, dried, short, thin crops flanking the road. A Saskatchewan I knew all too well and while absolutely in love with the beauty of the now heat-and-dust paled crops against the translucent sapphire of the endless sky, knowing what I knew about what this meant not only for the farmers, but for the entire province, I could only sigh.

Now, all my years in Saskatchewan, first at the edge of the boreal forest, then in small towns going south and south again and five years in a "big" small town from Grade 3 through Grade 7, slowly moving out of what we called north down to Saskatoon, which is also set in beautiful parklands, and down to the naturally treeless extreme southwest with its vast acres of grass, all of it went tumbling, upside down and sideways, through my mind. From the fifties, I remembered the deserted farmsteads with their decaying buildings, before that, the deafening whine of the bull saw, which terrified me as a little girl; the smell of cold, the rutted, muddy sometimes corduroy roads; little kids plodding through snowbanks on the way to school; the poverty on much of Saskatoon's west side, where we first lived and where I went to high school, and was stigmatized as a member of the city's underclass. Our technical school was designed to teach us to become the workers of the world, about which I'm still furious, all my years at the University of Saskatchewan, until I wanted to scream to get it to stop.

When, at eighty-three, I yearned sometimes for home, I wiped all that away and thought that home was the house in the Frenchman River Valley now lived in by another widow and everything changed so that I recognized only the lay of the land and the paint in one bedroom and the kitchen. What home? Where is home? In my heart, my sentimental self answered me, but my true heart was cold and stiff as a frozen hide hanging over a corral gate. Most of my life I felt it was better to keep it that way.

# TEN

# HADES

## I

In late afternoon we reached Saskatoon. I phoned my friend as we reached the city's outskirts to say I would call her when we were checked into our hotel and were ready to go to dinner. "I think we'll take Preston," I told her, a street that wasn't a freeway but would lead us through the area where I'd spent years of my life and finally across the South Saskatchewan River into downtown and our hotel. "Oh," she said, sounding dubious. I knew she was thinking it was late, this was hardly the fastest route, but I didn't care.

I wanted Lucinda to see something of the city, and we would not have time the next morning as we planned to leave early for our eight-to-ten-hour drive to Calgary. Lucinda, with a slight smile, ignored me, and, using her cell, headed down the freeway, and in minutes we were drawing up at the iconic Bessborough Hotel, built in the early thirties by the CNR on the riverbank in a European chateau style. It used to tower over the downtown. The only painting I had left from the days I saw myself as a visual artist was an oil I did in 1957, when I was seventeen, from the Nutana side of the river, capturing the evening's approaching thunderstorm, the sky nearly black in places and in others lit, shades of blue to white, the river indigo, and near the bottom of the painting, the city's downtown without a single high-rise, only "the Bess" on the painting's far left in shadow, painted in purple, charcoal, and navy under the alarming, fast-moving clouds so that, looking at the painting, at first you didn't see it. And the thin golden steeple of a church rising above the display, with a thread of the yellow rising into the sky.

I was mildly miffed by Lucinda's ignoring my direction, but did my best not to show it, knowing we were approaching the end of our journey, were both tired, anyone's temper would show strain. She didn't know why I'd suggested the way I did, and I didn't tell her. I was the one who wanted to drive down all those familiar streets, past the house I left with my parents to go to my first wedding, and the drugstore where we always filled prescriptions and bought, rarely, chocolate bars and notebooks, and past the university where I'd spent nine years of my life, five years the first time and after ten years had passed, another four, departing just before I would have finished my Master of Education to marry Peter and turn my life on its head. Then I thought I was leaving chaos behind to choose simplicity and beauty.



Not more than a half hour later Lucinda, my other friend, and I were strolling out of "the Bess" onto the street, discussing where we should go for supper. Dusk had come on by then, but it was still uncomfortably hot, and the two blocks leading toward the city's main street were crowded with young people standing in groups, laughing and chatting and not moving one millimetre for anybody who wanted to pass by. We gave up on the sidewalks and walked with others in the vehicle-free middle of the street. The air was thick with marijuana smoke and the various annoying scents of vaping. When I was in my late twenties and early thirties, I would have loved this scene, partly because it wasn't winter, but mostly because it would have felt so good to live in a city so full of life, everyone out on the street having a good time. I must have thought then, isn't this what cities are about?

But, if the scene appeared anarchic to Lucinda, now I found it so, too, and, as with many old people, wondered how having a good time had come to this, although nobody was knocking anybody over the head, we didn't hear ominous shouting, nor gunshots, and the loudest noise was the laughter of the young people. I had witnessed actual drug deals in downtown Calgary, and one afternoon when I was going to the main library, I followed a tall, lean drug dealer as he sauntered down the streets, followed by his acolyte, a tall, still skinny boy of not more than fifteen, wearing a too big, expensive black leather jacket. I trailed them for several blocks into the main floor of the library, where I stopped to see what would happen: shortly, nobody buying, they trailed back out again. I expect just about anything in downtown Calgary, but in Saskatoon? Now, yes, in Saskatoon, too.



At the time I was trailing the drug dealer and the boy, I wasn't even nervous. Nobody pays any attention to a five-foot-tall, otherwise unprepossessing older woman. Definitely not handsome, six foot, fortyish males of any kind, especially not drug dealers. As for the acolyte, pathetically, I thought, his eyes never left the back of the man's left shoulder, his pace slowing and quickening with the man's. I wondered with some pity if, being trained so young, the boy would become an El Chapo or an Escobar and one day die in a hail of police bullets. Or a lot sooner, of an overdose, or a bullet from another gangster. It was a scene designed for a writer whose main work is *noticing*, if only I had a place for drug dealers in my work. But I would have a place for that young boy, who seemed to me, appallingly, the entire time, to exude innocence.

On that street in Saskatoon, once there would have been a couple of patrolling police officers keeping a wary eye out. One evening when we were in our early thirties, all of us a bit drunk from sitting in the pub that used to be in the basement of the Bess, one of our number simply sat down on the curb, laughing, while the rest of us stood by her yakking, waiting for her to get up, when a beat cop came by and told her she had to get up and move on, whereupon she promptly fell in love with him.

But now, in the face of what looked like disorder to me, there wasn't a police officer to be seen. Finally, I realized that smoking marijuana in public was now legal, and I supposed it was also legal to vape on the street, so that those who weren't smoking were in danger of getting what used to be called a contact high.

Later, Lucinda confessed that the scene had made her uncomfortable. As for me, I'd enjoyed it, although everybody was younger than I was, and most of them were flaunting their deliberately thoughtless behaviour, daring older ladies to complain, deliberately not moving out of the way of anyone trying to pass. I, too, could have done without the smoke and vapour polluting the public space, so I have to admit that even for me the experience had an unpleasant edge.



And yet, thinking about that hot, smelly, uncomfortable evening back in July 2021, when I was about to turn eighty-one, I wonder if maybe that was the highlight of *my* trip, as, although I am guessing, finding the house of Lucinda's grandparents in Winnipeg was for her. I remember now that I was happy as we made our way down the street, and felt that somehow, even with the too-warm dusk, the unwelcome smells, the noisy laughter, nothing in the scene would become violent, and, for me, that was a kind of homecoming. I felt as if I were a ghost of the past walking down that noisy thoroughfare in the dusk, gazing around at the young people but invisible to them; they never guessing that the past was walking by.

And the whole time, I never thought once that I could remember that I should give up increasingly impossible (for an old woman on her own) Calgary, especially now that my family had been gone for several years, and move as I'd always planned to do, should anything happen to Peter, back to Saskatoon. I had thought about making that move often as the years passed but simply could not, ever, face the difficulty of doing it on my own. The last one had been too endlessly traumatic no matter what I said to others about it. I had felt unsure, too, that I could manage living in the midst of my youthful past.

My Saskatoon friend and I finally gave up trying to think of a restaurant and turned into a nearby café that both of us knew, I, at least, having gone to it when it first opened blocks away from where we stood that night, but close to the building where another friend and I, both grad students, once took a yoga class in the days when yoga was just becoming a thing in North America. We'd go hungry to the class, and afterward we'd go to the café and have a bowl of their thick nourishing soup. That was close to fifty years before. And my yoga-going friend remains my friend, although I rarely see her.



The café was packed and noisy but empty of familiar faces. The front area was full, tables nicely spaced, the air cool, the guests polite and nicely dressed. But the three of us were escorted into the back area whose booths were overcrowded with raucous young people. We were given the booth closest to the front, but definitely not in it, because the air conditioning had been turned off in our section, I can only guess to save money, or else it was, café owners being what they are, so that the rowdy people in the back would drink more. The night was very hot, the interior of buildings much hotter with the day's built-up heat, and soon sweat was pouring down our faces; Lucinda had to tell the waiter to tell the manager to turn on the air conditioner, which, to my amazement, he did.

**II**

I was still thinking of the days when on a weekend night the downtown was full of people coming and going from one club to another, each with its own band and its packed dance floor, usually people my friends and I knew. But one bright moonlit night in the early seventies, around midnight, I walked home alone the few blocks from a club where I had been with the half-dozen friends I usually went out with, the club not far from where we were presently sitting. Home then was a rented house where my son and I were living. My husband and I were separated, my son was spending the weekend with his father. When I left the club, a man I'd been introduced to, a stranger to all but the acquaintance who had brought him who said he was from another province, a man with whom I had danced with once and did not like, followed me out. He rushed up the half block to catch up with me. I asked him politely to leave, saying I was close to home and in the bright moonlight didn't need an escort, but he wouldn't go away, and, not knowing what else to do and never expecting what would happen next, I unlocked the door into my house and tried to shut the door on him. He shoved me inside, pushed his way in behind me, shoved me into the bedroom, threw me onto the bed, easily subdued my struggles to stop him, and raped me. Then he put on his pants and shoes, and without a word walked out of the bedroom into the front room, opened the door, walked out, and closed it behind him. The second I heard the door shut I jumped up, ran to it and quickly, loudly, snapped shut the dead bolt. It seemed to me that he, still on the other side of the door, halted for a second when he heard it. I have always thought that he did not realize the seriousness of what he had just done, that I might call the police, until he heard the lock thudding shut. First that hesitation, then I heard him walk briskly away, down the steps, down the sidewalk, and in seconds the sound had faded into those of the city night. I wonder if he went back to the club and sat back down at his table with his friends. If later he followed another woman home. If he did this often. Thinking back, once the accompanying emotion had faded, given his total lack of hesitation and his adeptness at subduing me, I believed that he did.

It was many years before I told a soul. Eventually I wrote a short story depicting a version of that night, which was published in *Story* magazine, likely in the nineties. I had a different last name by the time the story was published. I recall that *The New Yorker* turned it down, saying in its rejection letter something like, "We think it is not a story," meaning they thought it was a personal essay or maybe memoir. When I told this to the editor at *Story*, he was indignant at what he saw as a misjudgement about a piece of literature. But it was the young *Story* editor who informed me that a very bright moonlit night was a cliché, even though that's what it had been, and made me change it to a dark night—and that wasn't a cliché, I wondered? But getting published in the American magazine *Story* felt like such a coup that I decided against arguing.



Talking about *The New Yorker* editor's response, I told the *Story* editor that some years before that incident, in response to a question in a radio interview, I ended my reply by saying, "As soon as I write it down, it becomes a story." I stand by that to this day, along with saying in another interview somewhere and a long time ago, too, "For a real writer, there is no difference between fiction and nonfiction." I meant that we *choose* our written voice, which is already a couple of degrees away from the feel of the experience. Then we choose our words with a combination of our truth and our literary needs, we choose what details to tell, what bits to leave out, or add details, we *shape* the telling. Then we edit the prose. By the time we're done, what we've written as the truth is really only a likeness of the actual experience, which means that everything we write is to some degree fiction. Even in memoir, the real writer is, first and foremost, *creating a text.* What surprised me about both pronouncements, looking back from my early eighties, was that thirty or more years earlier I had already figured this out. It seemed to me now that I'd had to keep reminding myself of this, and, thinking of this manuscript I was working on, so often struggling with my memory and deciding what to put first and what to save for later, even though I told the truth as well as I could, I also held back, I reshaped my visceral reactions in favour of a less troubling aftermath on publication. And yet, at the same time, I stood by everything I'd written.



And yet, I didn't know why I didn't seem to rate having been raped in the classic evening-out-situation-by-a-stranger as one of my life's greatest traumas? Probably because when, many years later I finally wrote a version of it, I worked my way through its horror, or so I had always thought; but even though I could remember most of it in detail, I did not *think* about it, not really, I couldn't, not even when I was writing about it.

But now I remembered that in my first sexual experience, the man I was with became alarmed, saying that I was breathing so strangely he thought I would faint. That memory contributes to my sense that the sexual abuse I suffered as a small child was an attempted rape. I remember only the part where he carried me outside after and set me roughly down on the ground, where I screamed and screamed – and how the world had turned grey.

That is what I remember, never the violence, the violation itself. And people, including my mother, a sister or two, both my husbands, acquaintances, and sometimes myself, wonder why I have been, too often, difficult.

Later, when I was sixty and had realized what had happened when I was a baby, that final moment when all the pieces of the puzzle I had gathered clicked into place, I tried without the help of an analyst or hypnotist to remember that early incident itself. That darkness at the centre. For years this scene had inexplicably fascinated me: Dustin Hoffman in *Marathon Man* staring over and over again at the black-and-white film of an East African champion marathoner as he runs easily, well ahead of the pack, appearing not in the least physically stressed, in particular the moment when he glances back to check on the positions of the other runners, and his face shows the slightest touch of concern.

Then, as I struggled to remember, the African runner abruptly morphed into a young white man in bush clothes – heavy, dark work pants held up with suspenders over a thick tucked-in plaid work shirt, heavy work socks with something low for footwear over the socks, striding away from me, and as I screamed and did not stop screaming, turning his head to look back over his shoulder at me. That same look. The other new memory that I didn't know if I'd invented, if it was a metaphor, was that when he set me down so roughly on the dirt among the tree roots, I felt a violence in the placement, so hard that the physical shock of it in its full power went from my bottom all the way up through my body to the very crown of my head. At the time of whatever sexual violence had happened to me, I must have felt great pain, but I have no memory of pain. But then, I wonder, why was I screaming so hard, as if something truly terrible had happened to me, nothing like the usual crying of babies?

I lived in Saskatoon a total of something like twenty years and was married there twice and divorced once, gave birth to my only child there and buried my father, my mother, one sister, and one niece, and had a celebration of life there for another sister who had died there, as well as a relative or two on my father's side. But the event I chose to tell about here was the time I was raped and didn't tell a soul for I couldn't remember how many years. And I didn't know which was the more astonishing: that it happened or that I didn't tell anybody.

I pretended for years that the assault was nothing, that any adult could get past it, but now, in my last years, I thought about it often, especially about how very shamed I felt. As if I were to blame. Nations that allow, even quietly encourage, their soldiers to use rape as an act of war should be cast out of the human community. I think of Freud, who, in the late nineteenth century, finally began to accept that perhaps all the women and girls who had told him of sexual abuse, of rape they had experienced mostly at the hands of their fathers, but also of others – brothers, uncles, neighbours – were not deluded or hysterical, but were telling the truth, and he then backed away, recanted, stuck with his orthodoxy of their hysteria and their hysterical fantasies, and devised a new theory, apparently, in which their mothers could be blamed for the daughters' failure to behave like normal people.

And yet, that night I could not summon rage, the very thought of calling the police horrified me because of what I knew they would put me through, the questions they would ask, the assumptions about me they would make. The assault took place in the early seventies, when nearly all police officers were men. Maybe hovering in the background was the half-formed thought that they would find out that I was not a good woman, by which I didn't mean anything of a sexual nature, but something awful about me I must have thought I had successfully hidden from everyone.

When I could see finally that the assault was not my fault, not cosmic payback for all my failures, mistakes, and inadequacies, not a final affirmation of my essential worthlessness, I was able to begin to accept its having happened to me and its endless damage, and to write the story. Now, at eighty-three, it came back, and I thought too of how, when I was in mid-life, what happened to me as a baby at last came to me with certainty and then of the rage and despair that seized me and dragged me along as I paced our basement, up and down, up and down, breathing hard through the pain that had taken over my viscera, as my husband slept soundly upstairs, while downstairs in the cellar, not wanting to be sucked below into Hades' kingdom, I tried to find air to breathe. I didn't think. I paced. In the darkened house. I paced all the hours left of the night. And I did not cry. This was also what I had done the night the rape happened. I spent the rest of the night alone, without turning on lights, pacing, pacing, pacing in the dark.



Finally, I saw the darkness of the world; I felt rage at my first rapist who made me into a person my mother couldn't love and whom I myself couldn't like, the damage done to me not to be spoken of, not to anyone, ever. Even as I wrote this, I knew I would not be believed, not wholly, except to those who as children were also maimed this way, and by those who try to help them. And seeing that look on my mother's face as she neared death, something deeper than sorrow, I wished I knew what she knew then.

A whole chunk of my life that happened in Saskatoon now seemed brighter than it ever had at the time, when my life seemed constantly fraught, and my emotions wildly varying, the latter being what must have fogged my memory. But I had begun remembering things I had tried with all my being to erase forever. Oh, the horror of being a human being. Nothing, nothing is lost: It's still all there, unless you are comatose, brain-damaged or brain-dead. Some defiant and incorrigible part of you insists, *you must remember.* It is a wonder anybody survives at all, and as we all know, many people simply do not, preferring death or madness to remembering. Think of the Holocaust survivors, the survivors of the Ukrainian Holodomor, the Rwandan massacre survivors, or the returned soldiers of any war who refuse to or simply cannot speak of their experiences, all so much worse than anything I have undergone.

I think that, in the end, the main difference between fiction and memoirs is that we writers make a contract with the reader, that the first is made up, while the second purports to be the truth, and the reader engages with this contract in mind. Yet, as per the passage from "The Mark on the Wall," quoted in Chapter One, in 1917 Virginia Woolf wrote that "future novelists" would give up realism, "taking a knowledge of it for granted."



I was always the kind of writer who pursued descriptions of reality, wanting for once to get it right, wanting to explain the world from the point of view of an underprivileged, middle-aged, white Western-Canadian mostly rural woman, a point of view I thought not well enough represented and for the most part, when represented, not widely read. I believed that all of us had much to say to the world that we had been denied by the white males who governed everything and by, throughout my lifetime, the cult of youth that has followed the *children should be seen and not heard* world of my growing up and the white-gloved world of my teen years. That is why I have always loved George Eliot's *Middlemarch*, and Doris Lessing's and Margaret Drabble's novels. Alice Munro's middle and late work was a beacon to me, although emulating her turned out to be impossible, the very reason she is our Nobelist. Impossible to emulate her despite her upbringing closer to working class than to solidly middle-middle. As I've written, I wonder if that's where the toughness I see in her work comes from.

Now, forty-seven years after I began writing, the literary-academic world had moved on, and in their world, my work as a realist has become "old-fashioned." At past eighty, I turned back to Woolf's remarks, as a way of justifying what my writing had slowly, over the last forty-plus years, become or was still becoming. Those "reflections" she speaks of, "those are the depths they [novelists] will explore," I found myself there – lost in the depths of the reflections of what I thought was my life, but that I chose to call memoir instead of novel. So, when I read Virginia Woolf's musings about the real work of a novelist, I agreed with her, but glumly, uneasily.

I had always discounted irony as a trope. Disliked it and wouldn't use it unless by accident, because I thought that irony was a deliberate stopping of feeling, that it lent a writer a world-weary air that offended me who could not outgrow her own woundedness, did not for sixty years even recognize its source nor its narrative, and how it had changed ineradicably who I was.



### III

I would have to reread Sebald, I thought. I had read *The Emigrants, Vertigo, The Rings of Saturn, Austerlitz*, but the strange thing for me about reading Sebald was that the minute I finished reading any one of those books, I couldn't remember what they were about, not one of them; I couldn't remember the themes, the narrative arc – if there was one – I couldn't recall how he got from Point A to Point B, which he kept doing over and over again, when I'd lift my head and wonder, hadn't I been reading about X and now suddenly I was reading about M, and how did that happen? And what did my not noticing even in my too-intent reading mean? I guess I wanted the writer in him to seep into me; I wanted to become Sebald or become his writing.

I continued to read in wonder and awe, with a feeling that my chest had opened and wouldn't close throughout. Anthony Doerr, in *Four Seasons in Rome,* quoted Emerson as saying that every story seeks the "invisible and imponderable." I wondered why I so admired Sebald's work when I couldn't even remember what was in his books or what they sounded like. Never mind the puzzle of this very strange forgetfulness of mine.

Stymied, I got up from my desk, went to my bookshelf and put out my hand intending to grasp Sebald's *Austerlitz* to reread it; the tips of my fingers barely touched the volume or I think did not touch it at all, when in that instant, a full scene for my book flooded through my mind, more astonishing, the scene was entirely in Sebald's voice and in his style, both of which I'd been unable to remember. They were stored away in the tiny, hidden pleats and crevices of my brain, whole and exact, there all the time that I thought I could not remember a thing about his books beyond my admiration of them. I couldn't understand why I couldn't remember, and then, why I suddenly remembered all of it.



I raced for my computer, a scene from my life having risen, indelible, clear, and necessary. At my computer, I felt like the enormously gifted singer/composer/pianist Billy Joel, who told interviewer Fareed Zakaria on television how he sometimes feels at the piano: I, too, felt I could do anything; everything I knew about my art was there, immediately at hand.

I typed the scene; it is the first scene before I begin this book proper, although now edited and edited again, it has probably lost its echoes of Sebald's prose. It is the one thing I would not have thought belonged in any book, never mind Goethe or others who have reported the same experience. It sets the motif; it readies the reader for a text of sometimes unconventional considerations about one person's life as viewed from old age.

I read all of *Austerlitz* again; it was as if I had never read it before, but this time I watched carefully, saw how Sebald moved from A to R and S seamlessly, seemingly magically. I read, absorbing his tone that hung steadily behind the sentences and paragraphs, one out of the deepest pool of incurable pain. All of it so smooth, as if he is dreaming his book and can't wake up. While, in contrast, Salman Rushdie writes in intellectual exuberance, vigour, humour, and constant delight, his words and sentences pouring from him, unstoppable, no matter what his subject. A life-loving, intensely vigorous writer, in contrast to Sebald's never precisely stated but constant, acutely affecting grief.

I knew that I could go on being a realist, that being old-fashioned, applied to my recent work, had now lost its sting, made me want to laugh. I had proven at least, to my own satisfaction, that I knew how to do that and had done it sufficiently well to fulfill my original writer-dream, which was never to be experimental but to emulate the classical novelists whose work I so greatly prized. Plot had never mattered to me, only character, and regardless, plot as came out of character. Yet, isn't it true that readers love plot, and that nowadays many writers contort themselves into pretzels with their convoluted, tiringly endless plots? I was more interested in exploring consciousness as writers of serious fiction have always done, than I was in tricky, startling, and inventive plots or exploring information in equally endless depth, which the latter, according to Salman Rushdie, is the new subject of novels, because, he and others insist, the realist novel is done. But I had Flaubert's *Madame Bovary* as a model, because I chose to write about women's lives, but from a woman's point of view. Flaubert wrote to a friend, "Talent is long patience, and originality an effort of will and of intense observation." This, I understood.

I turned to Thomas Bernhard's memoir, *Gathering Evidence*, the book I'd been seeing mention of ever since it was published in 1985, but had always, after an irritated sigh at so many books to read, put off reading. After Woolf and Sebald, that book gave me permission to write this book, the partial story of my most ordinary of lives, even to its life-changing crises, and complete with "memories, dreams, reflections," the title of Carl Jung's 1963 autobiography.

Jung had verified that my inner world was not madness, but a wider sanity; it was another and a better definition of what was real and what was not; and by enlightening me in certain ways, it also affirmed a different set of values than the ones I had been pursuing, the ones circumstances, I thought, had forced me into. Nonetheless, I always passionately desired worldly success to prove, of course, that I existed and mattered, that I, too, had a worthwhile contribution to make.



Why had I been writing for over forty years, I asked myself? To keep repeating myself? To get cuter and cuter, more and more glib? As a writer I had always been on a journey to find my *real* journey and to learn to express it. All of us are writing to save our lives; now I would write to lose mine. I would make the story of this book the thoughts, dreams, reflections that travelling through the places where I had made my life invoked in me. I dreamt that if I did, I would drown in my past, but I believed that fully summoning all that had gone before, after a lifetime of stubbornly refusing to remember, would be worth the risk of losing my self.

Thomas Bernhard (1931–1989) led, throughout his youth and young manhood, a tragically troubled, difficult life, with the spectre of death through his constant ill health always hanging over him. In his book, he spares no one, blaming his teachers and caregivers, the medical experts whom he believed had not only exacerbated his misfortunes, but frequently also caused them. He is incandescent with rage. But he was also saturated in despair, daring to write in a no-holds-barred way about, for example, the many children in Salzberg who, he says, killed themselves. This, in Austria in the mid-twentieth century, not in Dickens' dark and wet nineteenth-century London. He says that every day he nearly did himself, because of the shameless cruelty they all suffered at the hands of their guardians and teachers, the ignorance of their absent parents or life-guardians who sent them to the city and its schools, then kept them there in boarding houses and dormitories as, without love or kindness, they sickened and grew bare-bones thin from malnutrition and hopelessness. Page after page of single-spaced, non-paragraphed prose, divided into sections with headings, and perhaps chapters, plotless in the conventional sense, prose that borders on stream of consciousness of the writer's passionate inner ravings, unadulterated, unmitigated, furious, and exact.



*Gathering Evidence* is a book that stuns the reader, which bears little resemble to Sebald's sophisticated prose, and never directly mentions the cause of his omnipresent angst that is the tone of his books. In his last years, Bernhard found major success both for his books but especially for his gifts as a singer, musician, and composer.

Why could I not write a book like that? Because I was not that angry, because my sufferings were mundane, although painful to me and causing me despair, because I was neither without fear nor quite so ruthless. Also, because I was not so brilliant to see what he saw. Nor did I always think he was right, probably because the first part of *Gathering Evidence* was published in 1972 when he would have been only forty-one (he died at fifty-eight), and writing this book, I am just nicely double that age.

His work is another signpost that began for me with Virginia Woolf's delicate excursions away from plot and into consciousness, leading through Sebald, who, despite giving the effect of a wandering of mind, is controlled and directed, to Bernhard who, in literary terms, appears to place no gates on his thoughts, nor ever to think in terms of plot, other than the few facts of his life as anchoring points. What is truly scandalous is not tales of murders, incest, rape, child pornography, or trafficking of humans, intolerable to civilization as they are, but instead, the contents, the workings, of the uncensored human mind. Every now and then I'm told that I say the unsayable. I suspect that the unsayable is all that is worth saying, at least in the writerly world that I have finally unlocked the sluicegates into. And I was warned by the dream of dripping water: *You will drown in the torrent.* Take John McGahern's *All Will Be Well*, his memory of an excruciatingly, inexcusably miserable childhood, told as an older man. Opening himself, at last, to his traumatic past.



I could never tell you the full truth about anything in my life, although I sometimes try: you cannot begin to imagine the things I have not said, and will not ever say: I am too ashamed, or the memory is too far in the past, a past that is more like a dream, and so very precious that I can only graze it for a quick brush with its beauty; I do have limits, concerning privacy, my own, and others.

But if you aspire to true artistry, and I always have, though claiming I didn't, from the moment in 1978 when I first started writing, in longhand in a notebook, gazing out the windows at the ranch over the low, grass-covered hills stretching, uninhabited for miles in three directions, the endless sky, and at night its blackness illuminated by trillions of hard, white, silver-glinting stars drilling their light down on the vast, nearly empty plains and the shack we lived in, living more outside than inside – if you aspire to artistry, you dissolve those barriers as much as you can, always stopping, you hope, before madness hits. This thought is not romanticism, although it will be judged as such by youthful writers, especially the ones who prize irony.

My narcissism doesn't like details: I avoid any but passing mention of sexual experience; I do not berate anybody except maybe, a little, my mother whom I loved, and who, in the end, loved me. The details do not count, especially if they are salacious and sensational; I find it impossible to more than point in the direction of certain terrible events in my life. My kind of memoirist hopes that our literary styles and voices, our humour, even our everyday diction will keep readers reading, and not the revelation of sordid detail.



I don't regret walking away from a life at the university that even today seems a madness to me, and even though I was reasonably good at it, and had a promising future in it. And I remember my remark to friends at the time when I left, that I quoted in the first memoir: "The university is killing all that is the best in me." Even if I didn't consciously know what the best in me was.

I do not to this day know how I knew that. I opened my mouth, and it came out and it was true and heartbreaking at the same time, given how hard it had been, what it had cost to get there, and the good things about it, including exercising my brain and feeling an equal for the first time in my life to all the other young women who were my dearest friends and acquaintances there. It had been a time, I realize now, when

I felt a full participant in life and not someone sitting on the sidelines watching but unable to enter it, the first time that I had felt competent and valued. I suppose I was remembering the day I realized that, if I stayed an art major and maintained my dream of becoming a visual artist, I would probably end by starving to death.

I didn't for a second doubt my lifelong drive to make art, but I must have thought it foolish and selfish given where I had come from and in the face of my desire to spend my adulthood in the middle class. So, thinking myself sensible, even wise, I switched to Education, and finally to the Education of Exceptional Children, where I already had a lot of years of experience, and which I enjoyed and seemed to have a gift for. Hardly an unusual story, but any other person whose most powerful desire is to make art and who doesn't follow it knows what happened to me when I made the decision to drop making art in favour of making a living. Life becomes bleak and unmanageable. Your soul starts to die.



I exchanged all of my life for another log house and a settler's shack, for long days in trucks and on horses, for cooking for crews and pouring endless cups of coffee and keeping my mouth shut, for years of feeling friendless and alone, and also, may I never forget, for, at last, Peter's steadiness to keep me upright, someone at last to lean on, something up to then I'd never had in my life except once in a while from my mother and, rarely, from my father; for a life lived in the wonders of nature, and for losing my dream of painting and the constant longing for my son living during the school year in his father's house in Saskatoon across the street from his high school: I did not want to finish raising him in the rural culture, he was already urban, I would not sacrifice him and his promise to my unreasonable needs even though the cost to us both was enormous.

And then, in late 2023, at least one full draft of this book completed, I had another dream that took place in a confused version of an old ramshackle house in Halifax in which my first husband, our baby, and I once lived. I had run upstairs to a room where the furnace, water heater, ducts, water pipes, and water supply, in real life located in basements, were placed. There I found a round, rusted tin basin, its edges sharp and raw, with straight sides, as if a barrel had been sawed off partway down. It was a much smaller version of the huge cisterns we small-town people, before municipal sewers and water systems, had in our cellars to collect rain and melted snow as our only water supply.

The basin was already full, but from a small tube fastened to its side, water continued to drip steadily, relentlessly, into it. In moments it would overflow and flood us all. Panicky, I ran downstairs and told my former husband, who went upstairs to look. Almost immediately he called downstairs or came back down or I went up and we cried in delighted astonishment: The drip has stopped!

The room grew brighter, as if someone had turned on a light.

# ELEVEN

# ARRIVAL

## I

After our dinner in that hot, crowded and noisy restaurant in Saskatoon, we strolled back to the Bessborough, where we said goodbye to my old friend as she got in her car and drove away, and Lucinda and I went to our air-conditioned rooms to bed. The next morning, once again not terribly early, with me at the wheel because I knew the way, we were on the road out of Saskatoon heading back to our Calgary lives.

The route we took, instead of south to Regina and then west on the Trans-Canada, was west through farmland dotted with small towns. At more than six hundred kilometres, the drive would take about eight hours, including stops for bathroom, food, and gas. I thought Lucinda simply wanted to see more of the province and had no idea that, on that route, there wasn't much to see that would interest somebody used to cities, ocean views, rainforests, or mountain ranges. But I didn't disagree; it was shorter; it was the reasonable route, and I was just glad that having to do it yet again, at least I had company.

I, though, made a mistake on the outskirts of the city and bypassed the turnoff I should have taken. We wound up heading out on back roads and eventually, trying to get back onto the right road, went through the town where I first taught school nearly sixty years earlier. I was married and pregnant, having signed my teaching contract on a Friday and the following Friday been informed of my pregnancy. All that winter my then-husband drove into the city every day to finish his degree at the university. Our baby was born on February 29, two weeks late. I had originally planned only to take off the last two weeks before the due date, and because Mother Nature does whatever she wants, the month I'd planned to take off after the baby was born turned into only two weeks.

Though my driving mistake meant that to get back on the right road we had to drive through that town, I didn't take us anywhere near the school where I'd worked, nor the house we'd lived in all that winter. I am one of those who would not go through my youth again for all the money in the world. Even old, awful as it is, is better, because at least you are not surprised



by the things that happen, and sometimes you even know why they happen, and might even have predicted them.

But I know very well that the year teaching school in that town was wonderful: the kids were great, farm kids nearly all of them, and the other teachers were great, too, a couple in particular being especially helpful to a new teacher who looked about twelve years old and was pregnant besides, and who, mid-year, left for six weeks to have a baby. I recall, especially, walking to the school and back again, listening to the meadowlarks singing in the field across from it, and I missed those meadowlarks more than anything else when we left. Once, walking down a narrow country road on the Shetland Islands with a half-dozen North American travellers, a skylark suddenly shot, singing, straight up perhaps twenty feet, out of the field of grass beside us, before dropping down again out of sight, while we halted in perfect shock, gasping, then laughing in delight. I choose larks over the raucous parrots in Australia or magnificent South American condors I've seen only on television, or the wild turkeys I saw in South Dakota, or the black swans in Tasmania, or the bright flamingos I saw on a lake in East Africa. Meadowlarks, a symbol of the Western prairie. That field where they sang each day is now covered with houses, sidewalks, and paved roads.

We would leave that town the next year to live in the lower mainland of British Columbia. There I taught in a large, overcrowded secondary school while my husband drove into Vancouver each day on a newly built freeway to work toward a master's degree. My chief memories of that year were my astonishment at the climate and the weather, so gentle and soft after Saskatchewan's extremes. That, and the time when I was on the second floor of the old hangar building that had been turned into an overcrowded high school, I could hear all the classroom doors up and down the halls slamming shut at the same time as the floor began to bounce up and down, so I could stay upright only by clinging to the narrow blackboard ledge with my fingertips, until the blackboard wall and the wall at the back of the room started whumping in and out so much I thought they would crack and split and the whole room would fall on us. I didn't know what was happening and had to ask the kids, who were hanging, white-knuckled, onto their desks, who half-whispered back as if their throats had closed with shock, "Earthquake!"



Funny how you remember things like that, that last maybe three minutes, and forget about being raped.

Then we passed through the town from my long-ago past and drove back on to the highway. I suppose we stopped in Kindersley where the highway starts to travel straight west about an hour from Rosetown. We would have been ready for lunch by then, so I'm guessing we ate there. It's an oil town, and that means lots of single young men needing fast-food places, motels, and gas stations, and a lot of trucks of every size. On one of my interminable solitary drives on the single lane highway from Calgary to Saskatoon, as the bumper-to-bumper traffic, mostly trucks and tanker trucks and big equipment heading west toward oil fields poured past me, as I headed east at a hundred kilometres per hour, a pair of maniacs – young males and I'll bet anything stoned, at the very least suicidal – pulled out of their lane and drove straight for me, head-on. For a miniscule part of a second, I simply couldn't believe it. But they didn't slide into an open spot in their lane – they kept coming straight at me. By then I was braking, then braking harder, and by now driving down the paved shoulder hanging onto the wheel until I came to a full stop. By then, they were far down the road behind me, I bet whooping and high-fiving while I was hyperventilating, my head ringing, dizzy with disbelief. Later, I heard from a friend that the same thing had happened to her on that stretch of road.



I said to Lucinda, a couple of times, but probably first at Kindersley after our fast-food lunch, that well into Alberta, there would be no Timmy's, no cafés, thus no bathrooms, few trees to hide behind if a bathroom were needed, no famous sights to look at, not even places to buy gas. But it took her asking me to do quick drives through two hamlets before she accepted what I said. Neither had even a grocery store, and there wasn't a soul to be seen in either of them. But that's what those tiny places are like, I probably said, and it was afternoon at the height of a too-hot summer day, seeding long done, weeks until harvest; anybody who could would be inside where it was cooler, if not at their cabin at a lake.

By the time we reached the Alberta border, we were both tired and eager to get back to Calgary. I must still have been driving, because I remember several hours later we were inching closer to the city, and the day was drawing on toward evening, Lucinda took the wheel, put her foot on the gas, and eventually headed out on the freeways that I would give my life never to drive on, and had me at my door by nine in the evening. We'd left the previous Sunday around nine or ten in the morning and over the past seven days, only five of which we spent in the car actually driving, had covered a total of something like 2,776 kilometres with the daytime temperature hovering all the way at around thirty degrees Celsius or eighty-six degrees Fahrenheit or higher, and not a drop of moisture falling the entire time.

Later, sometimes, recalling that trip, I wondered what we talked about as we drove through the unrelenting heat, past the crops that keep the province alive, through the tiny villages, or past them; I couldn't even remember gossip. There hadn't been a single quarrel or disagreement or even the unpleasant presentiment of one. Lucinda had been more than tolerant of my age-related limitations and had cheerily taken the lead whenever I would not or seemed to think I couldn't. Besides my stream of historical comment and the occasional – she might say it was more than occasional – telling of moments from my life related to what we were passing through, I think we talked a lot about books and writers and the writing we wanted to do. For me, the internal journey a thousand times more fraught than the outer one could ever reveal.

Every day, the incandescent sky, the white sun blazing down on us.

Writing this memoir, the ceaseless drip of memory took me to the edge of the abyss where I had struggled never to go, but was now glad to have gone; to the diminishing of the omnipresent wish for a fully lived life along with the realization, finally, that such a life is never fully achieved no matter what countries you travel to, nor what sights you see, not even by the bravest, boundaryless adventurer, but at last, to the vision of the ineradicable, amorphous, shifting needs of the unruly soul.

And yet, on a fine, warm fall day when the autumn leaves were at their most colourful, and having had a small psychological blow that nonetheless had shocked me despite my endless efforts not to be knocked askew by such minor upsets, I knew I needed to be in nature. I went to the park, and walked slowly down the trails looking at the colours and letting my thoughts meander as my feet were doing. I found a bench with, rather than the prized water view, a view of the island of deciduous trees and shrubs that grew in abundance in front of me, their autumn leaves shades of orange, yellow, and a red that moved through a soft, blushing pink to a fading scarlet, to a dusky wine.

Suddenly, as if I'd been carrying on a discussion with myself about this question, which I hadn't been doing at all, I said to myself, "Well then, if you don't believe in the various stories you've heard about what will happen when you die: not my deceased relatives welcoming me, not a choir of angels serenading me, not a miserable limbo, purgatory or bardo, not hellfire and eternal suffering, ask yourself what it is you would *like* to find on the other side when you are dead."

The answer came to me at once, directly, effortlessly: peace, clarity, kindness. By peace, I meant an absence of neuroses in me and everyone else that cause most of the suffering, the cruelty in the flesh and blood world. By clarity, I meant incisive direct thinking that would lead the way to the answers to the questions that follow us all our lives and are, on earth, unanswerable. By kindness: a world where kindness replaces rules, laws, and self-interest.

No trumpets sounded, no shining creatures descended, no celestial music filled the air. I thought I had perhaps at last conquered my tendency to grandiosity that, in the end, I saw as a pathetic impulse. It seemed to me that I'd known that answer all along, but the various teachings and ideas given me by others had confused me and had made me think I could not have a workable idea of my own.

I thought, now I can go home, and I began to rise from the bench, still contemplating the trees and shrubs.

A fog or a mist that had existed between me and the natural world had quietly dissolved. The fall leaves before and around me were brighter, their shapes clearer, the trees, too, the entire physical world shone, not on fire, not blazing, but appeared more acute and precise, their colours warmer in the new, clear light that, as I walked along the forest path, didn't fade and disappear but stayed on all the limbs, branches, and leaves. Contemplating them as I passed slowly by, I found that my inner world had, at last, stilled.



And yet, looking back on the months I spent writing this text, the weeks I spent not writing, pacing, thinking, the nights of fraught, sensual dreaming, the narrative threads I have caught and written down, finishing the rereading of this book, then settling back in an armchair, watching the snow come thickly down outside my window as I enumerate all the parts I've put into it, in dismay tinged with surprise, I think, but — *I've left out my life*. And then, again, or have I? I decide firmly that I have not. This is what matters.

## ACKNOWLEDGEMENTS

At the end of May 2024, in one of the most gruelling efforts of my life, I moved back to Saskatoon. After fifteen years in Calgary, my life in that city had grown, was continuing to grow narrower and narrower as the city expanded, built new freeways, designed a world which youth (males in particular) handled with ease and panache. Old ladies on their own did not. Not me, anyway. I felt more and more an alien, was more and more isolated as I grew old and I began to long for a place to live where I felt at home. Eventually, I made the big decision, and, in an effort almost too much for a woman past eighty, I gritted my teeth and moved. While I regret losing certain things about Calgary, mostly my few dear women friends there and the people in the literary world who did not forget me as I became an old woman, and the wonderful group of greatly talented writers who came to my condo every four weeks or so to talk about our work, Saskatoon is a city that generally I know how to navigate, where things are familiar instead of brand new and strange, and where I have memories in many corners and down many streets, memories that I utterly lacked in Calgary. Here, I know who I am.

I need to point out that, as with all people past eighty years, most people in this book, including myself, are either already dead or soon will be – tomorrow, a week, a year or two or five, or a few more – we will soon all be gone, or nearly all of us. "Lucinda," my companion and expedition leader, will be around for a long time yet, and may she go on many other journeys and find out a thousand new things and write stories and poems and books about them that will grip the readers' imaginations and leave them gasping with the wisdom and beauty found therein.

I haven't mentioned the many wonderful women friends I have across the country, although now chiefly in Saskatoon and

Calgary (Hamilton, Winnipeg, Regina, Victoria), but they have sustained and supported me in my larger journey of navigating old age's choppy, rarely placid surface and its deep currents and the riptides, and of helping me to face the inevitable and mostly dreaded although sometimes profoundly exciting "what comes next." There have been some beautiful men in there, too, not necessarily lovers or husbands, but friends, one or two rare ones, all of whom, each in their own way, have enriched my life.

Have I said enough about my family? Their story is my story; their grievances, desires and joys mine, too. They framed and made me, and I them, and the tumultuous and difficult times we had, we had together, and no matter what happened or happens and what I have written in this book, there exists and always has from the day our parents married and begot us, a current of the deepest love flowing through all of us. I can never say how deeply moved I was by the gentle, loving woman our mother became in her last years and I recall most days my warmest childhood memories of our father who loved us all and our sorrow that he has been gone for fifty years.

I have been fortunate enough to have lived nearly half my life in nature, and it is there that I found and still find spirit, whoever and whatever that may be, and so many times its presence saved my life. It is one of the sorrows of my old age that I no longer live in nature.

Thanks to my eternally beloved son especially who has always supported me and I him, to my two husbands, and my sisters always. Thanks to my agent, Marilyn Biderman, and to the people of Freehand Books, especially Naomi K. Lewis, my able editor, and Kelsey Attard, the hugely competent Managing Editor of Freehand Books who was always there when I needed her.

As for my own work, I will keep trying to write that book that will finally say what I have been for fifty years trying to say. This book, so far, is as close as I can get.

**SHARON BUTALA**, an Officer of the Order of Canada, is the award-winning author of twenty-three books of fiction and nonfiction and five produced plays. She has three times been a finalist for the Governor General's Literary Award, and is a recipient of the Glengarry Book Award, the Marian Engel Award, the Saskatchewan Order of Merit, the Cheryl and Henry Kloppenburg Award for Literary Excellence, the City of Calgary W.O. Mitchell Book Prize, and three honourary doctorates. She lives in Saskatoon.

sharonbutala.com